Exploring Disability

A SOCIOLOGICAL INTRODUCTION

Colin Barnes, Geof Mercer
and Tom Shakespeare

Polity

First published in 1999 by Polity Press in association with Blackwell Publishers Ltd.

Reprinted 2000

Editorial office:
Polity Press
65 Bridge Street
Cambridge CB2 1UR, UK

Marketing and production:
Blackwell Publishers Ltd
108 Cowley Road
Oxford OX4 1JF, UK

Published in the USA by
Blackwell Publishers Inc.
350 Main Street
Malden, MA 02148, USA

ISBN 0-7456-1477-9
ISBN 0-7456-1478-7 (pbk)

A catalogue record for this book is available from the British Library and has been applied for from the Library of Congress.

Typeset in 10 ½ on 12 ½ pt Palatino by Wearset, Boldon, Tyne & Wear.
Printed in Great Britain by TJ International, Padstow, Cornwall.

This book is printed on acid-free paper.

Contents

Acknowledgements

We are happy to recognize the inspiration of all those many disabled individuals and their allies who have, over the years, struggled to put disability on the political agenda, without whom this book would not have been produced.

Specific thanks to Polity Press and Rebecca Harkin for their patience and support.

For permission to reprint copyright material the authors gratefully acknowledge the following: Olive and John Brisenden, parents of the late Simon Brisenden for his poem, 'Scars', which is taken from S. Brisenden (1990) *Poems for Perfect People*, Hampshire: Hampshire Coalition of Disabled People; Micheline Mason for her poem, 'From the Inside', which is taken from M. Mason (1982) 'From the Inside', *In From The Cold*, Summer: 12–13; Open University Press for Box 5.1, in Louise Ackers and Pamela Abbott (1996) *Social Policy for Nurses and the Caring Professions*, Buckingham: Open University Press; and the University of California Press and Penguin for Table 20.14, in Peter Townsend (1979) *Poverty in the United Kingdom*, Harmondsworth: Penguin/Berkeley, California: University of California Press.

1

Introduction

As we enter the third millennium, concern about the social and political dimensions of disablement has intensified considerably. The exclusion of disabled people from the mainstream of economic and social life has been the subject of mounting political protest and mobilization. It has also become a major issue for policy-makers and politicians in richer and poorer countries alike, and a growing number have introduced some form of legislative framework in which to combat discrimination on the grounds of impairment or disability.

This new political focus on disability has also attracted increasing attention across a range of academic disciplines. There has been an unprecedented growth of 'disability studies' courses and specialist journals in America and Canada (Pfeiffer and Yoshida, 1995; Linton, 1998a), Britain (Barton and Oliver, 1997), and Australia and New Zealand (Sullivan and Munford, 1998). It has been complemented by a burgeoning literature on many different aspects of 'disability', including the process and experience of disablement and disability politics, culture and research. Recent British contributions include Oliver (1990), Barnes (1991), Morris (1991), Swain et al. (1993), French (1994), Hales (1996) and Barnes and Mercer (1997). This work has been a response to, and has itself stimulated, dramatic changes in public perceptions of disabled people, and the meaning and consequences of disability.

Equally important, where this transformation in the understanding of disability has occurred, and associated policy initiatives have been introduced, it has not been driven by traditional organizations 'for' disabled people, but primarily by the actions of grass-roots organizations controlled and run by disabled people themselves, referred to throughout this book as the 'disabled people's movement'. These changes have been further stimulated by a significant body of 'non-academic' writings produced by disabled and non-disabled people who are either associated with these organizations 'of' disabled people, or look to them for inspiration (e.g. Hunt, 1966; Bowe, 1978).

This pattern is demonstrated in various countries in Europe and North America, but it is particularly evident in the United Kingdom. Here, the activities of organizations directed by disabled people, notably the Union of the Physically Impaired Against Segregation (UPIAS) and the British Council of Disabled People (BCODP), formerly known as the British Council of Organisations of Disabled People, and the work of a small but influential group of disabled activists and writers, have generated an increasing body of knowledge and practice which has come to be known as the 'social model of disability'. This has exerted a crucial impact on disabled people's thinking and political campaigns. This 'model' should not be confused with a comprehensive social theory of disability; nevertheless, the necessary steps in that journey are being made, including such notable British contributions as the work of Paul Hunt (1966), Vic Finkelstein (1980), Jo Campling (1981), Mike Oliver (1983, 1990, 1996a), Paul Abberley (1987, 1991) and Jenny Morris (1991, 1993).

Drawing in varying degrees on sociological insights, this literature constitutes a direct challenge to conventional thinking and practice regarding disability. The traditional approach has concentrated on individual limitations as the principal cause of the multiple difficulties experienced by disabled people. In complete contrast, what has become known as 'disability theory' has argued that people with accredited (or perceived) impairments are disabled by society's blatant failure to accommodate their needs. The 'social model' does not deny the significance of impairment in people's lives but concentrates on those social barriers which are constructed 'on top of' impairment. Hence, disability is regarded as 'socially created' and the explanation of its changing character is located in the social and economic structure and culture of the society in which it is found. Instead of regarding disability as an individual limitation, the social model identifies society as 'the problem', and looks to fundamental social and political changes to provide the 'solutions'.

What is remarkable is not simply that this social interpretation of disability has gained such credibility and legitimacy in such a short period of time, but that it has been achieved with so little contribution from individual sociologists. Indeed, the discipline has more often presented a mixture of determined opposition from a few, and general apathy and indifference by the majority. Yet sociologists have prided themselves on their critical role in society: 'No sociologically sophisticated person can be unaware of the inequalities that exist in the world today, the lack of social justice in many social situations or the deprivations suffered by millions of people. It would be strange if sociologists did not take sides on practical issues . . .' (Giddens, 1993: 23). This has provided a traditional focus on social inequality and divisions associated with social class, and, more recently, gender and 'race'. Yet where sociologists have taken an interest in the process of disablement, they have typically not addressed this as an example of social exclusion or oppression, but followed instead what has variously been referred to as an 'individual', 'medical' or 'personal tragedy' model of disability. This has concentrated attention on those functional limitations which are attributed to disease, chronic illness or injury.

Studies by medical sociologists have taken centre stage, with disability approached pre-eminently from within an 'illness' perspective. A substantial body of work has been produced which distinguishes between the medical concern with disease as an abnormal bio-physical condition, and the sociological focus on 'sickness' and 'illness' as social states. The early stimulus was provided by Parsons' functionalist approach, which advanced a sociological interpretation of doctor and patient roles. His examination of 'sickness' as a social status and the rights and responsibilities associated with the 'sick role' exerted a considerable influence. However, this perspective has been largely overtaken by writings adopting a broadly interactionist and interpretative approach to the experience of illness. This extends from the impact of specific bio-physiological symptoms and changes to their social meanings. At the same time, there has been a continuing tradition of 'socio-medical' research which has been less guided by theoretical debates in sociology than by practical medical and health service concerns. The overall result is a rich theoretical and empirical resource documenting the prevalence and character of 'chronic illness and disability', as well as its impact on daily living, social relationships and people's sense of self and identity (Anderson and Bury, 1988; Radley, 1994; Bury, 1997).

The political mobilization of disabled people is a worldwide phenomenon (Coleridge, 1993; Rioux and Bach, 1994). It was activities in North America which first gained global attention, most notably with the growth and impact of the American Independent Living Movement (ILM) in the 1970s. At the same time, there has been an expanding American literature on disability which ranges from academic studies such as Robert Scott's *The Making of Blind Men* (1969) and Gary Albrecht's *The Sociology of Physical Disability and Rehabilitation* (1976) to Frank Bowe's more descriptive and populist account *Handicapping America* (1978) and Irving Zola's work bridging the concerns of disabled people and social science, illustrated by *Missing Pieces: A Chronicle of Living with a Disability* (1982). These writings drew attention to the disabling tendencies within medical rehabilitation programmes, as well as in American society generally. Nevertheless, this North American literature did not adopt the sharp distinction between impairment and disability that underpins the 'social model' approach. While pressing for improvements in the opportunities for disabled people, this was linked to the denial of civil rights to a minority group rather than a specific theoretical explanation of disability and the exclusion of disabled people from the mainstream of economic and social activity (Linton, 1998a, 1998b).

Nevertheless, in the last few years a contrary and more radical standpoint has been elaborated by a small but growing band of writers in North America and Australasia. They have made increasingly vocal calls for the development of a more critical and interdisciplinary field of enquiry. This has stimulated analyses of disability as a socio/political and cultural phenomenon (Rioux and Bach, 1994; Davis, 1996, 1997; Thomson, 1996, 1997; Gleeson, 1997; Meekosha and Dowse, 1997a; Linton, 1998a, 1998b). These initiatives provide increasingly common ground between disability theorists, including a growing international interest in the 'social model' approach as championed by British writers. At the same time, this is generating lively debates about the best ways forward for disability studies in general and for a sociology of disability in particular.

A principal factor in the worldwide spread of disability studies which take a social model approach has been the establishment of an expanding and dynamic community of disability teachers and researchers. A major stimulus was the publication, by Len Barton and Mike Oliver, in 1986 of the first international 'academic' journal devoted exclusively to the social dynamics of disability. Initially entitled *Disability, Handicap and Society*, but renamed *Disability and Society* in 1993, this journal has gone from strength to strength. It has expanded from three to five issues a year, with subscribers in over fifty nations (Barton and Oliver, 1997). A further feature has been the rapid expansion of a network of disability scholars and students pursuing disability issues by communication through the Internet. As an example, in 1995 the first 'disability research mailbase' was set up by two postgraduate research students at the University of Leeds, Mark Priestley and Emma Stone. Its aim has been to 'facilitate news, views and information amongst those interested in disability research – particularly those working within a social model of disablement' (Disability and Society, 1996: 136). From the outset it has attracted an audience from around the world, with an average of over 200 contributions and enquiries per week. There is therefore a growing constituency wanting to engage in debates on disability issues, as well as multiplying opportunities for participation by disabled people.

A recent feature of these debates has been the commitment to generate a sociology of disability which explores the insights and issues raised by those adopting very different starting-points. This is especially important given that there is a growing awareness among medical sociologists and disability theorists that their concerns in some respects overlap and are not necessarily mutually exclusive. Hence, each group stands to gain from an analysis which draws on both literatures (Barnes and Mercer, 1996; Barton, 1996; Oliver, 1996c; G. Williams, 1996). In addition, sociology generally has itself become more eclectic and drawn on the insights of other disciplines, which are reflected in its approach to disability. At the same time, the analysis of disability raises theoretical, methodological and empirical issues of wider relevance for mainstream sociology. Examples include biological determinism, social divisions, politics, power and welfare, the quality and meaning of life, 'care' and dependence, identity and difference. These are not simply fundamental to sociological enquiries more generally, but extend into other academic disciplines, as well as raising basic normative and ethical issues for society as a whole.

A brief word on terminology

Over recent decades there has been a growing recognition that our awareness of social issues is influenced by the concepts and language we use. Indeed, there have been continuing challenges to established prejudicial attitudes and stereotypes from disadvantaged groups including women, minority ethnic groups, older people, lesbians and gay men. Generally, sociologists and other social scientists have responded positively to these overtures, although there is little evidence that the same sensitivity has been displayed in writings on disability and disabled people.

Yet the debate over definitions and language has been central to the disabled people's movement's critique of traditional medical and academic social science approaches (see chapter 2). There is little doubt that if impairment is defined in negative terms, this reinforces disparaging attitudes towards disabled people, so that they are variously shunned and excluded from everyday life, or pitied and patronized as tragic victims. Nevertheless, the question of appropriate terminology remains a highly contested issue, even amongst disabled people and organizations controlled by them, not least because of the different meanings attached to key terms across linguistic and cultural boundaries.

For most disabled and non-disabled people throughout the English-speaking world, terms such as 'cripple', 'spastic', and 'mongol' have lost their original meaning and simply become terms of abuse. Similarly, although they appear regularly in the media and academic literature, words which depersonalize and objectify the disabled population are considered unacceptable. These include phrases such as 'the impaired', 'the disabled', 'the deaf' or 'the blind'. Yet whilst there is a growing consensus on the oppressive implications of the term 'handicap', mainly because of its historical allusions to 'cap in hand', begging and charity, divisions still remain with reference to the terms 'impairment' and 'disability'. For example, in some languages direct translation of the word 'impairment' has a profoundly negative meaning, so it tends to be avoided by disabled people and their organizations.

However, in this book we adopt the terminology of the British disabled people's movement which has remained unchanged since the formation of the BCODP in 1981 (apart from extending its remit beyond physical to sensory and intellectual impairments). This framework has recently been adopted by Disabled People's

International (DPI) Europe (DPI, 1994). It separates 'impairment', which refers to a medically classified condition, from 'disability', which is a generic term used to denote the social disadvantage experienced by people with an accredited impairment. We will avoid the phrase 'people with disabilities' (except in quotations from others) because it implies that the impairment defines the identity of the individual, blurs the crucial conceptual distinction between impairment and disability and avoids the question of causality. Although readers new to this literature may be bewildered by these exchanges, what is at issue is far more than a choice of words; the debate is about the best way to understand and contest disability and the multiple oppressions that are associated with it.

Overview of the book

Our starting-point is provided by the 'sociological imagination' (Wright Mills, 1970) which stresses the importance of investigating the interplay between an individual's everyday life and the wider society, and highlights comparative and historical perspectives. Chapter 2 continues with a brief overview of changing perceptions of disability and a comparison of the current sociological orthodoxy on disability and the more recent 'social model' approach articulated by disability theorists. This is followed by a discussion of the key issues and perspectives that will form the basis for building a sociologically informed account of disability.

Chapter 3 furnishes a broad overview of the medical sociology literature on 'chronic illness' and disability. It is argued that although medical sociologists have elaborated wide-ranging criticisms of bio-medical accounts of health and illness, it is interactionist and phenomenological approaches which have predominated in studies of 'chronic illness'. These are based on experiential accounts of illness and have too often ignored the impact of structural factors, or 'disabling barriers and attitudes'. However, that medical sociology literature which has focused on the medicalization of social problems and the impact of the self-serving nature of professional power has been given a fresh impetus by recent studies, much inspired by Foucault and his version of social constructionism, of 'madness' as well as theorizations of the body (Foucault, 1965, 1976).

Chapter 4 traces the emergence and development of what has

become known as disability theory and, in particular, the more structural or materialist account commonly associated with the 'social model of disability'. This chapter also draws attention to the relative absence of analysis within disability theory of important social divisions affecting disabled people's lives, including gender, minority ethnic status and 'race', age and sexuality. It will conclude by focusing on the perceived inadequacies of current 'social model' theorizing and the pressing need for a more comprehensive approach which draws on the insights of sociological studies, notably within medical sociology, and disability theory.

Chapter 5 turns from the theoretical to the empirical and focuses on the systematic exclusion of disabled people from the core institutions of contemporary society: in particular, family life and parenting, education, the labour market, and the built environment. It raises important moral issues concerning perceptions of the value and quality of life of disabled people which have hitherto been largely ignored by sociologists. These themes are developed further in chapter 6, which examines the role of social welfare policy in the lives of disabled people. It is argued that recent sociological and social policy studies of the changing nature of welfare have failed to take on board the issues raised by 'social model' theorists regarding the social exclusion of disabled people, and looks at how social policy might more positively contribute to undermining the process of disablement.

The next two chapters locate the emergence of these ideas within a political and cultural framework. Chapter 7 begins with an evaluation of the social forces precipitating the emergence of the disabled people's movement and subsequently explores the arguments, both theoretical and empirical, surrounding its role as a catalyst for meaningful social change. The role of culture, media and leisure in the social construction of disability and the significance of disability culture and art in forging a positive disabled identity are explored in chapter 8. Finally, in chapter 9, attention turns to recent initiatives to generate a distinctive 'emancipatory' disability research, which parallels the wider struggle by disabled people for social justice and greater control of their lives. We argue that the sociological analysis of disability has implications for both disabled and non-disabled people, in that it raises issues which must be confronted in any society.

Exploring Disability has been written primarily for students of sociology and associated disciplines, including social policy, political science and cultural studies. It is also designed as a broad-based introductory text for academics and researchers specializing in 'disability studies' and health-related disciplines, including medicine. It provides an introduction to the literature with a particular emphasis on the British experience, while demonstrating the 'global' character of disability and the issues raised. A central objective is that it should contribute to and stimulate these wider debates about the process of disablement in Britain and elsewhere, where social conditions (and the form and extent of disability) vary, to a lesser or greater degree. Our understanding of disability will be promoted as this comparative perspective on disability is advanced.

2

Understanding Disability

During the 1960s, the public perception of disabled people spanned 'imaginative concern, mawkish sentimentality, indifference, rejection and hostility' (Thomas, 1982: 4). To have an impairment was regarded as a 'personal tragedy' – a conclusion which united service providers, policy-makers and the wider public. It seemed to dictate a life as a passive 'victim' characterized by social exclusion and disadvantage, and by dependency on assistance from family and friends and a 'safety net' of state welfare benefits and services.

Social scientists did little to challenge these stereotypes and prejudices. Similarly, there were few attempts to explore whether the support given was adequate, effective, or what disabled people really wanted. While sociologists claimed to be in the vanguard of those exploring social hierarchies and inequalities, the condition of disabled people generated little research or theoretical interest. Although the social consequences of medical dominance of the health services attracted searching scrutiny and criticism, there was little inclination to develop comparable analyses of the professional control of disabled people's lives.

What a difference a decade makes!

Yet by the early 1970s a very different picture was emerging. The sense of grievance and weight of social disadvantage felt by disabled people had spilled over into political mobilization and social protest. People with impairments argued that they were subjected to a battery of disabling attitudes and barriers – from education to employment, through housing and transport, to sexuality and reproduction. Campaigns 'took off' around the world. The Disabled People's International (DPI), an international umbrella for organizations controlled and run by disabled people, attracted 4,000 delegates from over 120 countries – half of these from 'developing countries' of the majority world – to its third world congress in 1992. The United Nations (UN) nominated 1981 the International Year of Disabled People, and proclaimed 1983–1992 as the Decade of Disabled Persons. Governments in North America, Europe and Australasia began to respond to the heightened pressure to take legislative action to end the discrimination experienced by disabled people.

Disability was recognized as an issue which affects a significant proportion of the population. In the mid-1980s, a national survey estimated that there were more than 6 million people with impairments in Britain, or 14.2 per cent of the total population (Martin et al., 1988). A survey conducted by the United States Department of Commerce in 1991–2 reported that there were 48.9 million Americans with an impairment (or 19.4 per cent of the population). Statistics collected by the United Nations (1990) indicate that disabled people comprise a significant minority in most countries around the world, with the majority in the less industrialized countries, although disabled people make up a higher proportion of the population in the most industrialized countries. However, international comparisons must be approached with considerable caution because countries' use of very different measures and methods of data collection. Best 'guesstimates' suggest there are over 400 million disabled people, or around 10 per cent of the world's population (Helander, 1993). There is more agreement that this number will rise substantially over the next few years. This is mostly attributed to the rising number of people living to over 70 years of age – a group which contains a disproportionate number of those with impairments – as well as to medicine's enhanced capacity to prolong life. In addition, these numbers are typically matched by an equal number of 'carers' – neighbours, relatives, and friends – providing informal support. Nevertheless, policy responses towards disability have remained uncertain and diffuse.

In many Western countries, the accumulated impact of political campaigns and protest, coupled with the innovative analyses advanced by disabled activists, also began to make an impression on social scientists. A few sociologists, some disabled people themselves, began to rectify this lack of interest in disability (Albrecht, 1976; Zola, 1983a; Abberley, 1987; Barton, 1989a; Oliver, 1990). A primary aim of this volume is to explore their contributions and so demonstrate how a sociologically informed approach can make a positive contribution to understanding disability.

Our starting-point is provided by the 'sociological imagination'. This stresses the importance of investigating the interplay between an individual's everyday life and the wider society. It leads to a consideration of key issues and perspectives that will furnish a framework for a sociologically informed account of disability. These are presented as a comparison between the current orthodoxy on disability – what is termed the 'individual' (or 'individualistic medical') approach – and the 'social model of disability' which has been championed by disability theorists, particularly in Britain. Taking as its starting-point this emphasis on the social construction of disability, the following section highlights the importance of comparative and historical perspectives by reviewing how the perception of disability has varied across cultures and over time. The final introductory task is to outline a sociological framework for exploring disability.

Developing a sociological imagination

C. Wright Mills (1970), in his celebrated essay on the sociological imagination, argued that sociology has a particular contribution to make in helping us see how many seemingly 'personal troubles', which affect individuals and their immediate relations with others, are more appropriately understood as 'public issues' which link to the institutions of society as a whole (p. 14). Hence, it is a primary goal of the sociological imagination to detail the connections between personal biography and wider historical and political circumstances:

> Deeply immersed in our daily routines, though, we hardly ever pause to think about the meaning of what we have gone through; even less often have we the opportunity to compare our private experience with the fate of others, to see the *social* in the *individual*, the *general* in the *particular*; this is precisely what sociologists can do for us. We would expect them to show how our individual *bio-*

graphies intertwine with the *history* we share with fellow human beings. (Bauman, 1990: 10)

The potential of sociological enquiry is that it encourages us to explore how familiar or common-sense ways of thinking and behaving can be interpreted in novel ways. As Berger (1963) reflected: 'The fascination of sociology lies in the fact that its perspective makes us see in a new light the very world in which we have lived all our lives' (p. 21). It does not mean replacing 'error' with 'unquestionable truth', rather the intention is to critically scrutinize beliefs and practices otherwise maintained without examination (Bauman, 1990).

This highlights a key feature which distinguishes sociological approaches: namely, the contention that so many apparently 'natural' attitudes, institutions and structures which are perceived as 'unchanging' are in fact heavily influenced by social factors and therefore both sustained and modified by human action. The overall objective is to convey how biography, structure and history interact. For example, the failure of a disabled individual to find paid employment might be explained in terms of personal shortcomings. However, if the overall rate of unemployment for disabled people is much higher than that recorded for the rest of the population, this suggests structural discrimination in the sphere of employment against disabled people generally, as well as possible connections with other disabling barriers. What had been regarded as an individual inadequacy is perhaps more plausibly explained as a collective social disadvantage, and thus the object of sociological interest (and possible public action). In short, the sociological imagination involves the 'dynamic interplay of biography, context and the values informing sociological reflection' (Barton, 1996: 4).

In addition, the sociological imagination takes up the claim that attitudes and behaviour which seem 'natural' are more appropriately understood as a social product. A comparative approach has great merit exactly because it militates against falling into the ethnocentric trap of assuming that the prevailing view of disability in British (or Western) society is replicated elsewhere. It is equally important to recover the 'world we have lost' to examine how and why attitudes and practices towards disability have varied historically. Hence, applying the sociological imagination to disability entails a 'critique of existing forms of society' and prompts an awareness of 'alternative futures' (Giddens, 1982a: 26). From this perspective, 'Sociology cannot be a neutral intellectual endeavour, indifferent to the practical consequences of its analysis for those whose conduct forms its object of study' (Giddens, 1982b: p. vii).

Comparative and historical perspectives

A sociological approach suggests that the common meanings associated with impairment and disability emerge out of specific social and cultural contexts. Disability does not have a universal character. Indeed, in some cultures and languages, there is no term for 'disability', and social 'difference' is categorized in many different ways. Some of the most detailed recent anthropological evidence on the diversity of cultural attitudes on this subject is provided in Ingstad and Whyte's (1995) collection, *Disability and Culture*. The editors reference studies of social participation in the Tuareg, for example, which is affected by a number of factors: 'old age and immaturity (making one physically dependent), illegitimate birth (making one socially anomalous), and ugliness (rendering it difficult to marry)' (Ingstad and Whyte, 1995: 6). They note a variety of 'faults', including 'deafness, excessive freckles, protruding navel, absentmindedness, and flabby or small buttocks' (quoted in Ingstad and Whyte, 1995: 6). What makes or undermines 'personhood' demonstrates extraordinary cultural variation. For many traditional cultures, 'Instead of seeing impairment in terms of ability to perform specific tasks, they ask about personhood in relation to cosmology' (Ingstad and Whyte, 1995: 37).

The Masai people of Kenya generally view congenital impairments as caused by 'nature' or 'God' (and witchcraft) and not as a source of individual blame. The Songye people of Zaire distinguish three categories of abnormal children: ceremonial, bad, and faulty. Ceremonial children, who include those born feet first, or with the umbilical cord round the neck, are marked in a positive way. Bad children are not considered human beings, but supernatural, from the anti-world of sorcerers, and include albino, dwarf and hydrocephalic children. Faulty children – for example those with polio, cerebral palsy, club feet – have an indeterminate status. Here the focus is not on improving their situation, but on interpreting the fault. Potential sources include: the physical environment (failure of parents to respect food or sex taboos); family members (bad relationships leading to sorcery); ancestors (lack of respect); or divine intervention.

In Songye, Masai and also Punan Bah cultures, disabled people are not regarded as a distinct group, but are distinguished according to the explanation and implication of the particular condition. Among the Punan Bah, people with physical impairments are not separated from the household, and share in production and consumption with the family. Most impairments are not stigmatized, although ugliness is. Similarly, with the Masai people: 'Physically impaired persons marry, become parents, and participate in all communal activities to the best of their abilities' (Talle, 1995: 69).

In many traditional societies, such as the Masai and Punan Bah, the key 'disabling' condition is failure to have children: parenthood is the key to adult status. Those without children of their own, including people with physical impairments or learning difficulties, are sometimes given children by other members of their family, so that they can acquire full personhood. Among the Songye, a disabled woman may not marry, but can conceive a child, living with her parents until the child can perform household tasks. In contrast: 'physical and mental capacities are not culturally constructed as differences having implications for a person's fulfilment in life' (Talle, 1995: 70).

However, the impact of contact with industrial capitalism has enforced changes in these traditional cultures. Impairment has become a more important source of disability. The advent of Western capitalist social relations in Sarawak, with the arrival of logging companies, undermines the Punan Bah cosmology as well as its socio-economic arrangements. With young men increasingly involved in wage-labour, and the traditional economy severely curbed, personhood is being redefined. As a consequence, disabled and elderly people have suffered a diminution in status and become more dependent on others. Similarly, whereas the traditional community organization of Masai society ensured that impairment was not a major obstacle to activity, because mutual aid and co-operation were encouraged, this has been threatened by the increasing disintegration of residence patterns into one-family households. The interdependence of cultural and material factors is graphically illustrated – with outcomes that transform the link between impairment and disability.

There are those who argue, like Scheer and Groce (1988), that small-scale, traditional societies provide forms of social participation and support for people with impairments which contrast sharply with the situation in more complex, industrial societies. As a result, personal identity is far less linked to individual impairment. This picture is illustrated in Nora Groce's (1985) own study of Martha's Vineyard in Massachusetts. This explores a community that contained a high proportion of people born with congenital deafness. As a result, the majority of the population, both deaf and hearing, became bilingual in a sign language. The barriers to social interaction between deaf and hearing populations erected elsewhere did not exist. Those born deaf in Martha's Vineyard worked, married, held public office and participated in the community social life in ways similar to everyone else.

However, others provide ample evidence that there is considerable variation between traditional societies. Hanks and Hanks (1948/1980) ground this diversity in contrasting economic or material conditions. They argue that a primary constraint is the level of economic stability and viability of the society: that is, the demand for different types of labour, the amount of surplus generated, and how it is distributed. In turn, this is affected by social structure – whether it is hierarchical or egalitarian, how achievement is defined, perceptions of age and sex, its relations with neighbouring societies, its aesthetic values, 'and many more functionally related factors' (1948: 13).

Ingstad and Whyte (1995: 14–15) pinpoint three key questions to help understand the relationship between forms of organization and disability: 'First, what is the ability of the family to care for an infirm member?' (However, what constitutes the 'family', and the meaning given to 'care' and 'infirmity' are historically and culturally variable.) The general suggestion is that growing economic pressure on families tends to encourage separate provision for those with impairments. Second, 'How does the occupational structure of the society incorporate people with impairments?' Typically, a more complex occupational structure and labour market throws up more difficulties for those with impairments who want to find work. And third, how far are there 'special programmes, institutions, and organisations for disabled people?' These may provide more options for disabled people, including special, often residential, institutions, although they may also restrict them from entering new contexts.

The value of this cross-cultural perspective is that it challenges our universalist assumptions about what is 'normal' in respect of impairment. The presumption that impairment is a commonly agreed condition and that it automatically generates negative reactions is contradicted by comparative research. This demonstrates how the concept of disability is historically specific. How does the 'individual model of disability' contrast with previously dominant approaches?

Medieval Christianity and impairment as sin

Ancient Judaism regarded many impairments and diseases as signs of wrongdoing, and a justification for separating people because of their supposed uncleanness and ungodliness. Leviticus, in the Old Testament, catalogues those human impairments which precluded the possessor from participating in religious rituals – crooked nose, sores, missing limb, leprosy and skin diseases, and crushed testicles (Leviticus 21: 16–20). Yet Judaism also prohibited infanticide of newborn children with an impairment, and emphasized the importance of providing 'charity' for the 'sick' and less well off.

Christianity exhibited a similarly ambivalent response, viewing some of those with impairments as warranting healing and general support, while also interpreting impairment as a punishment for sin. Throughout the 'Dark Ages', those with impairments were expected to contribute to the domestic economy. Those rejected by their families had few alternatives to relying on the haphazard benefits of charity and alms-giving for subsistence. In England, by the sixteenth century, the combination of a decline in the wealth and power of the Church, and a growing vagrant population due to plagues, poor harvests, and immigration from Ireland and Wales, meant that there was rising demand for charity and poor relief (Stone, 1985). The English Poor Law of 1601 is the first official recognition of the need for state intervention to control people with impairments. It also formerly accepted the location of disabled people within the 'deserving' poor.

Nevertheless, the hold of the Church on the public imagination and moral beliefs remained very strong. St Augustine claimed that impairment was a 'punishment for the fall of Adam and other sins' (Ryan and Thomas, 1980: 87). People with impairments provided living proof of Satan's existence and of his power over ordinary mortals. Thus, visibly impaired infants were seen as 'changelings' – the Devil's substitutes for human children. Bloch (1965: vol. i) similarly reports there was an 'astonishing sensibility to what were believed to be supernatural manifestations. It made people's minds constantly and almost morbidly attentive to all manner of signs, dreams and hallucinations' (p. 73). The Malleus Maleficarum of 1487 declared that such children were the product of the mother's involvement with sorcery and witchcraft (Haffter, 1968). In the notes of guidance on questions to be asked during the examination of witches, one was whether she had given birth to a changeling. Impairment was a source of fear, ridicule and mockery. During the sixteenth century, the birth of an impaired child was accepted as proof that the parents were involved in witchcraft, sinful practices, or had simply had wicked thoughts. 'The deformed or otherwise abnormal child now became a cause of great fear and pangs of conscience: "have we offended against God?" It also became a shameful stigma in the eyes of society and a reason for isolation, ostracism and even persecution' (Haffter, 1968: 61). Medieval Christianity similarly explained the disordered mind in terms of demonic forces. Indeed, such ideas can still be found in current-day folklore.

Throughout this period there was an uneasy stand-off between religion and medicine. In popular medieval culture, shrines and pilgrimages were a traditional feature of healing, and there was a long record of conflict as the Church sought to maintain its regulation of medicine. There was opposition to medical charges (as contrary to the view of healing as Christian charity). Where religion saw impairment as part of God's design, medical intervention seemed to contradict this. And finally, the classical view of medicine was secular, and ran contrary to orthodox and popular religious beliefs about health and healing.

Industrialization and medicalization

The eighteenth century witnessed a significant intensification of the commercialization of land and agriculture, and the growth of industrialization and urbanization. The consequential impact on community and family life radically affected established social networks and social relationships. As far as disabled people were concerned, the speed of factory work, or working to the rhythms of machinery, often undertaking complex, dextrous tasks, the regimented discipline, and production demands '. . . were a highly unfavourable change from the slower, more self-determined methods of work into which many handicapped people had been integrated' (Ryan and Thomas, 1980: 101). What was tolerable for those with perceived impairments, which were perhaps not even acknowledged as such in the slower and more flexible pattern of agricultural or domestic production, became a source of friction and lost income within the new industrial system: 'The asylums of the nineteenth century were thus as much the result of far-reaching changes in work and family life, and corresponding methods of containing the poor, as they were the inspiration of philanthropists and scientists' (Ryan and Thomas, 1980: 101).

Oliver in *The Politics of Disablement* (1990) carries this materialist analysis further in exploring how people with impairments were categorized as a 'social problem' – no longer easily integrated into the economic system and a potential drain on social welfare. With the Poor Laws increasingly unable to cope with the demand for 'relief', reforms introduced in Britain in 1834 emphasized national uniformity of provision, denial of relief outside an institution, and deterrence as the basis for setting benefit levels. This was also a period when various institutional solutions were widely promoted.

The rise of the scientific medical profession at this time and its success in medicalizing illness and impairment gave legitimacy to radical shifts in the treatment of disabled people – characterized by professional dominance, and expanding segregation in institutions. There was an expectation of improvement in the condition of those with impairments, but in practice the establishment of scientific medicine imposed new forms of social surveillance and discipline for the disabled population. An increasing range of techniques was introduced to identify, classify, and regulate sick and disabled people. This heralded the 'therapeutic state' with its novel and polarized conceptions of normal and abnormal, sane and insane, healthy and sick.

In Britain, the new workhouse population included as one of its categories the 'aged and infirm'. The latter were subsequently separated from: the 'sick', the 'insane' and 'defectives' (Stone, 1985). The intention, although not always implemented, was that the 'sick' – a mixture of acutely and chronically ill people – should only be incarcerated if there was no alternative, in contrast to the 'insane', who were singled out for special institutional provision away from the mainstream of community life (Scull, 1984). Those defined as 'defectives' – initially those with visual, hearing or communication impairments, but extended in the early twentieth century to include those diagnosed as 'mentally subnormal' and those with epilepsy – attracted particular attention from philanthropic and charitable organizations. With concern at the rising costs of outdoor relief, the physical status of the working classes, and their capacity for military service, professionals were ever more involved in identifying and disciplining those elements in the population thought unable to contribute adequately to social and economic life.

Attempts to contain and confine proliferated: asylums for the mentally ill were the first to be built, followed by residential and educational facilities for those classified as 'blind', 'deaf', or as people with an intellectual impairment. The segregation, isolation, and infantilization of disabled patients became the way forward. The asylum population rose from 3 per 10,000 at the beginning of the nineteenth century to 30 per 10,000 at its end (Scull, 1979). A combination of medical, social and administrative reasons underpinned this trend (Parker, 1988). The new scientific and medical vocabulary took root. Further intellectual justification for divisions and hierarchies was generated by Social Darwinism and arguments for the 'survival of the fittest'. Those identified as 'abnormal' inspired wider fears of moral collapse, as illustrated by reports that intellectual impairment was linked to sexual and criminal deviance (Ryan and Thomas, 1980). Discussions of disability were also mediated by racist claims. Thus, the label 'mongolian idiot' became fixed in the 'mental deficiency' literature. The 'idiot' became an alien threat to civilized society.

Disabled people came increasingly to the attention of new medical specialisms and professionals. A whole new field of rehabilitative medicine and allied professional intervention was gradually established 'for' disabled people. It became the 'natural' way to deal with disabled people, just as impairment became the dominant explanation for what happened in their lives. The formal emphasis was on skills development and helping people to take care of themselves. The goal was to identify ways to help them fit in or cope with 'normal' life and expectations so that they did not become a burden on the rest of society. This medicalization of disability represented the establishment of an 'individual' model of disability that became the professional, policy and lay orthodoxy through the twentieth century.

A tale of two models

In this section, we will explore in more detail the dominant, individual, model of disability, and then contrast it with a social model of disability that was originally advanced by a small group of disabled activists, and which, without taking direct inspiration from any sociological perspective, emulates the critical approach endorsed by the sociological imagination thesis.

The individual model of disability

By the beginning of the twentieth century, the individual approach to disability – which sees its diagnosis and solution in medical knowledge – was securely entrenched. The focus is on bodily 'abnormality', disorder or deficiency, and the way in which this in turn 'causes' some degree of 'disability' or functional limitation. For example, people who have quadriplegia cannot use their arms and are therefore unable to wash or dress themselves. However, this functional 'incapacity' is used as the basis for a wider classification of the individual as (an) 'invalid'. Once they have been categorized in this way, the 'disability' becomes their defining characteristic and their incapacity is generalized. This forms the basis for a 'personal tragedy' approach, where the individual is regarded as a victim, and as someone who is in need of 'care and attention', and dependent on others – a perspective which has been at the heart of contemporary social welfare policies designed to help disabled people cope with 'their disability' (Oliver, 1983, 1990; Finkelstein, 1993a).

The recommended solution lies in curative and rehabilitative medical intervention, with an increasing involvement of allied health practitioners, psychologists and educationalists. To acquire an impairment is to become the object of professional attention. This 'expert' defines an individual's needs and how these should be met. The aim is to overcome, or at least minimize, the negative consequences of the individual's 'disability'. The rehabilitative focus has underpinned a growing range of policy initiatives designed by various professional 'experts' to address the 'special needs' and 'personal difficulties' of disabled individuals.

The basic medical concern is to diagnose the bodily or intellectual 'abnormality' and advise on appropriate treatment. There is an associated administrative and policy interest in translating the individual's 'disability' into specific needs – for welfare benefits and services (Albrecht, 1976). In Britain, this has stimulated a debate about the most appropriate definition and measure of 'disability'.

Initially, the individual's 'abnormality or loss' was translated into a particular level of incapacity. For example, the British National Insurance Benefit Regulations in the 1960s advised that the loss of fingers and a leg amputated below the knee constituted a 50 per cent disability, while the loss of three fingers and the amputation of a foot or the loss of an eye translated into a 30 per cent rating (Sainsbury, 1973: 26–7). Such a mechanistic approach (though still an element in the assessment process for the Severe Disablement Allowance) came under increasing criticism from policy-makers and social researchers. There was also a widening of the definition of 'disability' to include:

1   'anatomical, physiological or psychological abnormality or loss', such as those without an arm or a leg, or who are 'blind, or deaf or paralysed'; and
2   chronic illness which interferes with physiological or psychological processes, such as arthritis, epilepsy and schizophrenia. (Townsend, 1979: 686–7)

In addition, there was a reinterpretation of physical incapacity so that it was now defined in terms of the inability to perform essential activities of daily living. This approach underpinned the first national surveys of 'disability' in Britain conducted by the Office of Population Censuses and Surveys (OPCS – renamed the Office for National Statistics in 1997) in 1968–9 (Harris et al., 1971), and in the 1980s (Martin et al., 1988).

The focus of this debate was on technical, measurement issues about the best predictor of an individual's service needs, such as: the range of activities included; whether all should be equally weighted; whether allowance should be made for changing capacity over time and between social contexts, as well as across social groups (Sainsbury, 1973; Townsend, 1979). The trend has been to extend the range of activity restrictions beyond immediate self-care, such as washing and toileting, to include a range of other 'everyday' activities (Charlton et al., 1983). Equivalent indices have also been constructed for those with intellectual impairment and illness – for example the Psychiatric Status Schedule (Hertz et al., 1977).

The most influential intervention in these debates was the World Health Organization's (WHO) decision to complement its *International Classification of Disease* (WHO, 1976) with a scheme that detailed the consequences of disease. These discussions resulted in a threefold distinction in its new *International Classification of Impairments, Disabilities and Handicaps (ICIDH)* which was introduced in 1981. The explanatory document (WHO, 1980) defined the key terms as follows:

•   *Impairment* 'Any loss or abnormality of psychological, physiological or anatomical structure or function' (p. 27).

- *Disability* 'Any restriction or lack (resulting from an impairment) of ability to perform an activity in the manner or within the range considered normal for a human being' (p. 28).
- *Handicap* 'A disadvantage for a given individual, resulting from an impairment or disability, that limits or prevents the fulfilment of a role (depending on age, sex, social and cultural factors) for that individual' (p. 29).

In shorthand terms, 'impairment' includes those parts or systems of the body which do not work 'properly', and 'disability' centres on those things that people cannot do, primarily basic skills of everyday living. Most of the novelty of the WHO schema lies in the interpretation of 'handicap'. This extends the notion of 'consequences' to difficulties in carrying out social roles, while acknowledging that these vary across social groups and cultural contexts. The disablement process is represented in terms of distinctive but linked areas of consequences (WHO 1980: 30) (see diagram below).

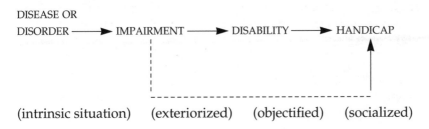

DISEASE OR
DISORDER ——▶ IMPAIRMENT ——▶ DISABILITY ——▶ HANDICAP

(intrinsic situation) (exteriorized) (objectified) (socialized)

There is a close correspondence between this *ICIDH* approach and that followed in the OPCS national surveys of disability conducted between 1985 and 1988. The latter selected as the main areas of functional limitation:

- Reaching and stretching
- Dexterity
- Seeing
- Hearing
- Personal care
- Continence
- Communication
- Locomotion
- Behaviour
- Intellectual functioning

An overall measure of ten levels of severity of 'disability' was constructed for the OPCS study based on the above activities. This emphasis on the individual's functional limitations has won international favour. As an illustration, the Americans with Disabilities Act of 1990 defines disability as an 'impairment that substantially limits one or more of the major life activities', with 'normal' functioning again the yardstick.

The OPCS survey was based on a sample of disabled adults and children who lived in both 'communal establishments' and private households. The 'entry criteria' were amended in comparison with its earlier study (Harris et al., 1971) to include those with a 'mental illness and handicap' and those with less severe impairments (Martin et al., 1988). As indicated in table 2.1, it was estimated that there were 6.2 million disabled adults in Britain. A majority of this disabled population was over 60 years of age, with more disabled women than men. Increasing age was also closely associated with 'severity of disability'. Almost a third of the total disabled population were ranked in the two 'least severe' categories.

The *ICIDH*/OPCS definitions and measurement of disability have generated considerable critical debate. First, this approach

Table 2.1 Estimates of numbers of disabled adults in Great Britain by age and severity category for women and men (thousands)

Severity category	Men				Women				Total population
	Age group				*Age group*				
				All				*All*	*Total*
	16–59	*60–74*	*75+*	*ages*	*16–59*	*60–74*	*75+*	*ages*	*population*
10	23	17	24	64	22	18	105	146	(210)
9	31	42	52	125	47	59	135	240	(365)
8	49	52	50	151	62	59	125	245	(396)
7	59	53	51	163	77	81	165	322	(485)
6	73	58	49	179	103	101	163	367	(546)
5	96	90	69	255	134	139	180	453	(708)
4	105	108	70	283	140	133	147	420	(703)
3	117	134	70	320	124	154	151	429	(749)
2	121	187	85	393	112	179	155	447	(840)
1	231	273	107	612	203	218	166	587	(1,189)
Total	904	1,014	627	2,544	1,023	1,139	1,494	3,656	(6,200)

'All ages' and 'Total population' figures may not add up because of rounding for individual age groups.

(10 = highest severity)

Source: adapted from Martin et al., 1988: table 3.6.

relies primarily on medical definitions, and use of a bio-physio-logical definition of 'normality'. Even then, the identification of boundary lines has been questioned: for example, at what point does blood pressure or body weight and shape move from 'normal' to 'pathological'? In practice, the meanings and consequences associated, for example, with having a visual or hearing impairment are not automatic but situationally and socially mediated. Spectacles are a necessary aid for many with a visual impairment, but they have been so 'normalized' that wearing glasses is no longer regarded as a mark of a disabled person – at least in most Western societies. The contemporary pressures to achieve specific standards of 'fitness' and 'competence' owe much to culturally generated criteria about what it means to be 'normal' or 'able-bodied'. Hence, the notion of 'normality' – as in the *ICIDH* definition of handicap – is heavily laden with able-bodied assumptions and prejudices – not least that everyone else should strive to become 'normal' like them. It also underpins the search for medical cures to 'disability': with 'magic bullet' advances represented as the saviour of disabled people to the exclusion of any other social intervention.

Second, in both the *ICIDH* schema and the OPCS studies 'impairment' is identified as the cause of both 'disability' and 'handicap'. Hence, the way to overcome 'disability' and social disadvantage is through appropriate medical and allied rehabilitative interventions. In contrast, the environment is represented as 'neutral', and any negative consequences of this approach for the person with an impairment are regarded as inevitable or acceptable rather than as disabling barriers. The possibility of a malleable environment, which can be altered by human action, is similarly ignored.

By regarding impairment as the 'cause' of disability and handicap, medical and therapeutic action is invested with primary significance. From another perspective, legislative changes to reform social policy, or guarantee disabled people full citizenship rights, are more appropriate. In the individual model, the definition of disability as a medical problem presumes a corresponding solution and so encourages the domination of disabled people's lives by a vast army of allied professionals.

Third, the individual model places people with an accredited impairment in a dependent position. Their condition is medicalized, and this ensures that they rely on professional experts and others to provide therapeutic and social support. Professional experts largely define disabled people's needs, and little weight is given to disabled people's own experiences.

The individual model presumes that disabled people are largely inert: acted upon rather than active. They can do no more than rely on others for 'care' or charity. Any intervention in their circumstances depends on policy-makers and service providers. They are encouraged to adapt and adjust as individuals to their 'disability'. This disadvantage is perceived as an individual, not a collective, matter. This further presumes an uninformed lay client deferring to a professional expert, and ignores the existence of power differentials and the possibility that lay and professional interests might diverge. The disabled person in the individual model is rendered childlike in their perceived inability to speak for themselves.

Fourth, the disabled person is expected to make every effort to make the best of their circumstances by individual adjustment and coping strategies. This subordination is further confirmed at the experiential level. The individual model presumes that the 'disability' takes over the individual's identity and constrains 'unrealistic' hopes and ambitions. Those with a perceived impairment accept being defined as not 'normal' and in some way 'defective'. Whether they are born with an accredited impairment, or whether it is acquired later in life, individuals are socialized into a traditional disabled role and identity, and expected to submit to professional intervention in order to facilitate their adjustment to their 'personal tragedy'. This has been a particular feature of psychological approaches to disability, and it has exerted a significant impact on the 'care' provided by a range of allied health and social welfare professionals.

This individualistic approach is also a feature of psychological studies which explore the impact of an impairment on a person's emotional and psychological well-being. For example, Weller and Miller (1977) outline a four-stage process of personal adjustment through which people accommodate to a severe spinal cord injury. The initial reaction of *shock* and horror is followed by *denial* or despair that any recovery is possible, leading to *anger* at others, and finally to *depression* as a necessary preliminary to coming to terms with their diminished circumstances. Hence, the presumption of a fifth stage, termed 'acceptance' or 'adjustment', which may not be reached until one or two years later. Equally significant, those who stray from this prescribed script – by not being depressed and/or in a state of denial – run the risk of being regarded as abnormal and in need of psychological guidance

(J. Oliver, 1995). The typical emphasis is on helping individuals to pass through a grieving process associated with their 'complex of losses'. In so doing, it sets aside the influence of social or material factors, including social policies, in helping an individual disabled person to 'cope' better, or to become more independent.

The criticism of the *ICIDH* advanced particularly by disabled people has led to the production of a revised version which is currently undergoing field testing in preparation for its final release in the year 2000. The '*ICIDH*-2' adopts a so-called 'biopsychosocial' model, which endeavours to synthesize the medical and social approaches to disablement. By separating 'impairments', 'activity limitations' and 'participation restrictions', it attempts to establish a framework which identifies those aspects which are properly the subject of medical intervention from other areas where social and environmental barriers are the major factors. However, the *ICIDH*-2 remains a classification of the consequences of health conditions, even if disablement is recast as an intrinsic part of the human condition rather than the polar opposite of 'normality'. The opposition to such a classification system (both generally and to specific instruments) is unlikely to be abated.

In summary, the central thrust of the individual model is to cast disability as a personal tragedy where the individual concerned must depend on others for support: 'Hence the assumption is, in health terms, that disability is a pathology and, in welfare terms, that disability is a social problem' (Oliver, 1996b: 30).

Towards a social model of disability

During the 1970s and 1980s, disabled activists and their organizations voiced increasing criticism of the individual, medical model of disability. In developing what became known as a social approach to disability, disabled people in Britain argued that it is society which disables people with impairments, and therefore any meaningful solution must be directed at societal change rather than individual adjustment and rehabilitation. The social model riposte to the individual, medical approach is that 'disability is not the measles' (Rioux and Bach, 1994).

The Union of the Physically Impaired Against Segregation (UPIAS) was in the vanguard of those calling for an alternative model of disability. In its manifesto document *Fundamental Principles* (1976), UPIAS placed the responsibility for disability squarely on society's failures: 'In our view it is society which disables physically impaired people. Disability is something imposed on top of our impairments by the way we are unnecessarily isolated and excluded from full participation in society. Disabled people are therefore an oppressed group in society' (UPIAS, 1976: 14).

The close connection between impairment, disability and handicap is rejected in the UPIAS model. While it broadly accepted the medical definition of impairment, the meaning of disability was turned on its head:

- *Impairment* Lacking part or all of a limb, or having a defective limb, organ or mechanism of the body.
- *Disability* The disadvantage or restriction of activity caused by a contemporary social organisation which takes no or little account of people who have physical impairments and thus excludes them from participation in the mainstream of social activities. (UPIAS, 1976: 3–4)

Subsequent discussions among disabled people and their organizations have amended the reference to 'physical impairments' so that any impairment (including sensory and intellectual examples) fall within the potential scope of disability.

Whereas impairment is regarded as an individual attribute, disability is not. Instead it is described as 'the outcome of an oppressive relationship between people with . . . impairments and the rest of society' (Finkelstein, 1980: 47). Once defined as a disabled person, the individual is stigmatized, and social expectations about how, for example, those with a visual or hearing impairment should behave, or what they are capable of doing, exert an influence independent of their impairment. The assumption is that the form of disability – that is, social oppression – is universal is rejected by those following a social approach who point to the cultural and historical variation which characterizes disability.

Similarly, from the social model perspective, the measurement of disability adopted by the OPCS disability surveys requires substantial refurbishment. It is about a focus on 'disabling barriers and attitudes'. Hence an alternative approach to measuring disability is required. An indication of how the survey researcher who adopts a social model approach would focus on different issues is illustrated by Mike Oliver's (1990: 7–8) alternative formulation of the questions used to assess 'disability' in the 1980s by OPCS:

1 OPCS: *'Can you tell me what is wrong with you?'*
Oliver: 'Can you tell me what is wrong with society?'

2 OPCS: *'What complaint causes your difficulty in holding, gripping or turning things?'*
Oliver: 'What defects in the design of everyday equipment like jars, bottles and tins causes you difficulty in holding, gripping or turning them?'

3 OPCS: *'Are your difficulties in understanding people mainly due to a hearing problem?'*
Oliver: 'Are your difficulties in understanding people mainly due to their inability to communicate with you?'

4 OPCS: *'Do you have a scar, blemish or deformity which limits your daily activities?'*
Oliver: 'Do other people's reactions to any scar, blemish or deformity you may have limit your daily activities?'

5 OPCS: *'Have you attended a special school because of a long-term health problem or disability?'*
Oliver: 'Have you attended a special school because of your education authority's policy of sending people with your health problem/disability to such places?'

6 OPCS: *'Does your health problem/disability prevent you from going out as often or as far as you would like?'*
Oliver: 'What is it about the local environment that makes it difficult for you to get about in your neighbourhood?'

7 OPCS: *'Does your health problem/disability make it difficult for you to travel by bus?'*
Oliver: 'Are there any transport or financial problems which prevent you from going out as often or as far as you would like?'

8 OPCS: *'Does your health problem/disability affect your work in any way at present?'*
Oliver: 'Do you have problems at work because of the physical environment or the attitudes of others?'

9 OPCS: *'Does your health problem/disability mean that you need to live with relatives or someone else who can help or look after you?'*
Oliver: 'Are community services so poor that you need to rely on relatives or someone else to provide you with the right level of personal assistance?'

10 OPCS: *'Does your present accommodation have any adaptations because of your health problem/disability?'*
Oliver: Did the poor design of your house mean that you had to have it adapted to suit your needs?'

The social model approach concentrates on a set of causes established externally: that is, as obstacles imposed on disabled people which limit their opportunities to participate in society. Hence, measures of disability should provide a way of monitoring the effects of physical, social and economic disabling barriers experienced by disabled people – their social exclusion – and the impact of anti-discrimination policies. In contrast, 'personal tragedy theory has served to individualize the problems of disability and hence leave social and economic structures untouched' (Oliver, 1986: 16).

In advancing a critique of the personal tragedy model, the disabled people's movement has generated a social model of disability which argues for a radical reformulation of our understanding of disability (table 2.2). It advances very different answers to key questions such as: 'What is the nature of disability? What causes it? How is it experienced?' (Oliver, 1996b: 29–30). This goes beyond a social model standpoint, to the development of a more comprehensive social *theory* of disability: 'the social model of disability is not a substitute for social theory, a materialist history of disability nor an explanation of the welfare state' (Oliver, 1996b: 41).

Of course, a 'materialist history' is but one among a range of theoretical explanations used by sociologists. It is here that a 'sociology of disability' must explore in detail the argument that 'society disables' people with impairments. Contributions to the

Table 2.2   Two models of disability

Individual model	*Social model*
personal tragedy theory	social oppression theory
personal problem	social problem
individual treatment	social action
medicalization	self-help
professional dominance	individual and collective responsibility
expertise	experience
individual identity	collective identity
prejudice	discrimination
care	rights
control	choice
policy	politics
individual adjustment	social change

Source: adapted from Oliver, 1996a: table 2.1.

development of a social theory of disability have ranged widely. It is important to consider work in allied areas, such as medical sociology and its analysis of what is termed 'chronic illness and disability' (Bury, 1997). In a similar way, the social model's references to 'disabling barriers' demands a more comprehensive examination of the processes and structures associated with social oppression and discrimination, whether at everyday levels, or in the workings of the state and social policy. Forms of domination also raise complex issues relating to culture and politics: not simply as sites of domination, but as arenas of resistance and challenge by disabled people.

The social model focuses on the experience of disability, but not as something which exists purely at the level of individual psychology, or even interpersonal relations. Instead, it considers a wide range of social and material factors and conditions, such as family circumstances, income and financial support, education, employment, housing, transport and the built environment, and more besides. At the same time, the individual and collective conditions of disabled people are not fixed, and the experience of disability therefore also demonstrates an 'emergent' and temporal character. This spans the individual's experience of disability, in the context of their overall biography, social relationships and life history, the wider circumstances of disabling barriers and attitudes in society, and the impact of state policies and welfare support systems.

Yet the claims of the social model should not be exaggerated:

> The social model is not about showing that every dysfunction in our bodies can be compensated for by a gadget, or good design, so that everybody can work an 8-hour day and play badminton in the evenings. It's a way of demonstrating that everyone – even someone who has no movement, no sensory function and who is going to die tomorrow – has the right to a certain standard of living and to be treated with respect. (Vasey, 1992a: 44)

Sociological issues and approaches

The central issues that have dominated theoretical debates in sociology may be summarized as follows:

> Firstly, sociology is concerned to understand the meaning of social action, that is the subjective perspective, emotions and feelings of

human agents as social individuals. Secondly, sociology is concerned with the relationship between agency and structure. Sociology attempts to explore the relationship between human action and the structural determination of social relations by certain constraining elements which in general we can describe as power relations. Thirdly, classical sociology has been organised around the problem of social order, that is the question of social integration through the presence of consensus and constraint in human life. Quite simply, sociology is concerned with the ultimate question of 'How is society possible?' Finally, sociology is about the analysis of the social processes and circumstances which constantly disrupt and disorganise the fragile order of social relations and social exchange. We can summarise this problem as the question of social inequality, because it is through an analysis of the unequal distribution of power (in terms of class, status and power) that we can begin to understand the de-stabilisation of social relations and social systems through organised conflict and individual resistance. (Turner, 1987: 3)

First, sociology concentrates on social action, that is, behaviour which has meaning to those involved. To understand the social world it is necessary to explore its meaning for social actors, and how its uncertainties and dilemmas are navigated. The focus is on people's subjective 'definition of the situation', their thoughts, feelings, and experiences. From an *interactionist* perspective, social life is possible because of communication and shared meanings, and the central task is to understand how people present themselves and negotiate social situations. In turn, the sociologist, as an observer of social action, attempts to 'tell it as it is' from the point of view of those being studied. This stands in direct contrast to a *positivist* tradition – which holds that there is one social reality, and it can only be revealed by adopting an objective approach associated with the methodology of the natural sciences, which includes testing hypotheses and quantitative data measurement.

Second, there is an assumption that human beings are reflective and have a capacity for choice or 'agency'. They can view their actions both as subjects and objects. That is, human beings are viewed as creative social actors. Nevertheless, individuals are also constrained in what they think and do. This has led to considerable debate about the relative importance of *agency* and *structure*. Those approaches which emphasize structural factors highlight the ways in which social behaviour is shaped and constrained. From this perspective, individual behaviour and attitudes have their bases in the social circumstances and the social groups to which people belong. In contrast, other approaches represent social action as far less certain and social interaction as more open to 'negotiation'.

Third, classical sociology initiated a debate about the maintenance of social order, and how potential disruption is contained. Again, sociological traditions tend to polarize, in this case over whether societies are characterized more by *consensus* or by *conflict*, and the structures and processes which underpin that situation. Consensus accounts argue that social stability is maintained because people generally accept the benefits of co-operation, while also recognizing the legitimacy of political regulation. Conversely, in conflict approaches, society is distinguished by diverse and frequently conflicting interests. The task for dominant social groups is to find ways to perpetuate and enhance their privileged position, while achieving the compliance of subordinate groups, whether by the use of covert influence or by exercising overt power. More specifically, this model considers what are the key institutional forms of social control, and how these contribute to the production and regulation of disability.

Finally, sociological debates have stressed the existence of inequalities and disadvantages generally in society. Inequalities of power and wealth are related to the perception and pattern of social conflict. The analysis of inequality has been particularly concerned with social class, but this has increasingly been supplemented by accounts which extend the bases for social exclusion and inequality to a much wider range of social divisions, including gender, 'race–ethnicity' and age. Moreover, disability has become a more salient and significant factor for a rising proportion of the population, particularly in the West. There is a growth in the number of people with accredited impairments, which cuts across other lines of social division. It is particularly related to an ageing population and the increasingly complex technological character of contemporary society. Hence, the importance of exploring the extent to which there is a parallel material and normative divide linked to disability that emulates more 'established' social divisions.

Theoretical levels and perspectives

How then do these general theoretical concerns translate into a sociological map for investigating disability? For analytical purposes, it is helpful to differentiate between individual, social (group) and societal levels of enquiry (Turner, 1987; Layder, 1997). Table 2.3 illustrates some of the potential applications of different sociological approaches to the study of disability and impairment. First, there should be a focus on exploring the experience of disability at the micro-level, with particular reference to the attitudes and feelings of the individual with an impairment. It is important to generate an account of how their self-identity links with everyday routines and behaviour, and how this has changed over time. There is an associated interest in face-to-face interaction, ranging broadly across more informal contexts such as the household, and more organized settings such as the workplace or residential institution. A number of interactionist and interpretative perspectives, such as symbolic interactionism (the study of the relationship between self and society that focuses on symbolic processes of communication) and phenomenology (the interpretation of the everyday activities and routines people employ to give meaning to social life), have been adopted at this level.

These 'experiential' and interactionist approaches are already widely favoured in studies of impairment and disability, with a concentration on the ways in which these constitute a threat to the individual's sense of self-identity. A similar focus might explore disability not as a permanent position but as a 'career' which is affected by changing personal and social circumstances and contexts, and interactions with others, including, most significantly, professional experts. The outcome may be compliance and reciprocity or conflict, but the crucial aspect for micro-level approaches is that the outcome is part of a negotiated and emergent, rather than fixed or determined, social process.

At the second level, attention turns to social roles and norms, and the social construction of concepts, such as disability, impairment and stigma, through which individuals are classified and regulated by the main institutions of social control. It also extends to the perception of the 'disabled body' itself as the product of social and cultural practices. This approach is widely used by medical sociologists to analyse illness as a social (rather than biological) state, by concentrating on entry into a specialized role which facilitates a person's adaptation and adjustment to their condition. If the 'sick role' is usually thought of as a temporary status, more complex questions are posed by the suggestions of a 'disabled' or 'impaired' role, which might imply longer-term and more substantial changes in people's lives. The emergence of specialized, bureaucratic institutions (spanning health, education and

Table 2.3 Levels of sociological analysis

Level	Topic	Perspective
Individual	Experience of disability and impairment	Phenomenology; (symbolic) interactionism
Social	Socio-cultural categories of disability; identity politics	Role theory; labelling theory; social constructionism
Societal	Social welfare systems; politics of disability	Functionalism; political economy, neo-Marxism

Source: adapted from Turner, 1987: figure 1.

welfare sectors) with interests in, and responsibilities for, disabled people provides a further dimension for sociological analysis. This identifies 'middle-range theory', where an attempt is made to bridge the gulf between general explanations of society and micro-level accounts of everyday life.

The third or 'societal' level of analysis encompasses studies of the overall organization of systems of health, education and social welfare for disabled people, how these link to the state, economy and social policy. It extends to issues of conflict and power, social disadvantage and discrimination. Society is seen as composed of social groups with diverse and competing interests. Social order is fragile and typically maintained by dominant social groups which force or persuade weaker social groups into a subordinate position. Inequalities in power and other valued resources provide the bases for dominance and conflict. In any society, one section has access to disproportionate power, economic resources and knowledge. However, social domination may be achieved by persuasion, overt control and constraint, as well as by more covert manipulation, or 'ideological domination'. At the same time, it is important to examine how far social order and relations are destabilized through individual resistance and collective mobilization.

These 'macro' issues have been addressed by a diverse group of structuralist and systems approaches associated with several theoretical perspectives, as diverse as functionalism and various 'political economy' accounts. Among the latter, neo-Marxist or 'materialist' analyses have been particularly influential in explaining the structural relationship between capitalism, power and inequality. This has raised specific questions about the institutional and policy links between the state and organized medicine, while its practitioners enjoy power, status and material rewards that rank them within the dominant classes. At the same time, there has been considerable criticism of the downgrading of social divisions other than social class, such as gender and 'race–ethnicity'.

A more recent influence on social theory has come from post-modernism. This has broken with the belief in a single, progressively evolving, reality or truth. Instead it has emphasized the existence of multiple realities, discontinuity and difference, while also challenging the notion of traditional authority and hierarchies of knowledge. This links with a parallel literature which has criticized the dominant interpretation of modern, industrial capitalist society and suggested that a significant transition to a postmodern society and culture is under way. This is evidenced by recent trends in industrialized societies towards greater diversity, new lines of social fragmentation, changing bases for social conflict and a more pluralist context generally. More specifically, there are claims of a transformation in such key areas as industrial organization, the class system, and cultural allegiances. The exact consequences for specific groups, such as disabled people, will vary and need to be explored in more detail.

While distinguishing these levels for analytical purposes, it is important to establish links across them – both in theory and in practice. A sociological framework for studying disability must be multi-level so that it incorporates analyses of the experience of disability at the individual level, the social construction of disability and associated 'middle-range' theorizing, together with the broader analysis of societal power and social inequalities. It should also be multi-dimensional in the sense that key concepts, such as power, will be integrated at all levels of analysis. For example, a major criticism of 'individual level' enquiries is that they tend to ignore or downplay issues surrounding social structure, power and social inequalities. Conversely, 'societal level' approaches are relatively indifferent to the ways in which individuals experience social oppression.

The sociological study of disability thus draws on a broad spectrum of competing theoretical perspectives and paradigms. The greatest stimulus to those engaged in studying disability has been generated by those working in one of the following broad areas: functionalism, interactionism, a political economy/conflict approach and, most recently, feminism and structuralism or social constructionism. However, since the 1970s, functionalism has been

a diminishing influence, while more recently, a social constructionist approach – now particularly associated with the writings of
Michel Foucault – has been influential in analysing the social creation of ideas about disease and the body – what had hitherto been
regarded as 'stable realities' (Nettleton, 1995). In practice, the sociological study of disability has not always mirrored trends in the
discipline more generally, but has been mediated through the sub-
specialism of medical sociology (the sociology of health and
illness), and the specific debates and theoretical approaches which
have exerted influence on its enquiries.

Our argument is for theoretical breadth in developing a sociological account of disability. This will comprise a study of the
experience of disability, and its variation across social contexts and
groups; an analysis of the social processes by which perceived
impairments become the basis for disablement; an analysis of how
people with impairments are dealt with by professional (and
other) agencies of social control; and a discussion of the political
economy of the structural conditions and policy responses which
produce impairment and sustain disability. Particular interest lies
in the impact of recent theoretical debates on sociology, notably
social constructionism and feminism, as well as the suggested shift
towards a postmodern society.

Review

A theoretically informed sociology will approach disability as a
social state rather than as biological difference. Attention is given
to the role of choice, meaning and agency in the experience of
impairment/disability. This links with analyses of the social construction of disability – across societies and over time – although
the complexity of this process should not be underestimated. If
disabled people are characterized by their separation from the
'normal' population, specific representations of disability may be
both contested and contradictory. The general trend since the nineteenth century, in Western societies, has entailed a medical take-
over of disability and the intervention of a multitude of allied
health and social welfare practitioners. Disabled people have been
effectively marginalized and excluded from the 'mainstream' of
social life; and this aspect of disabling society needs to be explored
in the context of unequal power and social resources.

Over the last two centuries, disabled people have been kept

more 'out of sight', and disability has almost been a 'taboo' subject. The fact that disability is now being subjected to social and political analysis is due, not to the work of sociologists, but to the pioneering studies of disabled people themselves. Recent decades are characterized by disabled people 'fighting back'. This is evident in their promotion of a social model in opposition to the traditional orthodoxy. It has been reinforced by a significant politicization of disabled people and their organizations, on an international scale, that can claim to be a disabled people's movement of social, cultural and political protest. This story continues in the next chapter with a review of sociological approaches to 'chronic illness and disability'.

3

Sociological Approaches to Chronic Illness and Disability

The aim of this chapter is to review the medical sociology literature on chronic illness and disability. Although sociologists have seen themselves as engaged in a wide-ranging critique of the bio-medical model of health and illness, disability theorists have charged that they have 'failed to challenge the individualization and medicalization of disability' (Oliver, 1996b: 18). This silence is attributed to the 'undoubted influence of American sociological theorists such as Parsons, Becker and Goffman on medical sociology in Britain' (Oliver, 1996b: 19). Certainly, medical sociologists have given little credence to the social model approach as it is elaborated by disability theorists (Bury, 1997). Nevertheless, most sociologists clearly differentiate their analyses of health and illness from a bio-medical perspective. One objective of this chapter is therefore to explore the key issues identified in sociological accounts. It will be argued that an emphasis on the divide between medical sociologists and disability theorists cuts off both 'camps' from debates of potentially mutual benefit. Furthermore, this dispute is not simply about the definition of disability, but also about the merits of different sociological perspectives. At the present time, disability theory in Britain is particularly influenced by neo-Marxist, structural analyses, whereas the sociology of chronic illness is largely under the sway of interactionist and interpretative approaches which concentrate on 'experiential' accounts.

Sick role behaviour

Until the 1950s, the (bio)medical model of disease and health was not deemed an appropriate subject for sociological enquiry. A change was signalled with the publication of *The Social System* by Talcott Parsons (1951), which included a chapter on modern medical practice. This is set within his consensualist explanation of how social order and the stability of the social system is maintained. To have a properly functioning society all its members must play their appropriate social roles. This is where the needs of the 'individual' and the 'system' intertwine. Health is defined as a 'normal' and stable state, and is associated with optimum capacity. In contrast, illness is regarded as a disruptive and 'abnormal' condition, which renders the individual unproductive and dependent. It is akin to a form of social deviance which, if not properly controlled, threatens the smooth functioning of the system as a whole, as well as effective role performance at the individual level.

How then does the social system 'manage' individual sickness? Parsons' answer is that the sick role provides a temporary and conditional alternative – a form of sanctioned social deviance. The sick role incorporates two responsibilities and two rights. First, at the point of becoming ill, the sick person is required to seek medical confirmation. The individual is then obligated to co-operate fully with the doctor in order to get better. Second, the sick person is expected to view their condition as both undesirable and 'abhorrent'. Third, once diagnosed as ill by the doctor, the individual is automatically relieved of all normal social role expectations and responsibilities. And fourth, individuals are not held responsible for their illness, nor are they expected to recover simply through an active decision of free will. From a societal point of view, the conditional legitimacy of the sick role is emphasized because of fears of 'motivated deviance' – that is, people might be reluctant to relinquish their social dependence and return to their 'normal' social roles and responsibilities (Gerhardt, 1989).

Thus, the medical profession has a crucial social control function in managing sickness. However, for Parsons, doctor–patient interaction is sustained by mutual advantages and shared goals. Indeed, the thrust of his functionalist analysis is that power is a generalized social resource which is based on legitimate authority. Differentials in power between the professional expert and the patient are necessary to serve the interests of society as a whole, by ensuring that the most able perform the most highly skilled roles. Hence the social control function exercised by the medical profession is regarded as wholly benign.

Chronic illness and the impaired role

Parsons' analysis of illness as a social state opened up the possibility for a sociology of health and illness, but has also attracted considerable criticism. Leaving aside attacks on his functionalist perspective, the sick role has been identified as an ideal-typical account based on acute illnesses which cannot be easily generalized to permanent or long-term conditions.

Kassebaum and Baumann (1965) argue that individuals who are chronically ill can usually only expect to retain a limited 'functional capability', which will result in a loss of income and resources which, in turn, makes eventual recovery even more difficult. As the illness becomes accepted as part of their 'normal' existence, so they must accept the social dependence prescribed by the sick role. The tolerance initially shown them may lapse the longer they remain in the sick role. This is the exact opposite of the Parsonian fear of social disorder or 'motivated deviance' because people see advantages in staying in the sick role. At the same time, the impairment becomes the defining feature of the disabled person's self-identity and expectations. Parsons (1975) responded that many of those patients for whom complete recovery was not a realistic possibility, such as people with diabetes, could be medically managed in ways that maintained a reasonable capacity to function 'normally' (p. 259).

Others, more interested in chronic illness and impairment, advanced the notion of an 'impaired role' (Gordon, 1966; Sieglar and Osmond, 1974). This is applied to the person whose condition is unlikely to change and who cannot 'recover' even if diligently following medical advice. By definition, the impaired role is difficult to leave and usually permanent (Gordon, 1966), and signifies a loss of 'full human status' and 'second-class citizenship' (Sieglar and Osmond, 1974: 116). A further variation is the 'rehabilitation role' (Safilios-Rothschild, 1970). Where the 'sickness' is recognized as not temporary, people seek ways to make the most out of their changed circumstances. The rehabilitation role obligates its occupants to resume as many of their previous roles as possible, or develop new capabilities. It is also expected that the person with the impairment will take their cue from rehabilitation profession-als and fully co-operate in attempts to develop ways to retrieve some element of 'normality'.

Where people become ill or acquire an impairment through no fault of their own, doctors, and (as Parsons recognized) other thera-peutic and rehabilitative personnel, work with the sick person to 'normalize' the disabling consequences of their illness/impairment and achieve some degree of social reintegration through changes in role expectations, counselling and other professional guidance. It is here also that psychological theories of adaptation to impair-ment have achieved such prominence. Emotional responses to 'losses' varying from visual impairment to limb amputation have inspired attempts to capture the phases through which disabled children go in adapting to life in a residential special school – dis-orientation, depression, anger and acceptance (Minde, 1972). However, as Gary Albrecht comments, this 'idealised process seems too facile' (1992: 74). The experience of many disabled people is that they are treated more as objects than as active participants in the treatment process, and 'manipulated' against their wishes into an 'abnormal' lifestyle.

This representation of chronic illness and impairment has broadly endured in rehabilitation practice although widely criticized by social scientists. There is considerable evidence that this account is contradicted by variation in practice: the stages are not followed sequentially; the view of adjustment is defined by, and progress evaluated in terms of, professional criteria and inter-ests; and it denies the subjective interpretation of the individual with the illness or impairment. It is 'the product of the "psycholog-ical imagination" constructed on a bedrock of "non-disabled" assumptions of what it is like to experience impairment' (Oliver, 1996b: 21).

Labelling theory

Parsons' references to illness as a form of social deviance, albeit temporary and legitimate, were soon picked up and elaborated in a very different way. There was a growing literature, initiated by those adopting a symbolic interactionist perspective, and more particularly labelling theory, which offered a novel analysis of the social process by which an act or attribute is deemed deviant. The initial emphasis was on the degree of social reaction, and whether the 'deviance' should be ranked as 'primary', which carries minimal consequences, or 'secondary', in which case the perceived deviance entails a transfer to a new social status and self-identity (Lemert, 1951). From this standpoint:

> deviance is not a quality of the act a person commits, but rather a consequence of the application by others of rules and sanctions to an 'offender' ... Deviance is not a quality that lies in the behaviour itself but in the interaction between the person who commits an act and those who respond to it. (Becker, 1963: 9)

The deviant is one to whom the label has been applied successfully. Once defined as deviant, that person is expected to play the deviant role.

Stigma

The potential for applying labelling theory to people with impairments is vividly illustrated in Erving Goffman's (1968) widely referenced study, *Stigma*. This explores how society's ways of categorizing people are established through social interaction. 'Stigma' is broadly defined to include: 'abominations of the body – the various physical deformities', 'blemishes of individual character', and 'the tribal stigma of race, nation and religion', plus, in Britain, social class (p. 14). Examples of the first category include the 'dwarf, the blind man, the disfigured, the homosexual . . . and the ex-mental patient'. In each case, 'undesired differentness' from 'the normals' provides the basis for the stigma. An associated feature is that this 'difference' is regarded as contagious so that close family and friends typically acquire a 'courtesy stigma' (p. 44).

Goffman suggests that the notion of 'normal human being' may have its origins in a medical approach or as a rationale for equal treatment by the state, but it is also very much a normative system of grading people. This categorization system to confer a social identity exists prior to social interaction, and is established by 'society' (p. 11). It is bolstered by an ideological justification for treating those with a perceived stigma as 'not quite human' (p. 15). In everyday interaction, 'specific stigma terms such as cripple, bastard and moron' are used to demean (pp. 15–16). Most controversially, he presumes a value consensus which unites both 'normals' and the 'stigmatized' in recognizing who is a 'normal human being' and who is not.

This means that the learning experiences and personal adjustments, or 'moral career' (pp. 45–55) of those with a stigma will vary, depending on whether the individual has an 'inborn stigma' or whether this is acquired (or learned about) later in life. A child born with a congenital impairment may be socialized into what to expect from early on, while another, with the same condition, may be protected by their parents from society's denial of their 'normal identity'. For the person who acquires a stigmatized condition later in life, the dilemma, for Goffman, is one of 're-identification', that their presumed identity is false, or that their former identity is no longer applicable. A final possibility arises where an individual is socialized into an 'alien community' and must then learn the norms and values of 'normal society'.

Nevertheless, there remains considerable scope for uncertainty in encounters between 'normals' and 'stigmatized' and Goffman pays considerable attention to the ways in which stigmatized individuals attempt to manage their 'spoiled identity'. He distinguishes those with a visible stigma, the 'discredited', from the 'discreditable', whose differentness is not immediately apparent. For those with a visible stigma, the dilemma is how to manage the tension involved in social encounters, and recover their status and identity. Responses range from plastic surgery (to remove skin conditions) to heroic feats (the blind person who learns to ski), although it is also possible to exploit the stigma for 'secondary gain' so that it becomes an excuse for not being able to do certain things. Conversely, the issue confronting the discreditable is how to control information about their 'differentness': 'To display or not to display; to tell or not to tell; to let on or not let on; to lie or not to lie; and in each case, to whom, how, when and where' (Goffman, 1968: 57).

Goffman references three strategies: passing, covering and withdrawal. 'Passing' is the 'management of undisclosed discrediting information about self' (p. 58). 'Covering' is a dilemma of the 'discredited with tension to manage' (p. 125), that is, where the stigma is known and every effort is made to ensure that it does not overwhelm social encounters. 'Withdrawal' entails removal from social activities with 'normals' altogether. For the stigmatized to adjust to their predicament presumes an attempt: first, 'to make the best of things', and cultivate a 'cheerful, outgoing manner'; second, not to go too far in 'normalization' lest these efforts embarrass 'normals', or be construed as an attempt to deny differentness; and third, to avoid self-pity or resentment (Goffman, 1968: 139–49; Burns, 1992: 225–6). If in doubt, the stigmatized person is advised to resume their 'resident alien' role: 'This means that the "good adjustment" of the handicapped is actually a quality granted to them by others. Then people say about them things like, "he's very brave", or "she's always so cheerful" ' (Radley, 1994: 158).

In a similar vein, Fred Davis illustrates how tension character-izes interaction between those with visible impairments and non-disabled people, due to ambiguity, embarrassment, and people's ignorance about the impairment. He explores how disabled people try to manipulate social encounters in order to present themselves as 'merely physically different but not socially deviant'. Like Goffman, he believes that their attempts at 'deviance disavowal' are unlikely to succeed (Davis, 1961).

Moral career as a mental patient

The discussion of the 'moral career' of those with a stigma con-tinues an earlier discussion in Goffman's (1961) book *Asylums* of the impact being placed in a 'total institution', such as a mental hospital, prison or monastic order. These offer greater opportun-ities to transform an inmate's identity and self-esteem by consoli-dating usually separate spheres of work, leisure, eating and sleeping into a single experience of 'batch living' – emulating factory farms.

The process starts with the 'mortification of self'. From the moment of entry into the institution, the patient is subjected to a series of 'degradation rituals' designed to induce docility and sub-missiveness. The old self is removed and a standardized, institu-tional alternative is provided. A process of stripping, washing and re-clothing removes almost all remembrances of their former life and produces a new identity. Permission is required to undertake even ordinary activities. The institution then engages in a 're-organization of the self' by supplying a new patient identity with appropriate social props such as standardized clothing and set routines. A 'privilege system' is operated to reward appropriate behaviour and punish wrongdoing so that inmates identify with the 'organization's goals and fate'.

Not that the aim of patient conformity is always achieved. Goffman identifies three possibilities: 'conversion', where the patient enthusiastically embraces their new identity; 'colonization', where the regime is broadly but unenthusiastically accepted; and 'withdrawal' or 'intransigence', where the institution's efforts are variously rejected. These secondary adjustments to batch living form the basis for an asylum subculture or 'underlife' where patients find mechanisms for distancing themselves from the institution by hiding possessions, and having illicit relationships, communication and meetings. This contrasts with his portrayal of the largely passive demeanour adopted by 'stigmatized' people in everyday social encounters (Goffman, 1968).

Goffman's picture of the social creation of the mental patient is emulated in Robert Scott's *The Making of Blind Men* (1969). He argues that 'blind men' are not born, 'they are made' by professionals. There is a broad continuum stretching from 'perfect' vision to total blindness, but the law defines blindness at a precise point (20/200). Scott then explores how those labelled as 'technically' blind are made 'socially' blind through the intervention of rehabilitation professionals and institutions. Even those with some vision are encouraged to learn the 'blind role' – with its learned incapacity, dependence and passivity. People defined as blind are rewarded for accepting the 'rehabilitator's' definition of their situation and, conversely, punished for clinging to contrary self-conceptions and behaviour patterns. Thus, 'blindness is a social role that people who have serious difficulty seeing or who cannot see at all must learn how to play' (Scott, 1969: 3).

Other research has supported Goffman's conclusions across a variety of less-extreme institutional and residential settings (Jones and Fowles, 1984). Patients have to conform to an institutional regime which renders them unfit for life in the outside world, where incarceration can lead to 'institutional neurosis' (Barton, 1959). Peter Townsend (1967) came to similar conclusions in his study of residential homes for older people. In response to such criticism, less 'disciplinary' regimes have been introduced and, for example, studies of residential care for children with learning difficulties have found that where it is child-oriented and displays a household type of informal organization and relationships, the 'inmates' do benefit (King et al., 1971). However, the general verdict is still that, as with residential homes for older people, there remains a 'massive uniformity of institutional life' – the wrapper may change, but not the contents (Booth, 1985).

Reviewing illness states

For critics, Goffman's account is obsessed with the defensive, anxiety-ridden and largely doomed manoeuvrings of stigmatized individuals, and of their acceptance of the negative label (Gussow and Tracy, 1968; Ablon, 1981). As a contrast, Paul Higgins' (1981) study of deaf people explores impairment as something which can be managed, openly and publicly. He argues that for many deaf people the main concern is to accomplish everyday activities rather than manage their 'spoiled identity'. Higgins found that much of the unease in encounters between stigmatized and non-stigmatized people stems from the latter's uncertainty about how they should treat the stigmatized person, rather than the other way round.

Studies of the public reaction to epilepsy, for example, have concluded that this emphasis on 'enacted' stigma or actual discrimination experienced is misleading in so far as it is less than the 'felt' stigma or anxiety about anticipated negative reactions by individual disabled people or, more especially, their other family members (Scambler and Hopkins, 1986; Scambler, 1989). The notion of 'felt stigma' parallels the notion of 'internal oppression' used by disability theorists (see chapter 4). In a variation on Goffman's (1968) notion of a 'moral career' for those with a stigmatized condition, some parents were fearful that their disabled child would be 'found out' and coached them to follow concealment and avoidance routines. Yet people also respond differently to negative evaluations, and whether they passively accept, or actively resist, requires examination. Several studies of people with learning difficulties, for example, suggest that negative labels and being treated as 'sub-human' are rebuffed (Bogdan and Taylor, 1987, 1989; Taylor and Bogdan, 1989; Booth and Booth, 1994).

Nevertheless, interactionist studies of 'stigma', and labelling theorists' emphasis on the social creation of deviance, have generated a substantial critique of the Parsonian standpoint. Eliot Freidson (1970a) points to the complex social reaction to illness, which also varies across social groups, in classifying illness/disability according to: (a) whether the individual is held responsible for their condition; (b) its imputed seriousness; and (c) the attributed legitimacy. These three dimensions are cross-classified to indicate whether individuals are labelled as deviant and whether there is any impact on their role obligations and eligibility for health and social services. Freidson emphasizes that public judgements are socially imputed rather than flowing directly from medical diagnoses. Thus, some illnesses, such as sexually transmitted conditions, are viewed in terms of individual responsibility and as a sign of a serious moral failing. Indeed, people who have a disease label attached to them are obliged to respond as much to its social meaning as to their biological symptoms: 'It is hardly possible to take up one's residence in the kingdom of the ill unprejudiced by the lurid metaphors with which it has been landscaped' (Sontag, 1991: 3).

These studies of the social creation of deviance raise important questions for the study of disability. Why is bodily and intellectual difference invested with such contrasting meanings? How far do disabled people resist being 'stigmatized'? Can they 'forge their own identities and manage their own lives?' (Albrecht, 1992: 78). Goffman's picture of US society in the 1950s and early 1960s cannot explain the later politicization of disabled people. Again, the concern with micro-level responses ignores the sources of labelling in the wider social structure. Interactionist studies do sometimes touch on power relations, but rarely make them a prime focus.

Experience of 'chronic illness and disability'

Where Parsons concentrated on the sick role, and interactionist-labelling approaches highlighted the ways in which some conditions are set apart as 'deviant' in some way, a fresh input was supplied by interpretative studies which have moved away from professional definitions of impairment and illness in order to explore the symbolic and material interaction between the individual and society, and how people make sense of health, illness and sickness (Radley, 1994). WHO's *International Classification of Impairments, Disabilities and Handicaps (1980) (ICIDH)* defined 'handicap' as a relational aspect of social disadvantage, which has been widely accepted in sociological studies of chronic illness and disability. It is the product of complex processes of interaction between an individual with an accredited impairment and the wider society (Williams and Wood, 1988).

An enduring theme in this medical sociology literature is the diversity of experience associated with 'chronic illness and disability'. It includes congenital and acquired physical impairments, 'mental illness and mental impairment' (although its medical status is questioned), stable and progressive (including terminal) conditions, temporary and permanent injuries, and a variety of 'disfiguring', though not always functional, impairments (from birthmarks, burns and scars to obesity and thinness). While the typical cultural representation of a disabled person is a wheelchair-user, or someone who is totally blind or profoundly deaf, the major categories identified in the OPCS survey had a mobility impairment associated with arthritis hearing impairment (Martin et al., 1988).

The initial emphasis was on the interactional difficulties of those with a chronic illness (Strauss and Glaser, 1975). In her study of those with rheumatoid arthritis, Carolyn Wiener (1975) noted strategies at the level of action and outlook to manage the uncertainty of symptoms and their severity creating particular dilemmas in everyday social and work activities. Echoing Goffman, her sample was keen to 'pass for normal' and disguise their condition, in order to minimize negative and stigmatizing consequences (Wiener, 1975: 80). The picture was of a continuing struggle to be in control of one's life and to present oneself successfully to others.

Mildred Blaxter's *The Meaning of Disability* (1976) was less preoccupied with these interactional difficulties than with examining the range of problems facing those with chronic illness and their families in such areas as medical care, money, employment and social relationships and difficulties. Professional responses and attitudes are a significant factor to negotiate, not least the conflicting social and administrative definitions of disability across health and social service agencies. These shape people's views of their problems and potential help-seeking strategies and solutions, with ample opportunities to exacerbate or improve the individual's situation: 'They have been fettered and constrained not only by their social environment but also by the two major systems of society with which their lives were structured: the system of medical care and the administrative system of welfare, employment and social security' (Blaxter, 1976: 246–7).

She offers considerable evidence that structural factors adversely affect disabled people – ranging from a lack of technical aids and adaptations and poor housing to the reliance of social services on the informal voluntary support of female relatives. This picture of a 'handicapping' environment is echoed in David Locker's (1983) study of people with rheumatoid arthritis. He stresses that barriers 'must be negotiated, consuming reserves of time, money and energy . . . or where the effort is such the person decides not to bother and retreats into an enforced passivity. It is also handicapping to the extent it leaves the individual with no option but to rely on the help of others' (Locker, 1983: 90).

Indeed, Blaxter emphasizes that 'disability is a social rather than a clinical fact' (1976: 39). Yet despite the detailed references to the problems created by state agencies and policies for disabled people, and Locker's conclusions that disabled people lack social support, neither writer follows through the bases for the professional and bureaucratic prejudices, nor questions what amount to 'disabling' social welfare policies. Instead, Blaxter extends her account to include an element of 'victim blaming': 'Whether impairment results in functional disability depends not only on the demands of the patient's usual environment and on his [*sic*] particular family and social circumstances, but also on the interaction of those with individual temperament and individual history' (Blaxter, 1976: 40). Subsequent studies in medical sociology have been largely preoccupied with developing this central theme of the interactional difficulties posed by chronic illness, with some giving more emphasis to professional and lay responses, and others concentrating on the meaning of 'disability' for those concerned.

In reviewing recent developments in this literature, Bury (1997) identifies three aspects of the experience of and response to chronic illness:

> First, is the *biographical disruption* brought about by such illness and the initial attempts to deal with the uncertainty it brings; second, there is the *impact of treatment* on everyday life, where this is relevant; and third, is the long-term *adaptation and management* of illness and disability which is undertaken as people respond and try to reconstruct normal life. (p. 123)

The onset of chronic illness carries a particular threat of 'biographical disruption' in a society which values an active and independent lifestyle exactly because it is perceived in terms of an assault on self-identity. Those with a chronic illness and impairment become particularly sensitive to the forfeit of previously valued and taken-for-granted aspects of self (Charmaz, 1983, 1987). This 'loss of self' revolves around four dilemmas: living a restricted life, existing in social isolation, experiencing discredited definitions of self, and becoming a burden (Charmaz, 1983). While some studies depict those with chronic illness as retreating from most social relationships, others suggest that this is exaggerated, and highlight the determination to 'fight' their illness, with often very little support.

Bury (1988, 1997: 124) distinguishes two types of meaning associated with having a chronic illness: first, as *'consequence'*, which refers to the impact it has on the person's roles and relationships in everyday life; and second, as *'significance'*, which relates to the cultural meanings and symbolic significance surrounding different sorts of illness and impairment.

With respect to the 'consequences' of chronic illness, studies across a broad spectrum of conditions have demonstrated how very different symptoms can interfere with everyday routines, ranging from self-care and close personal relationships to work and leisure activities. People experience difficulties in 'keeping up' with others, or undertaking tasks which have been taken for granted as part of 'normal' life (Anderson and Bury, 1988). A level of uncertainty is introduced about what our bodies can be expected to do. This has both practical consequences at the level of performance, and also extends into concerns about how the illness symptoms can best be managed. This calculation is made much more complex because of the unpredictability that goes with some conditions such as arthritis and multiple sclerosis. At the same time, with both symptoms and individual circumstances liable to change, meanings are equally flexible. Further uncertainties are introduced by symptoms or conditions such as pain, which are not visible, and not easily 'communicated' to others.

The second set of concerns and meanings identified by Bury centres on the 'significance' of illness. This focuses attention on the ways in which illnesses and impairments attract a different response across cultures and social groups. This is vividly illustrated by Susan Sontag (1991) in her studies of 'dread diseases', where she traces the particular symbolism attached in Western societies to conditions such as tuberculosis (TB), cancer and HIV/AIDS. There are immediate parallels in social perceptions of different impairments and the use of disability imagery to express heightened concerns of fear, pity or contempt. However, as already noted, the way in which a crucial distinction has been drawn between 'felt' and 'enacted' stigma suggests that the negative social reputation of some impairments exacerbates an already fraught experience (West, 1979; Schneider and Conrad, 1983; Scambler and Hopkins, 1986).

Biographical disruption can be mitigated in two ways (Bury, 1997: 125–6). First, by constructing an account of what has happened and why, so that it is possible to repair, or in some way incorporate, the threat posed to everyday routines and meanings (Williams, 1984b), and second, by according the condition some 'legitimacy', in the sense that the chronic illness is acknowledged as a part of the individual's changed lifestyle. This is seen as part of the process whereby individuals 'come to terms with' their condition (Corbin and Strauss, 1985). Nevertheless, there is considerable variation in response: some consolidate the condition into a new biography, while others continue to resist.

The impact of medical treatment on these processes has been of particular interest to medical sociologists. An illness may cause alterations in the body that mark or mutilate, with the side-effects of surgical and radiation treatment having a profound effect on a person's body image and social relationships (Herzlich and Pierret, 1987). Michael Kelly (1992a) explores this in the case of ileostomy patients. The changed body requires constant and delicate surveillance and regulation, often to keep things hidden from others. People who are permanently and severely impaired as a result of an accident or sudden illness, such as those with paraplegia and quadriplegia, experience a particularly disruptive transformation in the way they perceive their bodies and engage in everyday activities. Body maintenance activities that were once routine and private, such as cleaning one's teeth, washing, going to the toilet, become major hurdles to accomplish on a regular basis. Previously intimate or private tasks can now only be accomplished with help from others. The individual's identity and self-image must be reconceptualized to incorporate loss of physical sensation, dependence on others, and possible inability to conform to all aspects of stereotypical 'masculine' and 'feminine' roles.

These concerns underline attempts by those with a 'chronic illness and disability' to acquire some greater control over their lives and return to some sort of 'normality'. This has been cast in terms of exploring 'coping, strategy and style in adaptation (Bury, 1997: 129–33). The emphasis in medical sociology has shifted from the imposition of a stigmatized identity and passivity to a more active process of personal adaptation. In respect of 'coping', what is at issue is not the individual's personality but how far individuals use a range of 'problem-based' and 'emotional' approaches to retain a sense of 'competence' (Radley, 1994: 148). Coping mechanisms spill over into the strategies people adopt to manage their condition. Individuals are presented as making choices between different strategies in terms of what resources are available or required (social, financial, emotional). This has been linked to the development of different styles of managing chronic illness. The 'performance' that is required of people living with chronic illness and disability involves planning, rehearsal and evaluation of actions, undertaken with other people in mind, as people strive to accentuate the 'capable self' rather than the 'disabled self' (Corbin and Strauss, 1991).

The key tasks in coping with a chronic illness are listed by Kelly (1992b) as operating at four levels: the technical and practical management of the condition (such as a colostomy bag or medication); the management of thoughts and feelings (about one's sense of self-identity); the management of interpersonal relations (renegotiating long-established relationships, which perhaps involve new forms of support); and interpreting and making sense of the condition (so that individuals can carry on with their lives and not submit to negative features).

Choice of coping strategy is severely constrained by the lay and professional attitudes towards those with an impairment. For Murphy et al. (1988) impairment is viewed as a threat from which people want to distance themselves, thus establishing disabled people as outsiders or symbolic 'others'. A hierarchy of devaluation is suggested, which varies with 'severity and type of disability' or 'degree of departure from the standard human form' (Murphy, 1987: 132). Murphy uses the term 'liminality' to capture this 'problematic' status. It entails a state of 'social suspension' where disabled people are 'neither out of society nor wholly in it', where old roles and statuses have been lost, and nothing new has yet replaced them, so that 'they exist in partial isolation from society as undefined, ambiguous people' (p. 131).

Another trend in the medical sociology literature has been to move towards a more phenomenological emphasis on the subjectivity of the experience (G. Williams, 1996). This has directed attention to the reconstitution of the individual's self, and the negotiation and renegotiation of identity through talk (Sacks, 1984; Charmaz, 1987; Mathieson and Stam, 1995). These studies are characterized by the preoccupation with individual experience. If the body is usually unobtrusive and taken for granted, this is all changed by the onset of an illness or by an impairment. Such studies explore in great detail how the individual becomes aware that 'something is wrong', and generally much more 'body conscious' in reflecting on what is happening. Some of the most powerful phenomenological analyses come from individuals who explore the depths of their own experiences of cancer, neurological disease, and heart attack (Murphy, 1987; Frank, 1991).

However, it is exactly this sort of approach which distances itself from the material world that has attracted so much criticism from disability theorists. It is dismissed as both self-indulgent and as reinforcing 'tragic' stereotypes of disabled people. It also leaves many sociologists uneasy. Quite clearly, if there is to be a productive dialogue between medical sociology and disability theory, it needs to focus on further exploring the relationship between the environment and impairment. For the moment, there are clear contrasts in approach:

> Within rehabilitation, the environment has been defined for the most part as a physical phenomenon, a set of discrete obstacles or barriers, which add to and amplify the problems of impairment afflicting individuals. Within disability theory, the environment is regarded as the expression of power, a universe of discrimination and oppression within which disability is created. The sociological study of chronic illness and disability has tended to define the environment as something arising out of the symbolic and social interaction that takes place between individuals and their worlds as they negotiate their everyday lives. (G. Williams, 1996: 195)

As Gareth Williams (1996) and Mike Bury (1997) have both argued, disability theorists have underplayed the increasing overlap between chronic illness and impairment. First, the majority of cases of impairment in the latter part of the twentieth century are linked to chronic illness. In addition, most chronic illness emerges gradually, and is acquired later rather than earlier in life. This implies that the discrimination experienced by older disabled people is often very different to that associated with gender or ethnicity, although some research indicates that not all of this group are so 'tolerant' of discrimination on the basis of impairment (Zarb and Oliver, 1993). Second, most people can expect to have an impairment at some time in their lives, but particularly as they grow older. Disability is therefore an experience most people will encounter. Third, in similar terms to the argument of disabled feminists (Morris, 1991), it is suggested that impairment is a condition characterized with pain or other bodily or intellectual malaise (although disability critics argue that there are many instances of impairments which cannot be equated with ill health). It is not possible to separate these 'oppressive' qualities from the wider experience of disability.

Sociologists have criticized the medical model because it neglects the subjective experience of illness and impairment, and deflects attention away from the interactional and material difficulties that confront people with impairments. In its place, medical sociologists have given prominence to the interplay between different impairments, milieux and the wider structures of society (G. Williams, 1996: 204). In contrast, medical sociologists view disability theory accounts as presenting an 'oversocialised picture' (Bury, 1997: 138), and not moving beyond 'Marxist labelling' (p. 137). The 'sociology of chronic illness and disability' is in debate with itself, but there is a central message that the study of the experiences of those with a chronic illness or impairment can yield insights into the processes of disablement. The concern is that medical sociology may be deflected into ever more intensive studies of the 'subjectivity of experience' (Williams, 1996) and lose sight of disabling processes and structures (see chapter 4).

Social inequalities in impairment

One aspect of the sociology of chronic illness which does pay due attention to material and structural factors is the analysis of the social causes of morbidity and mortality. The social and economic origins of ill health have long been central themes in sociological and social policy debates, although most attention has been devoted to mortality patterns and causes. In contrast, where national studies have been undertaken of impairment (Harris et al., 1971; Martin et al., 1988), the primary focus has been on its extent, and on the policy implications of this, rather than on its causes, or indeed on social patterns in any detail beyond general figures on age and gender.

The inclusion of questions on limiting long-standing illness in the British Government's General Household Survey further demonstrated the relationship with socio-economic status (Townsend et al., 1988). Additional confirmation of the link between poverty and impairment was contained in Peter Townsend's (1979) study *Poverty in the United Kingdom* (see chapter 6). Ill health and impairment are causally related to industrial diseases and injuries, stress-related illnesses, poverty, poor housing, an unsafe environment, the sale of health-damaging goods and so forth. Class differences are pronounced and ubiquitous – with poorer people both sicker, having a higher incidence of impairments and more likely to die younger (Townsend et al., 1988; Patrick and Peach, 1989; Blaxter, 1990).

Equally evident is the way in which the amount and variety of impairment rises as a society becomes more technologically and economically complex and 'advanced'. In like fashion, the character of disability will vary across societies.

Medical and professional power

Parsons accepted medical authority as legitimate, and its social control function as essential to the smooth running of American society. However, this view has been strongly challenged by other sociologists who offer a very different view of professions, and particularly medicine – whether in terms of the organization and delivery of services or at the micro-level of doctor–patient interaction.

Most recent sociological writing now explains medicine's rise to dominance as a historically specific process which involved a power conflict with other interest groups. Crucially, state patronage established orthodox medicine in a dominant position. This has cemented a particular form of occupational control (over other practitioners and patients) within the health sector. However, medicine has had to engage in a continuing political struggle to retain its pre-eminent position, particularly in the health care 'division of labour', and its control over the 'determination of the substance of its work' (Freidson, 1970a: p. xvii).

According to Wilding, professional control is distinguished by a number of effects:

1 whatever the supposed priorities of policy-makers, the professionals can substantially determine the way in which the service actually operates . . .
2 services can be deployed for professional convenience rather than in line with client need . . .
3 professional control over resources negates planning and management . . .
4 professional control usurps the appropriate sphere of political decision making. (Wilding, 1982: 39–41)

Doctors are at the centre of an administrative–legal system for processing people within the welfare system, for sickness and disability benefits. Medicine, argues Vincente Navarro (1978), 'ameliorates or makes palatable those diswelfares generated by the economic system' (p. 214), and legitimates them in the eyes of the general population by translating health into an individual responsibility – a philosophy of 'victim blaming'. Some have talked about a medical–industrial complex to convey how medical and wider capitalist interests are linked (Navarro, 1978; Doyal, 1979). From this perspective, individuals with illness and impairments are viewed as incapable of productive work and excluded from mainstream society – in special institutions, or subjected to other means of social control to minimize their 'cost' to society.

Others have ignored this Marxist focus on capitalism, but still developed a wide-ranging critique of medical dominance (Freidson, 1970a). Medicine has been identified as an exemplar of those 'disabling professions' which emerged with late industrialization to dominate central areas of social and economic life (Illich, 1975).

Lay–practitioner relations

The characterization of lay–professional encounters in the Parsonian sick role model suggested a very unequal relationship, but one where both participants gained by observing their role responsibilities. Doctors (or other therapeutic experts) adhere to professional norms in applying their scientific expertise and knowledge, and patients benefit from 'a built-in institutionalized superiority of the professional roles, grounded in responsibility, competence, and occupational concern' (Parsons, 1975: 271). This consensual approach was further elaborated by Szasz and Hollender (1956), who linked different models of doctor–patient interaction primarily to the patient's illness. For patients with a chronic condition, 'mutual participation' is the characteristic form. This applies because the patient is more knowledgeable, while the doctor cannot deliver a 'cure', and so resorts to helping the sick person to help themselves.

This benign characterization of doctor–patient relations has attracted widespread criticism (Freidson, 1970a; Stimson and Webb, 1975). For many sociologists, the doctor–patient relationship is distinguished as much by a potential clash of interests as by reciprocity and mutual benefit (Bloor and Horobin, 1975). Interactionists have emphasized how participants employ various strategies to achieve desired ends in the consultation (Stimson and Webb, 1975; Bloor, 1976). However, an esoteric knowledge basis and a pre-eminent organizational position mean that doctors are far better placed to manage the interaction (McIntosh, 1976). In contrast to the 'mutual participation' model, research indicates that the more knowledgeable the patient, and the more clear their views about their condition – as often arises with chronic illness and impairment – the more likely it is that the participants will clash. Again, where the doctor is faced with clinical uncertainty, or lacks an effective treatment, then the doctor feels insecure, tends to communicate less and leaves the patient more dissatisfied (Calnan, 1984).

It has also been found that the character of encounters is affected by organizational settings (Fagerhaugh and Strauss, 1977). Generally, medical rather than surgical wards, and long-stay rather than acute care hospital settings, offer more opportunities for negotiation between patients and staff, notably in monitoring health status and treatments (Roth, 1963; 1984). Strong (1979a) also identified different types of 'role format', which vary across health care settings, although his conclusion was that 'medical control of the consultation was systematic, all pervasive and almost unquestioned' (p. 129).

The tensions in lay–practitioner relations are also suggested in professionals' tendency to differentiate between 'good' and 'bad' patients (Kelly and May, 1982). Life can be made very awkward for 'bad' clients. This category ranges from those who do not defer to professional expertise, to those whose conditions are medically uninteresting or resistant to treatment – which includes those with long-term impairments. Judgements are also made about patients on the basis of such factors as their gender, social class, ethnicity, and age (Lupton, 1994; Nettleton, 1995). Thus, male doctors dominate their female patients by treating them in stereotypical terms, as governed by their biology, and as mothers and housewives (Foster, 1989). Begum's (1996) research demonstrates that doctors are not immune from general social prejudices or prejudiced attitudes towards disabled people in general and disabled women in particular. Indeed, some preferred to talk about the individual's impairment than attend to their presenting condition.

From a conflict perspective, the doctor–patient encounter is set within a wider social context (Waitzkin, 1984, 1989). By equating the patient role with the sick role, Parsons ignored instances where individuals must seek medical authority for non-medical ends, such as examining an employee for sick leave or the extent of 'disability' for welfare benefits. Doctors are further charged with reinforcing capitalist relations by defining health in terms of the ability to work. These are often the circumstances which have necessitated a disabled person's encounter with a doctor. Conversely, when individuals become ill, the impact of social and environmental factors is downplayed (Doyal, 1979).

The shift in medical thinking towards consideration of the patient's point of view does not diminish medical authority – as more in the patient's world is brought into the consultation, the surveillance of the doctor is extended (Armstrong, 1984). The emphasis in recent professional training and practice on getting to know the 'whole person' has not diminished attempts to regulate the encounter with clients. As David Silverman (1987) notes, instead of being 'pounded into submission', patients are 'incited to speak' and so take more responsibility for their own condition:

> the greater involvement of the patient in the consultation is both emancipating and constraining. The mistake is to treat surveillance purely as a function of professionals treating patients as *objects* of the clinical gaze. Surveillance works no less efficiently when we are constituted as free *subjects* whose freedom includes the obligation to survey ourselves. (Silverman, 1987: 225)

These power relations are only effectively challenged where pressure comes from patients – for example by using private medicine, by the 'expertise' acquired as a chronically ill patient, medically qualified patients, or those who are terminally ill, or of a higher social class (Silverman, 1987: 131–2). However, most research suggests a conditional acceptance of medical authority, or 'deferential dialectic' (Gabe and Calnan, 1989), in which patients are both deferential and active in evaluating medical practice from their point of view.

Medicalization

For Ivan Illich (1975), this destruction of people's capacity for self-care and self-responsibility is attributed to a 'medicalisation of life'. He also claims that doctors mystify the real causes of ill health, and exaggerate their own capacity to provide solutions. This is the basis for the expanding power of medicine, as well as for its augmented role as an agency of social control. Illich holds that the public has been misled about medicine's 'iatrogenic' (that is, provider-induced) consequences. This iatrogenesis occurs at three levels: 'clinical' – modern-day treatments are ineffective and harmful; 'social' – with lay dependence on the health care system and providers; and 'structural' – individuals have been deprived of their ability to cope with pain, sickness and death. Illich's solution is a radical 'de-professionalisation' of medicine.

In less polemical terms, the 'medicalisation thesis' is elaborated by Freidson (1970a, 1970b) as the process whereby 'The medical profession has first claim to jurisdiction over the label of illness and anything to which it may be attached, irrespective of its capacity to deal with it effectively' (Friedson, 1970a: 251). Irving Zola (1972) also explores how this expansion of professional power beyond its immediate technical expertise enables medicine to replace other institutions of social control, such as the Church. Medicalization is an 'insidious and often undramatic phenomenon' which attaches the 'illness' label, and hence the medical interest, to an increasing part of human existence.

On the same tack, Conrad and Schneider (1980) note three factors. Firstly, the long-term trend for translating moral-social problems into the medical sphere. This transformation of problems from badness to sickness means that, for example, the drug addict and the alcoholic escape some moral condemnation – although the public may continue to stigmatize some diseases. Secondly, with the attribution of disease, the individual is delivered up to a new group of control agents and agencies – the (secular) 'experts' – physicians, psychiatrists, social workers. Thirdly, the effect of medicalizing social problems is their depoliticization. Thus, the trend towards 'blaming the victim' places the responsibility for health problems on individuals – so too with their resolution and treatment. In contrast, the social context in which alcoholism is 'encouraged' – for profits, tax revenues, and so forth – is disregarded, as are, for example, the pressures of 'alienating' work or of social relations.

However, not all sociologists are persuaded by these accounts of 'medical imperialism'. For example, Strong (1979b) counsels caution. He contends that the medicalization literature is located in a romanticized view of other cultures' ability to cope with pain, sickness or death. In some cases, instances of medicalization look more like 'reluctant imperialism', as with alcoholism, or reveal internal differences within medicine between competing specialisms. Again, Strong argues that the 'technical success of modern medicine in advancing the diagnosis, treatment and prevention of disease is under-estimated', particularly in respect of morbidity rates. At the same time, the public response presents contradictory signs, with many examples suggesting that the 'level of patient addiction' to medicine is exaggerated. Indeed there are instances of 'de-medicalization', although these represent the difficulties in assessing the medicalization thesis, since campaigns to get people to take more responsibility for their own health may also be interpreted as further medicalisation which creates a new category of 'worried well' (Crawford, 1977).

Mental illness as a myth

A key illustration of the critique of medicalization is demonstrated in the 'anti-psychiatry' literature which emerged in the 1960s and 1970s. One of its major exponents, Thomas Szasz, claimed that 'mental illness is a myth' (Szasz, 1970). In rejecting any physiological basis for this label, Szasz emphasizes its value-laden nature: 'we call people physically ill when their bodily functioning violates certain norms; similarly we call people mentally ill when their personal conduct violates certain ethical, political and social norms' (Szasz, 1970: 23). Szasz argues that 'mental illness' is a metaphor for what should, more accurately, be called 'problems in living' – behaviour that breaks social rules. Consequently, to talk of 'illness' mystifies what is in fact a moral judgement. By labelling someone as 'mentally ill' a wide range of coercive actions, including committal to a psychiatric hospital and compliance with a harsh treatment regime, are sanctioned. However, Szasz suggests that individuals may also invoke this medical diagnosis to their own advantage. He gives an example of a helicopter pilot who had served in Vietnam, who was charged with smuggling hashish. His defence was that he was suffering from 'Vietnam syndrome' which made him seek ways to 'relive the excitement he experienced in combat'. He was acquitted – the first in an increasing line of 'post-traumatic stress' defences.

Szasz contends that medicine has become the new religion of our society and that those labelled mentally ill, alcoholics or drug addicts are scapegoats, just as witches once were. He is adamant that 'Diagnoses are social constructs which vary from time to time and from culture to culture'. As an illustration, the Americans with Disabilities Act 1990 included as mental illnesses: 'claustrophobia, personality problems, and mental retardation', but excluded 'kleptomania, pyromania, compulsive gambling and transvestism'. This is an arbitrary division, increasingly evident in the twentieth century, as mental illness diagnoses are driven by economic, political, personal, legal and social considerations.

This argument opens up a sociological debate on two fronts relevant to disability theory. First, the argument that 'mental illness is a myth' challenges the decision by disability theorists to leave the definition of impairment to medical expertise. For many mental health system survivors, this initial classification of their difficulties as 'mental illness' and 'intellectual impairment' should be rejected (Beresford et al., 1996; Beresford and Wallcraft, 1997). Second, if one area of impairment is disputed as 'real', why should there not be a similar deconstruction of other medical categories within the impairment classificatory scheme? This is an argument for a social model of impairment, or recognition that a sociology of disability should extend the critique of medical power to consider the social construction of medical knowledge.

Towards a sociology of the disabled body?

Over the last two decades, social constructionist approaches to analysing the bio-medical model of health and illness have attracted significant interest among sociologists: 'Sociologists support, criticise, collude with, and conspire against those health professionals whose claim to expertise is their sophisticated knowledge of the body – but rarely if ever question or criticise their biological vision of that body' (Armstrong, 1987: 651).

Under Foucault's (1965, 1976) influence, medical concepts of disease have been analysed in terms of historically specific ways of viewing the body. He argued that the new scientific medicine which took root in the late eighteenth and early nineteenth centuries assumed a novel 'medical gaze'. It was encouraged by changes in methods of examination and observation, and the growth of hospital-based medicine (Jewson, 1976). A feature of bio-medicine was its fervour for developing empirical classificatory schemes, and establishing standards of 'normality'. Thus, medicine served a moral as well as a clinical function: 'it claimed to ensure the physical vigour and the moral cleanliness of the social body; it promised to eliminate defective individuals, degenerate and bastardised populations. In the name of biological and historical urgency, it justified the racisms of the state . . . It grounded them in "truth" ' (Foucault, 1979: 54).

The new way of looking at and treating the body is analysed in terms of a 'bio-politics' or 'political anatomy' (Armstrong, 1983). It encompassed the medicalization of illness and impairment. This knowledge–power linkage illustrates a contrast between sovereign and disciplinary power: the first resides in a single authority, the second is invested in a wider population. Disciplinary power is about hierarchical observation, or the ways in which bodies are understood, monitored and regulated in institutions such as the hospital. In tracing the history of madness, Foucault argues that the reasons underlying the development of a more humane medicine, with moral replacing physical treatment, were less 'progressive' than imagined. Psychiatry was viewed as a key part of the apparatus of regulation and control. New specialisms emerged, such as rehabilitation medicine and, later, epidemiology, which also claimed parts of chronic illness as their territory. What developed was a new form of authority characterized by individualized responsibility: where individuals were induced to watch over their own behaviour.

With technological change in the production and termination of life, the state has become increasingly involved in legal and ethical disputes over life and the quality of existence. These are issues of mounting concern to disabled people. According to Foucault, since the 1960s, 'industrial societies could content themselves with much looser forms of power over the body' (Foucault, 1980: 58), but in respect of medicine at least, this development can be placed earlier, albeit gathering momentum in recent years, with the rise of public health medicine and epidemiology, as well as the 'patient-centred' discourse of general practice (Armstrong, 1983).

A further influence was exerted by anthropological studies of body symbolism in small-scale societies, and the ways in which the social body constrains how the physical body is perceived (Douglas, 1966, 1970). According to Scheper-Hughes and Lock (1987) there are three bodies, which align with different analytical concerns: first, the individual body, understood as lived experience of the body-self; second, the social body, or the symbolic, representational uses of the body – 'a crippled economy'; and third, a societal bio-politics of the body, where the concern is with the social regulation of individual and collective bodies to promote social stability. Medical sociology has demonstrated a particular interest in how the state engages in the regulation of bodies (and minds), and how, in turn, individuals accept the importance of self-discipline and self-control of their bodies. Turner (1992) has captured this trend in his reference to an emerging 'somatic society' in which the body is a central metaphor for social, political and cultural activities and anxieties.

Deborah Lupton supplies an instructive review of this literature in her book *Medicine as Culture* (1994). Theorizing of the body is linked to the developing consumer society and culture. Body maintenance becomes a central objective, with regular care and servicing essential. It becomes a 'text' which conveys specific messages (Scott and Morgan, 1993). There is enhanced emphasis on 'looking good':

> The rise of commodity culture to prominence in western societies has resulted in the ageing body and the disabled body becoming sources of great anxiety. A body that does not function 'normally' or appear 'normal', that is confined to a wheel-chair or bed, is both visually and conceptually out-of-place, as evidenced by the lack of public facilities for people with disabilities or the elderly. It is no longer acceptable to allow one's body to age gracefully, for age has become a negative cultural value. (Lupton, 1994: 38)

From this perspective, the body is surrounded by new possibilities – medical technology offers organ replacement and bodily reshaping and design, genetic structures of the unborn can be modified, while health promotion and healthy lifestyle campaigns have highlighted the importance of body maintenance and bodily self-discipline. Conversely, consumerism demonstrates a corresponding rejection or avoidance of weak, distorted and sickly bodies. Interpretations of 'able-bodied' normality in terms of body shape and capacities become intertwined with moral and social virtues. This is further linked to the growth of a 'risk discourse' in contemporary society, which encourages individuals to seek ways to minimize potential sources of harm and ill health – through a focus on diet, exercise, not smoking, and generally adopting preventive strategies (Nettleton, 1995). Again, 'able-bodied' and healthy 'normality' is equated with virtuousness. Those minds and bodies which are not well maintained are translated into objects of shame and scorn.

In like manner, disabled bodies contravene notions of the 'civilizing process' – with its emphasis on greater self-control over body functions and emotions, allied to a heightened sense of shame and delicacy about what is acceptable behaviour in the public arena (Elias, 1978). This has particular implications for those assisting disabled people with personal and intimate tasks. This requires negotiation of social and cultural boundaries to manage any shame or embarrassment experienced by either party (Nettleton, 1995). A system of working has to be agreed to deal with the ways in which the 'carer' invades another's personal space (Lawler, 1991). An already sensitive relationship is made more tense because most of those providing support are women, and male power over women has traditionally been enacted through body relationships and codes.

Just as feminist writers have argued that analyses of the body are 'gendered', so too there is a growing recognition that the body is infused with 'able-bodied' notions. The thrust of social constructionism, and many recent feminist contributions, has been to disregard medical accounts of the body as 'capturing' its underlying reality, and to explore instead how meaning is created by use of a particular language (or discourse) and for what purpose. Hence, the emphasis on 'reclaiming' bodies (impairment) from their medical or biological location and subjecting them to a socio-cultural analysis. The bio-medical model of the body, like any discourse, restricts what can be seen or said, while also opening up new possibilities. For these sociological critics, disability theory has not broken away from the bio-medical or non-social representation of the body: 'The definition of impairment proposed by the social model of disability recapitulates the biomedical "faulty machine" model of the body' (Hughes and Paterson, 1997: 329).

Medical sociology has developed from the position that illness/impairment is not simply a medical issue. Hence, 'body issues' should represent a meeting-point for sociological and disability theory, and the development of a sociology of impairment as central to a sociology of disability (Abberley, 1987; Shakespeare and Watson, 1995; Hughes and Paterson, 1997). At the same time, 'cyborg' images of part-human, part-machine beings are explored within a postmodern discourse where individual physical, sensory and intellectual capacities are replaced or enhanced by use of the new technology. Nevertheless, the impression given by post-structuralist analysis is that new discourses generate their own meanings without regard to material circumstances. Accounts inspired by Foucault (1980) have responded by demonstrating how the medical discourse (like any other) is grounded in specific power relations and ideological interests, and in turn contributes to them.

Review

In this chapter we have examined sociological approaches to 'chronic illness and disability'. If the starting-point was Parsons and structural functionalism, the two key aspects of the Parsonian approach – analysing illness as a social state, and medical authority as a system of social control – have been the subject of extensive criticism since the late 1960s. Initially, this was associated with two broad perspectives within the medical sociology literature. First, studies that adopted interactionist approaches which explored the social and moral 'career' and individual experiences of 'chronic illness and disability', and second, a conflict approach, that focused on professional and medical dominance and social inequalities in health.

Since the 1980s, social constructionism has offered a novel perspective within the sociology of health and illness that has been characterized by a critical approach to bio-medicine's claims to scientific objectivity – for example, in its approach to 'madness' and intellectual impairment. As the variety and intensity of sociological debates demonstrates, medical sociologists do not hunt as a pack. And yet, from a social barriers point of view, the sociological literature is barely distinguishable from the medical in the way it accepts 'disability' as an individual health or medical matter. Moreover, it has until recently ignored the competing analyses offered by disabled activists and disability theorists.

Notwithstanding this divide between medical sociologists and disability theorists, there are areas where a constructive dialogue should be possible. As the social model develops from a sociopolitical programme into a sociology of disability, the complexities in the relationship between environment/society and impairment/disability will have to be confronted. Nor should all the emphasis be placed on a 'medical sociology' versus 'disability theory' confrontation: there are emerging signs of growing diversity within each tradition as much as between them, although, as we shall see in chapter 4, disability theorists remain more united in their view of the necessary relationship between theory and political action.

4

Enter Disability Theory

In this chapter we will trace the emergence of what has become known as disability theory, and its central inspiration – what has been termed a 'social model of disability'. This has its origins in campaigns by disabled people against the discrimination, isolation and dependency which characterized their lives. It is built on a basic rejection of the individual or medical approach, which puts the fate of disabled people solely in the hands of professional experts, particularly doctors, rehabilitation and social care staff. From this perspective, 'disability' is interpreted through the prism of 'personal tragedy theory' and refers to an experience unique to each individual and always determined by their impairment. In contrast, a social model of disability is informed by a socio-political approach. It highlights the barriers and constraints erected by disabling society.

A 'social model' or 'social barriers' approach has obvious over-laps with sociological perspectives, but they are not the same thing. Moreover, just as there are very different theoretical strands within sociology, so too there are contrasting emphases within dis-ability theory. This discussion will first trace the gathering criti-cism of the 'individual model'; second, illustrate how this has informed debates that gave substance to an alternative social model approach; and third, review the different ways in which its exponents have sought to develop a more comprehensive social theory of disability.

New ways of analysing disability

Scattered initiatives in exploring the process of 'disablement' have appeared throughout the second half of the twentieth century – including a volume of the US-based *Journal of Social Issues* in 1948 devoted entirely to this subject – but it was not until the 1960s that a discernible literature on disability studies took shape. The spur was the politicization of disabled people, in different countries, including the growth of the Independent Living Movement (ILM) in the United States (see chapter 7), the self-advocacy movement in Sweden, and struggles by disabled people in British residential institutions for greater control of their lives. A range of issues was identified: the social disadvantages experienced by disabled people, their politicization through civil rights and equal opportunities campaigns, and social policy responses.

The Independent Living Movement

The first writers (employing a sociological framework) to argue that a qualitative shift was taking place in the perception of disabled people, both of themselves and by others, emerged as a result of a growing movement of social protest among disabled people in North America in the late 1960s and 1970s. Constantina Safilios-Rothschild (1976) and Gerben DeJong (1981) both describe the remarkable change taking place within the disabled population, with some rejecting the disabled stereotype role and decrying their low socio-economic expectations. The new awareness among disabled people was triggered by specific factors such as the return of disabled casualties from the Vietnam War and the general political climate stressing civil rights and social protest. This generated sporadic protest actions and, most conspicuously, sparked off the Independent Living Movement in America. It rejected the behavioural expectations of child-like dependency assumed by professional rehabilitation experts, which gained full force in institutional settings. Instead, it was argued that environmental factors are at least as important as impairment-related variables in assessing the capacity of a disabled person to live independently. This heralded a new paradigm of disability, in which the emphasis on self-help and de-medicalization went hand in hand with de-institutionalization, 'mainstreaming' and 'normalization' – leading to new opportunities – while also exposing them to the 'possibility of failure' which goes with living in an 'open market' (DeJong, 1981).

The activities of the ILM broke new ground for disabled people by drawing on the philosophical and political traditions of 'radical consumerism'. This linked with key ideological virtues in capitalist America: namely, consumer sovereignty, self-reliance, and economic and political freedom. The avowed aim was to facilitate the reclamation of disabled people's individual autonomy through opposition to self-serving professional domination and inept bureaucratic administration of welfare. In its place, the ILM followed other political movements which swept America during this period by pursuing the interests of disabled people through the economic and political marketplace (DeJong, 1983).

However, this attack on professional control and maladministration tended to ignore other structural factors, as well as exaggerate the opportunities that the free market economy would deliver to disadvantaged groups such as disabled people. A contrary interpretation was offered by medical sociologists, such as Gareth Williams (1984a), who argued that state-sponsored welfare systems emerged as a response to the failures of the marketplace to satisfy deprived people's needs. The ILM's picture of 'an abstract individual battling against a sanitised environment' (p. 1009) was both implausible sociologically and, politically, the embrace of market forces would favour the relatively advantaged minority of the disabled population, such as young, well-educated, middle-class, white Americans, rather than the mass of poorer disabled people. It might even have the unintended consequence of encouraging state welfare providers to withdraw their support for disabled people (Blaxter, 1984).

Disability policy and the state

The work of Deborah A. Stone (1985), an American political scientist, marks a further advance by exploring the development of disability policy in the context of the growth of industrialization. In short, she argues that disability is socially constructed in the sense that 'disability' is what policy-makers define it to be. Her account presumes that all societies have two distributive systems: one based on work, the other on need. The key question posed is: how can redistribution based on need be accomplished without undermining the principle of distribution according to work? This constitutes the 'fundamental distributive dilemma': 'When should need be allowed to supersede other rules as a principle for distribution?' (Stone, 1985: 18). Successful resolution of this dilemma requires rules that are generally accepted and validated, and which do not undermine the pre-eminence of the work system. In advanced capitalist societies, the welfare state provides generally accepted answers to these issues. It specifies 'categorical exemptions from the labour market' (p. 21), including 'sickness' and 'disability'. Stone's analysis concentrates on the emergence of disability as an administrative category, which entitles those so classified to certain 'privileges and exemptions' – welfare payments and not having to work – although disabled people are also liable to be stigmatized and to experience economic deprivation.

For administrative purposes, an objective way of validating 'disability' must be found. Stone argues that historically the category of 'disability' has been open to deception. It is here that the link between medicine and 'disability' has been so crucial, exactly because it has provided a means of separating 'genuine' and 'artificial' claims to impairment. More generally, one sign that a society is in crisis is when the criteria for entry to the needs-based system are disputed, or it is argued that they have become too lax or easily manipulated. Stone also maintains that the disability category was essential to the development of the workforce in early capitalism, and remains indispensable 'as an instrument of the state in controlling labour supply' (Stone, 1985: 179).

Hitherto, the crises around 'disability' have been resolved because it has been relatively easy to redefine. However, Stone argues that in the late twentieth century this is less so. There are several reasons for this: first, the standards for eligibility have become more detailed; second, once certain groups are accepted into the category they cannot be ejected from it; third, people are socialized into the 'disabled' role; and fourth, categorization is legitimated by the medical and welfare bureaucracies. This has caused a crisis in disability policy which may not be resolved by categorical adjustment alone. It also means that political alliances with other groups, and general sympathy for disabled people's campaigns, as well as the solidarity within the disabled people's movement, all become more uncertain.

Stone's argument furthers the understanding of 'disability' as a distributive category within state welfare bureaucracies. She also demonstrates how the ascription of the disability category is a 'highly political issue', indeed a social construction, which is transformed into a formal administrative category, and made 'objective' by the involvement of the medical profession. However, her 'statist' account concentrates on the broad mechanisms and processes which preclude people from participation in the labour market, and bring them into the needs-based system, without exploring the wider disabling barriers erected within both systems against people with impairments.

A new minority group?

A notable feature of North American studies of disability has been the conceptualization of disabled people as a 'disadvantaged or minority group' akin to black people, other minority ethnic groups, or old and poor people (Albrecht, 1976; Safilios-Rothschild, 1976). Membership of such groups signifies an imposed second-class, or deviant, position, and a denial of 'majority status' rights. These issues have been explored in detail by the American political scientist Harlan Hahn (1985, 1986). He argues that the emergence of disabled people as a 'new minority group' is complemented by a novel socio-political analysis that offers a direct challenge to the dominant 'functional limitations' paradigm, which informs medical rehabilitation and economic policies for disabled people. In contrast, the socio-political model articulates a very different definition and analysis of disability (including its causes and positive policy responses).

Hahn notes that medical definitions emerged out of the need to distinguish between the 'deserving' and 'undeserving' poor. In America, their foundations lie in late eighteenth- and nineteenth-century compensation programmes for disabled ex-soldiers and workers. These medical definitions convey professional assumptions about the functional consequences of impairment which may prove little more than a 'cultural invention' (Hahn, 1986: 131). Since professional wisdom suggests that structural causes are of no consequence, and that solutions are individually, rather than collectively based, important issues are depoliticized.

This ignores the impact of broader economic policies on creating and sustaining higher levels of unemployment among disabled people. Instead, individually based 'deficiencies' are accentuated, which then justify professionally orchestrated 'rehabilitation' programmes. Hahn suggests that such policies are not only disadvantageous to disabled workers but fail to address the needs of a 'post-industrial society'. They place an exaggerated emphasis on training for low-grade, 'entry level' jobs and manual labour. Apart from sidestepping the crucial issue of employer bias against workers with impairments in the labour market, such an approach prevents disabled people from 'upgrading their skills' for the type of work increasingly available in a technically advanced, service sector economy (Hahn, 1986).

Hahn identifies a new politics of disability in the growing challenge to medical and economic definitions of disability by disabled people's groups in America. He emulates studies of contemporary political protest to argue that the distinguishing physical and behavioural features of disabled people, their growing collective awareness, and their differential treatment, secure their redefinition as a 'minority group'. This signifies their common interest with other oppressed minorities, and heralds their embrace of the struggle for legal and civil rights. Hahn insists that traditional approaches have adopted an analysis which denies that disability is properly the subject of public policy intervention. In contrast, the socio-political approach advances a justification for exploring an alternative environment shaped by political protest by disabled people and imaginative and radical, policy changes.

This route has been widely endorsed by American disabled activists. However, it has attracted criticism from those who feel that disabled people's rights are at risk of becoming submerged in a grand bargaining process involving many different special interest groups. Others have doubted whether a 'minority group' approach goes far enough in challenging the organizing structures and values of a disabling society. Hahn's analysis tends to assume that legislative action will be sufficient to eradicate the underlying causes of disability. The 'minority group' route may then accord disabled people's demands a degree of political legitimacy they do not have at present, but without eradicating the causes of their disablement (Liggett, 1988).

In contrast to definitions of disability which reflect professional criteria, Hahn argues that the 'minority group' perspective embodies the social meaning of disability derived from the lived experience of disabled men and women. Such an approach is based on an explicit recognition that 'discriminatory attitudes', rather than functional impairments, lie at the heart of disability. Hence the importance of active participation in the struggle for disabled people's civil rights. Hahn believes that 'in a fundamental sense, the ultimate origins of the problems facing disabled citizens probably can be traced to the nature of economic systems' (1986: 133), although he does not offer a detailed political economy of capitalism, or analyse the different forms of 'disability' across modes of production. Nor does he provide a detailed analysis of the similarities and differences in the oppression of disabled people compared with other 'minority groups'.

Growth of the human service industries

Another radical break with earlier theorizing on disability was advanced by the Canadian social scientist Wolf Wolfensberger. His analysis is based on the emergence of what he calls a 'post-primary production economy' – a version of 'post-industrial society' – with a projected fall in employment in primary industries (agriculture, fishing and forestry) by the year 2000 to only 10 per cent of the US workforce, compared with a massive increase in employment in the 'human service industries' in the post-1945 period. With other Western industrial economies following suit, this heralds two major problems for global capitalism: first, an uneven distribution of resources, with only a minority of producers responsible for the lion's share of the nation's wealth; and second, unprecedented levels of unemployment. Wolfensberger (1980) maintains that industrial economies have resolved these problems 'largely unconsciously' by keeping food prices and the cost of other essential goods artificially low, creating unproductive employment – examples include the armaments and advertising industries – and by generating a large human services industry whose growth has been based on more and more (disabled) people becoming dependent on an expanding range of health, education and social welfare services.

Wolfensberger focuses on the 'organisational dynamics' of the human service industries, with special reference to professional groups such as teachers, social workers and rehabilitation experts. He draws a contrast between agencies' manifest or stated purposes and their latent or unacknowledged functions. In a 'post primary production economy' the latent function of human service industries has been to create and sustain large numbers of dependent and devalued people in order to secure employment for others. This is in marked contrast to their stated function, which is to 'cure' or 'rehabilitate' such people back into the community.

In parallel, Wolfensberger was extremely influential in the early development of the service principle of 'normalization' or as it subsequently became 'social role valorisation' (Wolfensberger, 1983). This has been applied particularly, but not exclusively, to people with intellectual impairments or 'learning difficulties'. The concept of normalization first gained ground in Denmark in the late 1950s, and soon spread to other Scandinavian countries. It was the basis for egalitarian initiatives to generate an environment for people with learning difficulties that offered as 'normal' a life as possible, although this did not necessarily mean their removal from segregated institutions (Emerson, 1992). Ten years later, Wolfensberger pronounced his aim to 'North Americanize, sociologize, and universalize the Scandinavian formulations' (Wolfensberger, 1980: 7). He started by emphasizing 'culturally normative' means and practices, but later shifted his focus to the impact of discrimination on disabled people and the need to concentrate attention on achieving 'socially valued' roles (Chappell, 1992). He follows labelling and social reaction theory in explaining how people with learning difficulties find themselves locked into a spiral of devaluation. Wolfensberger's suggested alternative is based on strategies and policies which highlight personal competencies and good practices. This is captured in a subsequent shift in emphasis in his writing from a focus on 'normalization' to what he terms 'social role valorization'. This is defined as the 'creation, support, and defence of valued social roles for people who risk devaluation' (Wolfensberger, 1983: 234) including 'socially valued life conditions' (Wolfensberger and Thomas, 1983: 24).

In contrast to earlier fears about professional dominance, such experts are now accorded a central role in 'interpreting' disabled people's socially valued roles and activities. Critics have suggested that whatever 'normalization' achieves for disabled people, it facilitates professionals' adaptation to new policies on de-institutionalization and community-based service provision. 'Normalization' does not challenge the legitimacy of the professional role in the lives of disabled people, but guarantees its continued authority. The whole focus of this approach is on changing disabled people to make them more like 'normal' people rather than challenging that ideal of 'normality'. Moreover, Wolfensberger's technological determinist approach contains little explanation of the historical relationship between industrial capitalism, the state, professions and disability. Thus, it fails to address the interaction between material and cultural forces and how these precipitate, maintain, or undermine general approaches to disability or professional policies towards disabled people.

The disability business

A more extensive historical analysis of the social construction of disability and the accompanying growth of a massive rehabilitation industry is provided by Gary Albrecht, in *The Disability Business: Rehabilitation in America* (1992). He offers a 'political economy of physical disability and rehabilitation' in America which links 'democracy, social legislation and advanced capitalism' (p. 13). It includes an ecological model of disease and impairment 'production, interpretation and treatment' (p. 39):

> A person's position in society affects the type of physical disability one is likely to experience and more importantly the likelihood that he or she is likely to receive rehabilitation services. Indeed, the political economy of a community dictates what debilitating health conditions will be produced, how and under what circumstances they will be defined as disabling, and ultimately who will receive the services. (Albrecht, 1992: 14)

He identifies five types of subsistence strategy: hunting and gathering, pastoral, horticultural, agrarian and industrial societies. The latter includes both industrial and post-industrial or postmodern stages. Each of these demonstrates a specific level and type of impairment as well as differing social responses to those with impairments and 'disabilities'.

As a society becomes more technologically and socially complex, so the number of people with impairments increases, as does the degree of severity of impairments. In industrial societies, for example, health status and impairment levels are linked to four interrelated elements: the workplace, the environment, war, and lifestyle. Examples include industrial accidents and work-related diseases, the effects of pollution, the impact of modern weaponry, and the misuse of drugs. Albrecht argues that, in modern America, 'disability' and 'rehabilitation' have been commodified and transformed into a commercial enterprise due to the growth of the human service sector and the politicization of disability by the disabled people's movement,.

His approach, like that of DeJong, discussed above, is grounded in a minority group approach invested with the rhetoric of radical consumerism: 'the challenge is to create a social policy and realistic programme based upon the existing political economy of the rehabilitation business that serves the needs of all people with disabilities' (Albrecht, 1992: 317). Albrecht raises key issues in understanding the production of impairment, as well as the consequential social responses. He acknowledges that structural factors like poverty, 'race', gender and age are significant in the creation of disability, but the links are not explored in detail. Similarly, he offers a political economy of industrial society without dwelling on specifically capitalist interests and values, nor the ways in which the cultural representation of disabled people sustains a particular form of disability. Nevertheless, he sets out a highly instructive analysis of the legislative response and the legal framework surrounding 'disability' in America, as well as the self-serving character of the 'disability business'.

What each of these contributions from North American writers illustrates is the emerging challenge, from a variety of theoretical starting-points, to the traditional medical approach to disability. These writings have acted as a considerable stimulus to subsequent debates and contributions. Key issues are raised, including: the relationship between disability and the evolution of industrial society; the role of material and cultural factors in the development of contrasting forms of disability; the professional domination of disability; and the growth of social protest and political struggles by disabled people. Yet, in comparison with the British literature, the discussion of the disadvantages experienced by disabled people is not developed into a theoretical analysis of disability as a form of social and cultural oppression. Instead, the American version of a social model approach concentrates on 'disability' as an administrative issue arising out of the interaction between an impairment and a range of environmental and socio-economic characteristics such as gender, ethnicity, age and education (Zola, 1994). It was sustained by continuing civil rights struggles to achieve 'majority status' rights and entitlements.

Developing a social theory of disability

Theoretical analyses of disability in Britain, as in America, have their roots in political action and struggles by disabled people in the late 1960s and 1970s, including specific campaigns for greater autonomy and control by disabled people in residential institutions (Finkelstein, 1991), and for a comprehensive disability income and new living options (Oliver and Zarb, 1989). In this climate of social and political change, the unprecedented politicization of disabled people runs parallel to the formulation of radical social analyses of disability. A paradoxical feature of the North American literature is that it references the changing status of disabled people in other parts of the world but ignores the debates about developing a social model of disability in Europe or elsewhere. A further contrast is that North American analyses tend to be dominated by academic writers, whereas in Europe disabled activists outside academe have provided a significant input.

Confronting 'able-bodied' society

As an illustration of the impact of disabled activists rather than academics on writings about disability, one of the first books to challenge the 'able-bodied' orthodoxy was Paul Hunt's edited collection *Stigma: The Experience of Disability* (1966). It comprises twelve personal accounts of disability from six disabled women and six disabled men. These were chosen by Hunt from over sixty responses to a letter he had placed in several national newspapers and magazines. The significance of this contribution is that it is not the work of established academic writers but of disabled activists. The aim was to avoid 'sentimental autobiography' or preoccupation with 'the medical and practical details of a particular affliction'. He argues that 'the problem of disability lies not only in the impairment of function and its effects on us individually, but also, more importantly, in the area of our relationship with "normal" people' (Hunt, 1966: 146). Disabled people 'are set apart from the ordinary' in ways which see them as posing a direct 'challenge' to commonly held societal values by appearing as 'unfortunate, useless, different, oppressed and sick' (Hunt, 1966: 146). For Hunt, disabled people are perceived as 'unfortunate' because it is assumed that they are unable to 'enjoy' the social and material benefits of modern living. These include the opportunity for marriage, parenthood, social status, independence and freedom, employment, 'a house and a car – these things and plenty more are denied us'. When, despite these deprivations, disabled individuals appear happy, they are lauded for their 'exceptional courage'. Apart from devaluing other disabled people who may not respond to their situation in the same way, this encourages non-disabled people to see disablement as a 'personal tragedy'.

Hunt further observes that disabled people are viewed as 'useless' because they are deemed unable to contribute to the 'economic good of the community'. This marks them out as 'abnormal' and 'different', or members of a 'minority group' in a similar position to other oppressed groups such as black or gay people. Moreover, 'people's shocked reactions to the "obvious deviant" stimulates their own deepest fears and difficulties, their failure to accept themselves as they really are and the other person simply as "other"' (Hunt, 1966: 152). Hence the 'prejudice which expresses itself in discrimination and oppression' (p. 152) encountered by disabled people. The last aspect of disabled people's 'challenge' to 'able-bodied' values is that they are 'sick, suffering, diseased, in pain'; in short, they represent everything that the 'normal world' most fears – 'tragedy, loss, dark, and the unknown' (p. 155). Although he explains prejudice in terms of an instinctive fear of difference, the relationship between material considerations and cultural perceptions of disabled people is central to Hunt's understanding of the experience of impairment and disability.

Nevertheless, there are the beginnings of a growing collective consciousness: 'We are challenging society to take account of us, to listen to what we have to say, to acknowledge us as an integral part of society itself. We do not want ourselves, or anyone else, treated as second class citizens, and put away out of sight and mind (Hunt, 1966: 158). Hunt was also a key figure in the formation of political organizations controlled and run by disabled people such as the Union of the Physically Impaired Against Segregation (UPIAS). Its 'manifesto' – *Fundamental Principles of Disability* (1976) – has been a major influence on the development of the disabled people's movement and disability theory. It criticizes 'disability' organizations controlled and run by non-disabled 'experts' for their failure to address the causes of disability and the exclusion of disabled people from mainstream economic and social activity, and for their lack of accountability to the disabled community.

The assertion that 'it is society which disables physically impaired people' (UPIAS, 1976: 14), has become the defining statement for a social model approach. As already noted in chapter 2, the traditional causal link which traced disability back to impairment is demolished. Disability is now redefined as 'the disadvantage or restriction of activity caused by a contemporary social organisation which takes no or little account of people who have physical impairments and thus excludes them from participation in the mainstream of social activities' (UPIAS, 1976: 14). Disability is represented in terms of social barriers. The 'reality' of impairment is not denied. Instead, the emphasis is on the ways in which society goes out of its way to render people with impairments dependent and unable to engage in many social and economic activities.

Disability as social oppression

If UPIAS set down the broad outlines for understanding disability as a form of social oppression, it has been left to others to amplify this statement into a social theory of disability. Paul Abberley's work represents some of the most sophisticated discussion of what this might entail. He looked to develop an approach to disability which draws on comparable work on sexism and racism while also identifying what was specific about the situation and experiences of disabled people. Abberley emphasizes that a theoretically informed account must recognize the historical specificity of the experience of disability (Abberley, 1987: 6).

In his account, oppression is an all-inclusive concept which is located in hierarchical social relations and divisions. Historically, biological arguments have been used to justify the oppression of both women and black people. In the nineteenth century, for example, women's 'maternal instincts' were believed to suffer if they were over-educated (Sayers, 1982), and 'scientific' evidence was brought forward to suggest that black people were genetically and intellectually inferior to white people (Kevles, 1985).

This is replicated in the social history of disability. However, Abberley argues that the biological element in disabled people's oppression – impairment – is far more 'real' than its counterparts for women and black people – sex and skin colour. Indeed, for many disabled people 'the biological difference . . . is itself a part of the oppression' (Abberley, 1987: 7). Impairment, by definition, is functionally limiting, whereas sex and 'race' are not. This means that many disabled people, because they cannot conform to a 'non-disabled' ideal, experience low self-esteem (French, 1994) or 'inter-nalised oppression' (Rieser, 1990b) – which resembles the notion of 'felt stigma' used by medical sociologists (see chapter 3). Hence, a social oppression theory of disability must address this material rather than socially constructed difference and 'very real inferior-ity' for at least two reasons. First, it comprises the bedrock upon which conventional views of disability are based. Second, the extent of internalized oppression forms a major barrier to the development of a 'political consciousness among disabled people' (Abberley, 1987: 6).

A social oppression theory of disability must confront a number

of other concerns. First, as a group, people with perceived impairments encounter economic and social deprivation. Second, these
disadvantages are the consequence of a particular ideology or
ideologies which justify and perpetuate them. Third, this situation
is neither natural nor inevitable. And finally, Abberley suggests,
there must be some beneficiary of this state of affairs.

Abberley also raises these issues in a later study, 'Disabled
People and Normality' (1993), where he explores how the perception of impairments is affected by material forces. Thus, in industrialized societies, impairment is associated with 'abnormality'
because many disabled people are prevented from striving to
achieve a 'normal' standard of living: for example, an inaccessible
working environment excludes workers with impairments, as does
a welfare system which does not offer disabled people a reasonable income. Disabled people are oppressed because they are
denied full participation in social life.

Abberley elaborates the experience of disabled people as an
oppressed group. He notes the material disadvantages in terms of
poverty and unemployment which accompany impairment
(Townsend, 1979), and attributes these to social relations rather
than biological features. He also links this with the cultural
representation of disability and of a disabled identity as 'abnormal'
which pervades Western societies. He is less specific about who
benefits from disabled people's oppression, apart from suggesting
that the 'present social order, more accurately, capitalism in
particular historical and national forms' (Abberley, 1987: 16)
emerges the winner. To empower and enable disabled people to be
less dependent runs counter to the whole individualizing process
associated with industrial capitalism, in which reward is an
outcome of work, and social needs are irrelevant to the ultimate
distribution of goods and resources.

The challenge to analyse disability as a form of social oppression
has scarcely been acknowledged within academic social science
writings. Equally, within disability theory, the issue has been little
debated and mostly dominated by those influenced by neo-Marxist
concerns, at least until feminist approaches made an impact on the
disability literature, and raised questions about the specific circumstances of disabled women, which academic writers (rather than
writings by other disabled people) had largely ignored (Morris,
1989, 1991). One of the most influential of recent contributions to
debates about oppression and difference has been the study by the
American social theorist Iris Young entitled *Justice and the Politics of*

Difference (1990). Although not written from the standpoint of disability or sociological theory, it offers an instructive account which a sociology of disability might profitably build upon.

Young notes how the demand for social justice has shifted from distributive aims to a wider canvas of decision-making, division of labour and culture as well as 'the importance of social group differences in structuring social relations and oppression' (Young, 1990: 3). In her account, oppression comprises five different dimensions: exploitation, marginalization, powerlessness, cultural imperialism, and violence. It is viewed not only in terms of coercion by the state apparatuses, but as something structural, which is located in everyday routines, values and norms, and institutional practices. Indeed, following Foucault (1980), there is not necessarily an easily identified, oppressive sovereign power. Instead, liberal institutions such as education, health and welfare services and the production and distribution of consumer goods are all listed as instruments for domination.

Her interest is in exploring the diverse forms in which oppression is experienced. *Exploitation* is taken from the Marxist theory of class relations and conflict. However, she judges that exploitation is not easily transposed to other disadvantaged groups. Some feminists have argued that women's unpaid labour is appropriated by men, who enjoy relatively greater power, status and autonomy as a result. While disabled people are similarly exploited as wage-labourers, or rendered more dependent because of their greater exclusion from the labour market, there is (as yet) no disability equivalent of the feminist concept of 'domestic labour' (Abberley, 1987).

In contrast, Young argues that the isolation and exclusion associated with *marginalization* form central elements in the experience of disabled people. She terms this the 'most dangerous' form of oppression because of the risk of their removal from social life through their education and accommodation in special institutions. 'Even extermination' is on the agenda, with examples of infanticide and abortion, forced sterilization of women with intellectual impairments, and Nazi genocide programmes. Relative, and often significant, material deprivation confirms disabled people's marginal status. The welfare state system supplies a safety net of financial and other support, but rarely at an appropriate level. Moreover, assistance from the state is often double-edged: 'Being dependent in our society implies being legitimately subject to the often arbitrary and invasive authority of social service providers and other public and private administrators, who enforce rules with which the marginal must comply, and otherwise exercise power over the conditions of their lives' (Young, 1990: 54).

Powerlessness is an adjunct of exploitation. However, Young suggests that the relevance of powerlessness extends beyond its association with a capitalist class structure. She highlights how those employed in the professions enjoy opportunities to exercise authority and autonomy in their work. The form of occupational control which they enjoy contrasts with the lack of 'authority, status and sense of self' experienced by the mass of those in the workforce – the 'powerless'. For many disabled people this is a routine experience, not simply because a relatively high proportion are employed, if at all, in 'manual' rather than 'mental' labour, but also because their lives are saturated by unequal encounters with professionals.

Cultural imperialism takes the argument away from the social division of labour and concrete power relations to what the Italian Marxist Antonio Gramsci (1971, 1985) termed 'hegemony' – i.e. the achievement of dominance through the willing consent of the subordinate population. Such ideological pre-eminence is achieved by treating the dominant group's way of looking at the world, its values and institutions, as 'natural' or commonsensical. Disability is infused with 'able-bodied' norms and values. What is contentious is any suggestion that contrary views and interests are thereby eradicated, or that the dominant culture is completely internalized by the subordinate group. More plausibly, alternative subcultures survive, though not openly celebrated, and may be the basis for future protest and opposition.

The final dimension identified by Young is *violence*. This may take the form of random physical attacks, sexual assaults or 'mental' harassment, intimidation and ridicule. Such acts are widely experienced by some oppressed groups. In the case of disabled people, sexual abuse, particularly affecting children and women in institutions, has been widespread (Westcott and Cross, 1996; Rioux et al., 1997). There is also the systematic violence practised on disabled foetuses through abortion, and the ridicule and disgust shown towards people who 'look different': 'In its identification of some groups with despised or ugly bodies, rationalistic culture contributes to the oppressions of cultural imperialism and violence' (Young, 1990: 11).

Young's 'five faces of oppression' are not always easily distinguished in practice, but her account promotes a framework for exploring how far disability compares and contrasts with other forms of social discrimination, as well as a basis for analysing the diverse experiences within the disabled population.

Materialist accounts of disability

In 1980, Vic Finkelstein, a disabled activist and social psychologist, published *Attitudes and Disabled People*. This is the first major attempt at a historical materialist account of disability. He analyses disability as a social problem that is directly linked to the changing 'mode of production' (in the Marxist sense of distinctive stages of development in the division of labour and forms of ownership, which takes into account political and ideological factors).

Finkelstein identifies three separate, sequential historical stages. In Phase One, the pre-industrial period, economic activity was agrarian or cottage-based. This mode of production and the social relations associated with it did not preclude people with impairments from economic participation. Disabled people were nevertheless at the bottom of the social hierarchy along with the poor and unemployed. Phase Two is equated by Finkelstein with the onset of industrial capitalism in the nineteenth century in western Europe and North America. People with accredited impairments were increasingly excluded from paid employment on the grounds that they were unable to keep pace with the 'disciplinary power' of the new mechanized, factory-based production system. This exclusion from the mainstream of economic and social activity was the justification for segregating individuals with impairments in a variety of residential institutions, defining them as in need of care and supervision. 'Phase Two was inaugurated with the growth of hospital-based medicine and the creation of large asylums' (Finkelstein, 1980: 10). The number of disabled people grew and so too did the number of professionals concerned with their care and rehabilitation. What Finkelstein terms Phase Three is only just taking shape. It corresponds with the emergence of post-industrial society, and sees developing technology as the harbinger of social and economic revolution. This will facilitate the liberation of disabled people as people with impairments work with others in society to achieve common goals based on general human needs. For Finkelstein, the new technology will enable 'the most severely physically impaired people to operate environmental controls which can enable them to live relatively independently in the community' (p. 11). Phase Three signals the struggle for the reintegration of disabled people in society.

Finkelstein's analysis has been criticized for offering a 'mechanical' account of the relationship between the mode of production and people's perceptions and experiences of disability. Technological determinism submerges its Marxist inspiration. The account also overlooks the fact that the experience of technology can be both empowering and disempowering. The development of advanced information technology enables many people with impairments to enter the labour market (Albrecht, 1992). Conversely, other disabled people, particularly those with learning difficulties and those in older age groups, are marginalized by recent technological changes (Barnes, 1995; Roulstone, 1998). The benefits of technological development are unevenly distributed: many people with mobility-related impairments are unable to afford or obtain motorized wheelchairs (Lamb and Layzell, 1994, 1995). Again, new technology may simply shift disabled people's dependence from one set of experts to another. Notwithstanding these shortcomings, and the lack of empirical illustration, Finkelstein's account has inspired other disability theorists to explore the historical development of disability.

Mike Oliver's *The Politics of Disablement* (1990) advances the most compelling statement of a materialist history of disability yet produced by a disability theorist. He argues that definitions of disability, as of other perceived social problems, are related both to economic and social structures and to the central values of particular modes of production. He explains the emergence of the individualistic and medicalized approach to disability in terms of the functional needs of capital, especially the need for a workforce that is physically and intellectually able to conform to the demands of industrialization. But it is not simply the mode of production which precipitated the development of personal tragedy theories of disability, but also the 'mode of thought' and the relationship between the two.

The rise of capitalism brought profound economic changes to the organization of work which in turn affected social relations and attitudes, both of which had significant implications for family life. These factors, in conjunction with the unprecedented population growth, constituted a potential threat to the established social order. It is not that disability arrives with the development of capitalism, but rather that it takes a specific form (the personal tragedy model) and the social oppression becomes more acute.

Thus feudal society

> did not preclude the great majority of disabled people from partici-
> pating in the production process, and even where they could not
> participate fully, they were still able to make a contribution. In this
> era disabled people were regarded as individually unfortunate and
> not segregated from the rest of society. (Oliver, 1990: 27)

It is with the onset of industrial capitalism that the institution
became the major means of social control. It is manifested in the
proliferation of prisons, asylums, workhouses, industrial schools
and colonies. The institution embodied both 'repressive' and 'ideological' mechanisms of social control:

> It was repressive in that it offered the possibility of forced removal
> from the community for anyone who refused to conform to the new
> order. But it was ideological also, in that it acted as a visible monu-
> ment, replacing the public spectacle of the stocks, the pillory and the
> gallows, to the fate of those who would not or could not conform.
> (Oliver, 1990: 48)

The effect was to segregate and isolate disabled people from the
mainstream of community life.

Two factors are central to Oliver's account of the role of ideology – a set of values and beliefs underpinning social practice – in
the social creation of disability. First, there were the individualizing tendencies associated with the emergence of capital and, most
notably, the growth of the free market economy and the spread of
wage labour. Second, there was a medicalization of the mechanisms of social control, in particular, the medical profession's rise to
prominence within institutions for sick and disabled people, which
precipitated the development of notions of an 'able-bodied individual' (Oliver, 1990: 79).

'Able-bodiedness' became the benchmark against which physical and intellectual 'normality' was judged. This enabled the
medical profession to focus its 'disciplinary gaze' on both acute
and chronic conditions and, as a consequence, expand its sphere of
influence to cover 'rehabilitation'. This 'medicalization of disability' transformed the lives of disabled people. The medical interest
was extended to include the selection of educational provision for
disabled children, the assessment and allocation of work for

disabled adults, the determination of eligibility for welfare payments, and the prescription of technical aids and equipment.

At the same time, this period saw the increasing portrayal of disabled people as 'less than human'. Such cultural imagery permeates Victorian literature (Oliver, 1990: 89). These essentially negative images are reinforced by professional conceptions of disability as adjustment to tragedy and stigma. The outcome, Oliver maintains, is the acceptance of a personal tragedy approach in Western society, even among disabled people. However, in the economic and political crises of the 1970s and 1980s, the attempted 'restructuring' of the British welfare state hit disabled people particularly hard. One unintended consequence of the failure of traditional welfare policies and government cutbacks has been the politicization of disability, and the generation of a disabled people's movement.

This account locates the creation of disability firmly within the context of the material and ideological changes which accompanied the emergence of industrial capitalism. It presents a sophisticated review of the social creation of dependency and disability, although it has been taken to task by some Marxists for allowing too much ground to cultural factors (Gleeson, 1997). It also offers little analysis of disability in non- or pre-capitalist societies. From another theoretical direction, Oliver's emphasis on the mechanisms and structures which create disability and dependence has been criticized for excluding the experience of disablement – particularly with reference to marginalized groups within the disabled population – as well as the role of impairment in the disabling process.

Gender and disability

Disabled women have written on disability since the formative years of the disabled people's movement – as the even division between female and male contributors to Hunt's (1966) pioneering collection illustrates. However, there has been a slowness to explore the relationship between gender – what it means to be a woman/feminine or a man/masculine – and disability. Disabled feminists have attributed this 'silence' to 'male-dominated sociological' accounts of disability, which have largely ignored or misrepresented the experiences of disabled women. For Morris (1991), the disabled people's movement, as with other political movements, has been dominated by men – both as theorists and as holders of important leadership and organizational posts. At the same time, non-disabled feminists are criticized for a failure to address disability issues or for simply repeating disablist ideas (Morris, 1991; Begum, 1992b).

One of the earliest attempts to relate women's experience was Jo Campling's *Better Lives for Disabled Women* (1979), followed shortly after by her innovative collection of essays *Images of Ourselves: Women with Disabilities Talking* (1981). Although grounded in an individual perspective, these stressed common concerns about personal relationships, sexuality, motherhood, education, employment and culture. These highlighted specific ways in which disabled women were oppressed: 'In a society where physical attractiveness in women is valued so highly, especially through the mass media, a negative value is placed on a physical defect, and a damaged or distorted self image results' (Campling, 1979: 198).

One of the first attempts to set these experiences within a wider theoretical framework was made by two American writers, Michelle Fine and Adrienne Asch (1985). They found that disabled women experienced a similar, but more acute, pattern of discrimination to women generally, and without receiving the 'ostensible rewards' of the 'pedestal' on which non-disabled women have been set. Moreover, the dominant, patriarchal value-system has encouraged disabled men to oppose the stigma associated with impairment, and thus aspire to 'normal' male roles. In comparison, disabled women have lost out, being 'perceived as inadequate for economically productive roles (traditionally considered appropriate for males) and for the nurturant, reproductive roles considered appropriate for women' (Fine and Asch, 1985: 6). Fine and Asch maintain that disabled women experience a 'double disadvantage', so that they fare worse than either disabled men or non-disabled women 'economically, socially and psychologically'. This oppression is the outcome of structural forces: 'The combined forces of a hostile economy, a discriminating society and a negative self-image contribute to a systematic rolelessness for disabled women' (Fine and Asch, 1985: 9).

Studies in Britain have also explored the level and character of social oppression encountered by disabled women. Susan Lonsdale's *Women and Disability* (1990) documents a range of social and economic disadvantages which largely replicate gender divisions in the general population. Jenny Morris' edited collection *Able Lives: Women's Experience of Paralysis* (1989) takes a more specific focus by exploring the experiences of female members of the

Spinal Injuries Association. She illustrates the male bias in rehabilitation programmes, including: the unequal opportunities in education and employment; the priority given to sport in Spinal Cord
Injury Units; and the approach to family and sexual relationships.
In addition, there is a significant emphasis on the personal
experience of impairment in terms of physical difficulties, incontinence, pain and ageing.

This feminist critique is developed further in Morris' later work
Pride Against Prejudice (1991). The 'personal is political' maxim provides a central thread to her analysis. This brings 'private' issues to
do with sexual and marital relationships, housework, abuse and
violence on to the political agenda. In contrast, the typical focus of
(male) disability theorists has concentrated on structural factors
and the 'public domain' of, for example, work, and the built
environment. This has relegated the 'private' domain issue to a
lesser status, where it remains marginalized in both disability
theory and political campaigns. Yet non-disabled feminist writers
are also condemned for excluding disabled women's experience
from their accounts (Fine and Asch, 1985).

The disregard for the specific interests and priorities of disabled
women is illustrated in feminist criticism of gender stereotyping. A
central concern of many disabled women has been that they have
been denied participation in 'female roles' such as being a wife or
mother. Instead of rejoicing in their liberation from such oppressive stereotypes, disabled women complain that they have not had
any choice in whether or not to aspire to the 'goals of womanhood'
(Begum, 1992b: 74). The widespread prejudice against disabled
women is that they are incapable of performing, or should not be
allowed to take up, these roles because of presumed individual
incapacities. In the same way, feminist criticism of the 'burden of
care' in looking after other family members, which falls disproportionately on women, has led to calls for a more 'collectivist'
approach to service provision, which includes the greater use of
residential-type services (Dalley, 1988). For disabled writers, such
arguments convey no appreciation of the experiences of disabled
people in residential institutions. They also ignore the ways in
which disabled people's dependence is socially created (Morris,
1991, 1993).

The circumstances of disabled women's oppression indicate that
it is not simply environmental and social barriers that preclude
them from social participation, but also 'the knowledge that each
entry into the public world will be dominated by stares, by conde-

scension, by pity and by hostility' (Morris, 1991: 25). This anxiety is intensified by the way in which self-identity and body image have been merged in modern Western society. The dominant body ideal places a high importance on perceived 'feminine' qualities. This has obvious negative implications for many disabled women. Use of a wheelchair is, for example, very difficult to reconcile with representations of femininity. There is a further distancing of non-disabled people from the idea of 'defective bodies' engaging in sexual activities as 'unwholesome, repulsive and comical' (Begum, 1992b: 78). This form of oppression is particularly experienced by people with intellectual impairments, with a widespread presumption that a disabled woman can only expect to marry another disabled person, if at all. Moreover, those in same-sex relationships find themselves viewed in disablist terms by non-disabled lesbians and gay men (Hearn, 1991). Indeed, there is a relative absence of studies of sexuality and disability (Gillespie-Sells, 1993; Shakespeare et al., 1996).

The relative silence on gender divisions in disability theory, at least until the last decade, has given way to a rapid growth in studies of the experiences of disabled women. Much of this writing has gone beyond bringing disabled women into disability theory, to consider more radical revisions in a social barriers approach. More specifically, it is argued that disability theory should extend its analysis to include the 'personal experience of physical or intellectual restrictions' (Morris, 1991: 10). A division has then appeared in approaches to disability theory, with a growing number of disabled feminists strongly arguing that more weight must be given to the experiential world of impairment in understanding disability.

'Race', ethnicity and disability

The critique of disability theory for ignoring gender has been extended to its failure to address the experience of black disabled people (and other minorities, including disabled lesbians and gay men). There has been very little conceptual or empirical work on the subject of 'race' and minority ethnic status (Atkin and Rollins, 1991; Begum, 1993) as these impact on the experience of disability and a disabled identity.

With regard to 'race' and minority ethnic status, a black disabled identity is generally approached within the context of 'institutional racism'. This has been defined by the Confederation of

Indian Organisations as: 'all attitudes, procedures and patterns – social and economic – whose effect, though not necessarily whose conscious attention, is to create and maintain the power, influence and well-being of white people at the expense of black people' (Confederation of Indian Organisations, 1987: 2). For some black disabled people, institutional racism combines with disablism to form a 'double discrimination' (McDonald, 1991). The extent of this oppression means that black disabled people form 'a discrete minority within a minority' and often face 'exclusion and marginalisation even within disabled communities and the disability movement' (Hill, 1994: 74).

However, according to Ossie Stuart, the concept of 'double discrimination' is an inadequate framework within which to understand racism and disability. Instead, he adopts the concept of 'simultaneous oppression' (Stuart, 1993: 94). This was first used by the black feminist Helen Carby (1982) to argue that black women's experience of oppression differs substantially from that of their white peers. Carby maintained that attempts to juxtapose simultaneous oppressions renders the experience of black women both marginal and invisible. Following this course, Stuart (1993) argues that black disabled people do have different experiences – most obviously because they are viewed as 'outsiders'. In addition, the resistance by non-disabled black groups to white oppression reinforces a sense of black identity which marginalizes black disabled people.

Extending this analysis to include the experience of disabled lesbians and disabled gay men, Nasa Begum (Begum et al., 1994), argues that the process of identifying and acknowledging the impact of racism, disablism, sexism and heterosexism can be extremely difficult and painful. In fact, black disabled people's experience is much more complex, and needs to be reflected in its development of resistance strategies and alliances with other oppressed groups. Some work with white disabled people to challenge disability, while others ally themselves with black people to fight racism.

References to 'double oppression' misleadingly suggest a hierarchy of oppressed groups. Again, simply 'adding on' one form of oppression to another generates a false picture which does not help understand how, for example, disability is mediated through the experience of being black: 'As a black disabled woman, I cannot compartmentalise or separate aspects of my identity in this way. The collective experience of my race, disability and gender are what shape and inform my life' (Hill, 1994: 7). Moreover, the different systems of oppression can only be challenged through empowerment and politicization, and by black disabled people developing a 'political analysis which addresses our reality. For it is only by black disabled people acknowledging the synthesis of race, gender, sexuality, disability and so on, that we can prevent others from distorting our differences and defining it in their terms' (Begum et al., 1994: 36).

Bringing impairment in?

Although the early formulations of a social barriers approach to disability (UPIAS, 1976) were adamant about the significance of separating out the different worlds of impairment and disability, an increasing number of disabled people have voiced their doubts about this strategy (Abberley, 1987). This has been emphasized most vividly by some disabled feminist writers, who link the exclusion of impairment from a social model approach with a general criticism of disability theory for ignoring personal experience:

> there is a tendency within the social model of disability to deny the experience of our own bodies, insisting that our physical differences and restrictions are *entirely* socially created. While environmental barriers and social attitudes are a crucial part of our experience of disability – and do indeed disable us – to suggest that this is all there is to it is to deny the personal experience of physical or intellectual restrictions, of illness, of the fear of dying. (Morris, 1991: 10)

It is noteworthy how this literature parallels, although it rarely references, the considerable range of studies by medical sociologists exploring experiential accounts of 'chronic illness and disability'. For example, both Liz Crow (1992) and Sally French (1993) argue that the 'social model of disability' needs to recognize that impairment is part of the experience of disability, and further that, even when social barriers are removed, some impairments will continue to exclude disabled people from specific activities. Drawing on her own experience, French states:

> I believe that some of the most profound problems experienced by people with certain impairments are difficult, if not impossible, to solve by social manipulation. Viewing a mobility problem as caused

by the presence of steps rather than by the inability to walk is easy
to comprehend ... However, various profound social problems that
I encounter as a visually impaired person which impinge upon my
life far more than indecipherable notices or the lack of bleeper cross-
ings, are more difficult to regard as entirely socially produced or
amenable to social action. (French, 1993: 16)

She cites as examples her inability to recognize people only a short
distance away, being 'nearly blinded' in sunlight, and not being
able to receive non-verbal cues nor emit them correctly. No strategy is offered for incorporating impairment into a social model
approach, but both Crow and French maintain that a shift in direction by disability theory is vital in order to win the broadest
possible support from disabled people.

The main targets of this critique respond that, by blurring the
distinction between impairment and disability, 'bringing impairment in' clouds the crucial question of causality, and the source of
disability, as well as obscuring the most appropriate targets for
political action (Finkelstein, 1996; Oliver, 1996c). They acknowledge that impairments have diverse origins – such as disease, accident and injury – and that disabled people, like non-disabled
people, experience illness at various points in their lives. In such
cases, medical interventions are quite appropriate. Far from
denying the 'reality' of impairment and its impact on disabled
people's lives, their emphasis on separating impairment and disability has been 'a pragmatic attempt to identify and address
issues that can be changed through collective action, rather than
medical or other professional treatment' (Oliver, 1996c: 48). This
emphasis on holding to the UPIAS formulation for reasons of
political strategy is echoed by others: 'to mention biology, to admit
pain, to confront our impairments, has been to risk the oppressors
seizing on evidence that disability is really about physical limitation after all' (Shakespeare, 1992: 40).

Oliver (1996c) further points out that, as a wheelchair-user, he is
sometimes more restricted than non-disabled people when moving
around at parties. However, other people may find this type of
interaction difficult too, but for other reasons – such as shyness. He
argues that disability theory should not be seen as an attempt to
deal with the personal restrictions of impairment, but rather the
environmental and social barriers that constitute disability.
However, this introduces a distinction between the 'private' and
'public' domains which seems to reinforce his feminist critics' fears

that disabled men still do not accept or understand their argument that the 'personal is political'.

There remains a basic disagreement about the ways in which experience is properly integrated into a social model perspective. There is no dispute that experience is central, but writers divide on whether the focus should be restricted to disability or extend to impairment as well. Indeed, for the 'critics', the experience of impairment and disability cannot be compartmentalized; instead it 'is to experience the frailty of the human body' (Morris, 1991: 181).

Social constructionism and the disabled body

These calls for an embodied notion of disability – which links in to the experience of impairment – run parallel to another literature influenced by social constructionist analyses of the body. While sociologists have been slow to recognize the 'disabled body' (Turner, 1984, 1992; Scott and Morgan, 1993; Shilling, 1993), disability theorists have been equally reluctant, if for different reasons. Again the concern has been that this will allow impairment back in. Nevertheless, over the last decade, particularly in North America, there has been a surge of interest in the cultural representation of disability and the disabled body.

This literature has rejected the proposition that impairment is simply a medical concern. The perception of the body has changed: it has a history. Over the past two centuries it has been medicalized and, more recently, it has become the source of all manner of anxieties, a site for struggle, and part of a malleable process of identity construction (Turner, 1984; Shilling, 1993). It is an experience, and it is represented in ways which offer scope for social analysis.

The attempt to generate an embodied notion of disability is particularly evident in a post-modernist project – using cultural and literary representations – as illustrated by Rosemarie Garland Thomson in *Extraordinary Bodies* (1997). She challenges the widespread belief that 'able-bodiedness' and 'disability' are 'self-evident physical conditions' (p. 6). Instead, she explores how the 'physically disabled body' becomes 'a repository for social anxieties about such troubling concerns as vulnerability, control, and identity' (p. 6). Her objective is to remove the disabled body from medical discourse and recast disabled people as a disadvantaged minority in the tradition of American writings. She demonstrates how there are hierarchies of embodiment which decide valued and devalued identities: 'In this economy of visual difference, those bodies deemed inferior become spectacles of otherness while the unmarked are sheltered in the neutral space of normalcy' (p. 8). To explore this hierarchy or difference, it is necessary to deconstruct not simply notions of what is regarded as deviant, but also what is deemed normal. In this regard, there are many similarities between the social meanings attributed to female bodies and those attributed to disabled bodies (p. 19) – both are seen as deviant and inferior, denied full participation in economic and public life, and contrast to the (male/'able-bodied') norm. This presumes a normative body hierarchy, in which some bodies are perceived 'as ugly, disgusting, or degenerate' (Young, 1990: 11).

Once again, feminist writings on gender suggest a way forward for the analysis of disability:

> (both) challenge existing social relations; both resist interpretations of certain bodily configurations and functioning as deviant; both question the ways that differences are invested with meaning; both examine the enforcement of universalising norms; both interrogate the politics of appearance; both explore the politics of naming; both forge positive identities. (Thomson, 1996: 22)

Thomson further illustrates the body's historical journey in the context of a detailed study of 'freakery' or 'cultural spectacles of the extraordinary body' which flourished into the early twentieth century. She argues that 'enfreakment' (Hevey, 1992) has a cultural significance in the way in which it stylizes, silences, differentiates, and distances bodily difference: 'By constituting the freak as an icon of generalised embodied deviance, the exhibitions also simultaneously reinscribed gender, race, sexual aberrance, ethnicity, and disability as inextricable yet particular exclusionary systems legitimated by bodily variation' (Thomson, 1996: 10).

Social constructionist studies have sought to analyse how the categories of 'impairment' and 'disability' are being constantly rewritten as part of a wider politics of the body. To this extent, they offer further ammunition to the social model critique of impairment as necessarily a personal tragedy. Hence, the main thrust is to demonstrate how the presumed personal inadequacies are socially produced (Thomson, 1996). At the same time, there is a risk that this line of analysis mystifies the social and economic consequences of disability. A disabled body and identity do have a 'material reality'. Disability is the source of wide-ranging exclusion from participation in mainstream society. To an extent no longer as true of gender and 'race', disability is still regarded as a 'natural' difference and inferiority. A denial of the material body seems a contradiction for many disabled people. However, if politics is increasingly as much about 'aesthetics as it is about economic and public life' (Hughes and Paterson, 1997: 337), then the argument for including cultural depictions of impairment within disability theory is reinforced.

Review

This chapter has focused on the emergence of disability theory. The generation of a social model of disability has opened up a wholly new way of conceptualizing disability. Its impact in focusing disabled people's attention on 'social barriers' is not in question, and this forms the entry point into chapter 5. At the same time, different theoretical and political emphases have emerged. Some writers have argued for a materialist approach, which highlights structural factors in the social creation of disability and dependency, while others offer accounts which privilege personal experience. Such diversity is to be expected given the many different disciplinary and political backgrounds represented in these debates.

In the next chapter, the discussion moves on from these conceptual debates to consider disabled people's experience of a broad range of social disadvantages and discrimination, which apply throughout the life course from birth (and before) through to old age, and across a range of areas that are central to disabled people's everyday lives.

5

Disabling Barriers

In this chapter, the discussion turns from theoretical debates to consider empirical illustrations of the diverse structural barriers to disabled people's meaningful participation in mainstream society. Attention will focus on key sociological concerns such as family life, education, employment, and the built environment, all areas where, it will be argued, people with accredited impairments are denied the same rights and opportunities as their non-disabled peers.

The failure of sociologists to seriously address these issues is all the more remarkable when it is remembered that since the initial politicization of disability in the 1960s, several studies and reports, both in America and the United Kingdom, have examined the various environmental and social forces which contribute to the oppression and exclusion of disabled people and their families. An outstanding, early example is Frank Bowe's *Handicapping America*. (1978). Bowe identifies six main barriers to disabled people's inclusion into American society: architectural, attitudinal, educational, occupational, legal and personal. Although he does not advance a detailed theoretical explanation as to why America 'handicaps' people with accredited impairments, Bowe offers a thorough and carefully scripted account of the exclusionary features of a disabling society. In the same year, in the UK, the Silver Jubilee Access Committee (SJAC), under the chairmanship of Lord Snowdon, published its report *Can the Disabled Go Where You Go?*

(SJAC, 1979), which expressed similar concerns about the inaccessible and discriminatory environment in Britain.

Shortly afterwards, 1981 was designated the United Nations (UN) International Year of Disabled People, and also witnessed the formation of Disabled People's International (DPI). These concentrated international attention on the denial of basic human rights to the world's ever-growing disabled population. At its inaugural meeting, DPI delegates identified seven basic human rights which were judged as essential to enable disabled people to participate fully in contemporary society: education, employment, economic security, services, independence, culture and recreation, and influence or political participation (DPI, 1982). Subsequently, the 'right to life' and the 'right to parenthood' were added to this list at a meeting of disabled people across Europe (CSCE, 1992).

This expanding activity around disability stimulated the publication of a number of studies by social policy analysts which drew attention to the various economic and social problems faced by people with accredited impairments. In the UK important examples include Eda Topliss' (1979) *Provision for the Disabled* and Alan Walker and Peter Townsend's edited collection (1981) *Disability in Britain: A Manifesto of Rights*. However, none of these studies engaged with the theoretical and conceptual issues raised by disability theorists (reviewed in chapter 4). This discussion seeks to rectify this omission in order to generate a plausible sociology of disability. It begins by considering disability in the context of family life.

The disabled family

Family life is a central institution in the lives of most people. However, the 'romantic' view of the family as a harmonious and stable institution resting on agreed values, norms and roles has been widely criticized. Over the last century, there have been important changes in family life and organization. There are more reconstituted families, following divorce and remarriage, more lone-parent households, fewer children per household, and many more older people. Sociological studies have indicated that there are significant inequalities in the household division of labour as well as in the level and form of consumption (Giddens, 1989). For the most part, the family is characterized by a distinctive 'sexual division of labour'. The family is a place where a great deal of (unpaid) work is performed – largely by the female members. This ranges from cleaning and cooking, through to child care and emotional support. At the same time, resources in the family tend to be distributed unequally, with men usually having greater access to both 'free time' and money. The ideal of 'family life' is further contradicted by the level of domestic violence and abuse experienced by female members, as well as the levels of 'psycho-social malaise' among women with younger children.

It is only recently that analyses of the 'disabled family' have attracted the attention of social researchers. So when impairment occurs within the family, how are the lives and relationships of family members influenced by disablism? According to Eda Topliss:

⁎ Although the precise impact upon family life depends upon the position within the family of the disabled person, a growing body of literature suggests that whether it is a disabled husband, wife, child or elderly person who is affected, disablement has an important effect on the relationship and opportunities of the family as a whole. (Topliss, 1979: 129)

Subsequent research has confirmed this general conclusion, although many effects of disability on the family have yet to be fully researched. There has been a particular focus on families with a disabled child, but surprisingly little attention given to households where one (or both) of the adult partners has an impairment. A notable exception is Gillian Parker's (1993) *With this Body*. She takes issue with those who have suggested that 'the management of disability in marriage is smoothed by ageing and the suspension of conventions pertaining to bodily care' (Borsay, 1990). As Parker points out, many disabled adults are 'both married and young', and it is important to explore how far disabled spouses engage in 'cross-sex help' (Parker, 1993: 6). The picture she paints is more complex. The married couples interviewed indicate their uncertainties in giving and receiving support with personal tasks. Marriage does not make it easier to negotiate a course. Indeed, it might make the situation more problematic: 'Some spouses found receiving personal care from their partners difficult; but others, particularly men, found the idea of care from an outsider even more so' (p. 21).

The situation is compounded because of the low level of service provision. Where this leads to the non-disabled spouse stopping work to look after their disabled partner, a downward cycle is set in motion, as the household is left without a regular income. This creates additional strains in the couple's relationship. These are likely to be much greater if the impairment is acquired while the couple are still young. The presence of young children increases these difficulties, since couples where one (or both) of the partners has an impairment, tend to have a smaller informal network of contacts who might help the disabled spouse. In addition, such help is often thought inappropriate. Providing intimate care may actually be harder for those in a close sexual relationship, or, alternatively, where sexual relations have been restricted.

Parker further concludes that 'women can be more disabled than men in comparable situations' (Parker, 1993: 125) – not only do they earn less, they are subjected to indirect discrimination in the benefits system, and service providers generally give a lower priority to their support needs. In addition, service provision is often arranged in ways that replace the woman's role in the house-hold, instead of enabling her to retain control of domestic arrange-ments. Thus an unequal power relationship in marriage means that the woman who acquires an impairment often experiences considerable difficulty in asserting her needs. Nevertheless, while clear differences in 'care-giving' existed between male and female spouses, Parker concludes that these are not as substantial as previous studies have suggested.

Outside of this study of the marital relationship, men's contribu-tion to informal caring in families is widely represented as minimal. Studies of families with a disabled child agree that responsibility for looking after that child rests overwhelmingly with the mother (Baldwin and Glendinning, 1981). In addition, where it is a disabled mother looking after a child, there is little significant shift in the traditional division of domestic tasks, except in cases of very severe impairment (C. Thomas, 1997). A similar conclusion emerges from studies of informal support for older parents, and the overall conclusion seems to be that where a man is involved, he is the exception who proves the rule (Dalley, 1988).

There has been a trend for more disabled children to live with their families, with less than 2 per cent of the estimated 360,000 total living in institutions (Smyth and Robus, 1989). There has also been an increase in life expectancy for many children with severe impairments, so that the demands on families and community-based services is rising. A direct consequence of having a disabled child is that the mother's participation in the paid labour market is severely constrained. Given that there are additional costs associated with having an impairment, the impact on the family can be far-reaching (Baldwin, 1985; Smyth and Robus, 1989).

A child with a severe impairment also typically extends the physical and emotional effort which is involved in day-to-day parenting. While all child care entails routine 'servicing', the parents of a severely disabled child feel that they are engaged disproportionately in routine tasks, with independence delayed beyond what was originally anticipated or never achieved (Baldwin and Glendinning, 1981: 55). It is also often the case that the child with a severe impairment is frequently ill, resulting in more time spent at hospitals and clinics. However, 'many women with severely disabled children derive substantial rewards from this specialized task' (Baldwin and Glendinning, 1981: 56).

Nevertheless, commentators reach a consistent conclusion that support given by the array of professionals – including health visitors, social workers and educational psychologists – is inadequate (Voysey, 1975). Despite abundant evidence of unmet need – only 5 per cent of children living at home had access to respite services – family support lacked coherence:

> Parents consistently pointed out how the onus lay with them to initiate such contacts as and when they felt they needed to. This often causes them considerable difficulty . . . Parents were reluctant to be seen to need help, and were unsure about how that expressed need would be judged by professionals or administrative officials. (Glendinning, 1986: 13)

The lack of adequate levels of service provision, particularly for women in the family, has been linked in Britain to the redefinition of 'care *in* the community' to mean 'care *by* the community' (DHSS, 1981a). The official emphasis was on the importance of the informal provision of 'care' for disabled people. While informal carers acquired a new policy significance – see for example the Disabled Persons (Services, Representation and Consultation) Act 1986 and the National Health Service and Community Care Act 1990 – there was little debate about why this reliance was necessary (Twigg, 1989). As the recent British literature on 'young carers' demonstrates, there is a presumption that even children will provide unpaid assistance to a disabled parent (Keith and Morris, 1996).

What might have been regarded as a failure of statutory services to supply the necessary support for households with a disabled member was turned into an attack on disabled people's rights to independent/integrated living choices. Although there has been a developing emphasis by service providers on giving disabled people more support (see chapter 6), there has been considerable ambivalence about, if not resistance to, sustaining disabled women in households 'to look after children, to run a home, to look after parents or others who need help themselves' (Morris, 1996: 10).

The issue of reproductive rights is a further pressing concern for disabled families and households. How disability enters this arena is illuminated by Carol Thomas (1997) in her study of the 'journey through conception, pregnancy, childbirth and early motherhood' (p. 624). Her interviews with disabled women identified three central themes: a 'risk' discourse; a pressure to appear as a 'good enough mother'; and the dubious experience of being 'helped' by health and social support staff. The 'risk' issue involved both concerns about whether the disabled woman would exacerbate her impairment by having a child, as well as the general question of whether they were likely to transmit their impairment to their children. The changing medical knowledge surrounding genetic counselling and prenatal screening, along with 'normalizing' technologies, has placed prospective disabled parents under ever more intensive strain. (Selective abortion on the basis of impairment, and euthanasia, are considered further in chapter 9.) The women interviewed described a pattern of endless pressure (from professionals and family members) to follow medical advice and not take risks. This medical discourse was embedded within a wider disabling ideology that disabled people's lives are 'not worth living'.

The pressure to be 'good enough mothers' was also very acute: from friends and family, as well as from health and social welfare professionals. It is reinforced by an oft-repeated material consideration: that bringing up a disabled child would be more demanding in terms of the parents' time and resources. Again, disabled women reported feeling very vulnerable:

> Living with the fear of losing the right to care for their children forces some mothers to go to great lengths to 'present' themselves and their children as managing 'normally' – often at great personal cost in terms of comfort, and emotional and physical well-being. One consequence is that assistance may not be requested when it is needed because the mother feels that her request may be interpreted to mean that she is not capable. (C. Thomas: 1997: 635)

Disabled mothers felt a greater sense of 'surveillance' and of being evaluated by others, certainly than is expressed by non-disabled mothers. This is understandable given the much greater possibility that disabled mothers will have to submit to professional regulation, including even the loss of the right to parent.

The interaction with service providers is a further issue. The perception by disabled mothers of those formally providing 'help' was often, but not always, critical. Thomas's respondents were concerned that the lay–practitioner relationship was one-sided. Professionals feel obliged to 'take over'. However, this 'help' was often perceived as inadequate or inappropriate. In many instances, the professionals seemed less than fully informed about the woman's impairment or about her particular needs, including information and advice on technological aids or support with household tasks. Indeed, there was a clear sense that the professionals had not bothered to ask the women what their needs were and what form of assistance they would prefer. While the disabled women wanted to be regarded as 'good mothers', the professionals tended to regard them not as 'care givers' but as more appropriately 'cared for' (Morris, 1991). A disabled mother seemed necessarily 'dependent' and this strongly influenced lay–practitioner encounters, but where the 'help' offered was so inappropriate it was experienced as 'intrusive and disempowering' (C. Thomas, 1997: 640). Thomas concludes: 'disabled women's reproductive journeys are strewn with social barriers of an attitudinal, ideological and material kind' (p. 640).

Disability interacts with other forms of discrimination – as with families with a disabled child from a minority ethnic background. The traditional view has been that disabled children (and adults) are well catered for within the context of the extended family, and that welfare support was therefore not in such demand. However, recent work by black disabled researchers, such as Nasa Begum's *Something to be Proud of: The Lives of Asian Disabled People in Waltham Forest* (1992a), illustrates how myth becomes a justification for depriving black families of support services.

The effects of having a disabled child on family life depend on the family's existing relationships and circumstances, with some able to draw on more resources and support than others. However, for most families, having an impaired member is associated with having fewer material resources and social isolation. The nature of the impairment will also have an influence: with experiences reported as more difficult where the child's condition is deteriorating, or where the child has a communication impairment, or demonstrates 'challenging behaviour' (NCHAFC, 1994: 19–20). These factors sometimes result in family breakdown and divorce. For example, McCormack (1992) reports a divorce rate among British couples with children with learning difficulties ten times higher than the national average. Disabled children are more likely to be abandoned by their parents, they have less chance of being adopted (Burrell, 1989), and they are more prone to physical and sexual abuse (Kennedy, 1996; Westcott and Cross, 1996) than their non-disabled peers. For some parents, the determination to look after and 'protect' their disabled child may result in neglect of or jealousy from siblings (Meredith Davies, 1982). For some the notion of a 'disabled family' is very real, but not all parents view the birth of a disabled child as a disaster – as the contributors to Morris's (1992a) collection *Alone Together* demonstrate. Similarly, of those parents surveyed by the Office of Population Censuses and Surveys (OPCS), 45 per cent indicated that having a disabled child had affected their relationship, although responses were almost equally divided between those who thought they had become closer and those who identified heightened stresses and strains (Smyth and Robus, 1989).

The ways in which disability is manifested in families reinforces their exclusion from participating in social life. Disabled people are either denied a 'normal' family life, or subjected to endless pressure to demonstrate that they can really 'do the job'. And yet the service support which they may need is often inadequate or inappropriate. The social and ideological barriers to inclusion are once again clearly illustrated, even if the family can still supply 'a safe haven and support base for people with disabilities shunned by social institutions and locked out by discriminatory processes' (Meekosha and Dowse, 1997a: 53).

Education

In sociological terms, the growth of formal education is associated with industrialization and the increasingly complex division of labour which has required the development of specialized institutions: first, to facilitate the acquisition of the technical and social skills necessary for the workplace and adult life more generally; and second, to enable the selection and allocation of young people for different types of schooling and levels of achievement (Bowles and Gintis, 1976). Historically, children with perceived impairments were socialized into low expectations of success in education and work. Their educational provision has been dominated by an ideology of 'special educational needs' and a segregated education system. However, this has come under mounting scrutiny from a variety of sources, including disabled people's organizations, parents' groups, educationalists and sociologists.

There are several possible sociological explanations for the development and persistence of the special education system. A conventional 'functionalist' perspective suggests that disabled children need 'special' support which cannot be supplied in the mainstream sector, and that the system emerged as a largely philanthropic response to this perceived need (Warnock, 1978). Adopting a conflict perspective, Sally Tomlinson (1982) argues that it is primarily the outcome of professional vested interests, with teachers in the mainstream sector concerned to exclude those children considered particularly demanding and disruptive. Subsequent trends were shaped by power struggles between a range of professionals including doctors, educational psychologists and special-school teachers. A neo-Marxist approach maintains that the development and maintenance of the special-school system, particularly that which is concerned with 'problem behaviour' is little more than 'a pernicious system of social control' (Ford et al., 1982: 82).

This latter view has been widely echoed by disability theorists, who argue that the special education system is a key element in the creation and perpetuation of the social oppression of disabled people, and one of

> the main channels for disseminating able-bodied/minded perceptions of the world and ensuring that disabled school leavers are socially immature and isolated. This isolation results in passive acceptance of social discrimination, lack of skills in facing the tasks of adulthood and ignorance about the main social issues of our time. (BCODP, 1986: 6)

What has been at issue in the post-1945 years is the quality of education received by disabled children, whether this is advanced or hindered by the special education system, and how far the mainstream sector would be affected by the latter's abolition?

The British 1944 Education Act flattered to deceive. In a radical break with previous practice, the Act stated that, as far as possible, disabled children should be educated in mainstream schools. However, in practice, it encouraged local education authorities (LEAs) to make separate provision for children with selected impairments (Tomlinson, 1982). LEAs were required to deliver universal education according to 'age, aptitude and ability'.

The numbers attending special schools in England stood at 38,499 in 1945, rising to 58,034 in 1955. Apart from a slight decline in the early 1980s, the expansion in the number of special-school pupils continued steadily into the 1990s, although local practice started to demonstrate more variation, with some LEAs reducing their segregated placements (Audit Commission, 1992a, 1992b; Norwich, 1994). Across the whole of the UK, there were 114,000 children in special schools in the early 1990s (CSIE, 1997). Within these totals, those classified as having moderate learning difficulties are an increasing proportion. In the mid-1980s, OPCS estimated that two-thirds of disabled children under 16 living in residential homes and over a third of those living in private households had experienced education in segregated environments (Meltzer et al., 1989).

Until 1971, special schools in Britain were controlled and run by the (then) Department of Health and Social Security (DHSS). This confirmed the predominance of medical and psychological definitions of what was deemed in the best educational interests of the child. This bias is further reflected in the categories used to classify children within segregated facilities such as 'subnormal', 'severely subnormal', 'delicate' and 'maladjusted' (Tomlinson, 1982). Such labels served to reinforce the perceived inadequacies and pathology of the individual child (Apple, 1990). Psychological notions of intelligence and intelligence testing, and the construction of definitions of 'ability' and 'need', confirmed the disabled pupil's demeaned status (Barton, 1995).

However, there was growing concern that the segregated system of special education was not delivering on either its educational or social promises to be in the best interests of disabled children. In response, the British government set up a committee chaired by Lady Mary Warnock to consider this matter. The Warnock Report (Warnock, 1978) argued for special provision within the mainstream. However, it distinguished three main forms which such integration might take: *locational* – special units or classrooms on the same site as an 'ordinary' school; *social* – where locational integration is complemented by social interaction; and *functional* – in which 'special needs' children join their peers on either a part- or full-time basis. The report also referenced a continuum from complete segregation through to short periods of exclusion from other schools. It argued that: 'all children embark on a shared educational journey towards independence' (Warnock, 1978: 52). In addition, the report recommended abolition of statutory categories of 'handicap' in favour of the term 'special educational needs' (SEN), while those classified as educationally subnormal were relabelled as having 'learning difficulties'.

These proposals had a considerable influence on the 1981 Education Act and subsequent legislation. However, pupils with severe learning difficulties remain apart; while both hearing and visually impaired children have also largely been excluded from these initiatives. Moreover, LEAs and schools have found ways to frustrate the integration of SEN children, by identifying circumstances which allowed for exceptions. Such thinking has prevailed into the 1990s, with education specifically omitted from the 1995 Disability Discrimination Act.

The 1981 Act further required LEAs to assess the special educational needs of children with an accredited impairment. The process of obtaining a 'statement' on a child meant that a child's needs would be identified and appropriate educational support – such as special teachers and teaching – made available by the school/LEA. Although advanced as a particular gain for SEN children, obtaining a statement has proved contentious. It is orchestrated by professionals, while local authorities have a vested interest in avoiding its potential resource consequences (Audit Commission, 1992a, 1992b). The 1993 Education Reform Act attempted to address some of these criticisms by extending the parental right of appeal.

A number of arguments have been used by policy-makers, professionals and parents to argue that segregated special provision is in the disabled child's best interest. First, the type of education and protection disabled children need can only be located in the special-school environment. Second, special schools are staffed by teachers with the appropriate expertise, qualities and skills needed to teach disabled children. Third, only in the segregated school environment are teachers able to offer pupils a curriculum flexible enough to prepare them for the rigours of life in the adult world. And finally, by concentrating expensive resources such as specialist teachers and equipment in one place, separate provision is justified on the grounds of administrative and economic efficiency and effectiveness (Barton, 1995).

The support for special schooling by a significant number of parents of disabled children, and also some disabled children, has been crucial. Their argument has been that mainstream schools fail to prepare adequately for a disabled child's educational, care and social needs (Saunders, 1994). Too often, only lip-service is paid to 'integration' – whether in the classroom and curriculum, or in wider school activities. Hence, the disabled child is educationally and socially isolated. This is contrasted with special education, where professional support is often much more in evidence. This greater personal and technical support is reinforced by a more accessible environment, and an enlightened peer culture.

Most conspicuously, Deaf people and their organizations have consistently argued that Deaf children need regular contact with their disabled peer group and disabled adult role models in order to combat internal oppression and develop a positive self-identity. (In this and subsequent chapters, capitalizing 'Deaf' refers to those people with a severe hearing impairment who self-define as a distinct linguistic and cultural group.) Attending a School for the Deaf is the only way in which children can be sure to learn British Sign Language and thus overcome the disadvantages of having to compete in a hearing culture, whether inside school or in the wider society (Ladd, 1988; Gregory and Hartley, 1991). Otherwise children with a hearing impairment who attend mainstream schools, where they have to use 'high-tech' aids to hear, are denied access to the Deaf community and its culture (Rieser, 1990b).

The contrary argument from within the disabled people's movement is that the special education system is fundamental to the disabling process and therefore must be abolished. There are a number of reasons advanced for this. These centre on the claim that, notwithstanding the humanitarian rhetoric, there is compelling evidence that the educational attainment of disabled children in separate school environments is inferior to that of the general population in mainstream schools. Youngsters defined as having special educational needs experience a narrower curriculum, while other factors, not least teachers' lower expectations, often constrain their performance (Rutter, 1979; Wade and Moore, 1993). One outcome is that disabled children leave school with fewer academic qualifications and skills than their peers. 'Special schools' enter less than a third of their pupils for GCSE examinations, and just 4 per cent attain grades between A and C, a situation described as a 'denial of examination opportunities' (G. Thomas, 1997: 3). According to British government statistics,

41 per cent of disabled people of working age have no educational qualifications, compared with 18 per cent of non-disabled people (*Department of Employment Gazette*, 1995).

Again, much of the further education undertaken by disabled students concentrates on 'social training', 'general life skills', and specialist disability skills such as lip-reading and Braille rather than work-related skills. While all non-disabled young people in Britain aged 16 or 17 are eligible for a place on a Youth Training course, disabled young people can be refused entry on the grounds that they are unlikely to get a job. The end result is that a lack of formal qualifications, higher unemployment, social isolation and dependence on services are especially pronounced among disabled young people. 'Special' schools and colleges perpetuate the subordination of disabled people. They pander to the fear and ignorance surrounding impairment among the general population (Rieser and Mason, 1990; Barnes, 1991). Paradoxically, special provision is a 'bonus' for the mainstream sector in so far as it takes 'difficult' and 'uneducable' or 'unwanted' pupils – with those defined as having 'behavioural difficulties' a growing proportion. All of which confirms special education as an important mechanism of social control (Oliver, 1986; Barton, 1995; Tomlinson, 1996).

It is questionable how far the educational policies implemented over the last ten years will significantly facilitate a shift away from special schooling in Britain. The 1988 Education Reform Act promoted the introduction of a national curriculum (which has potentially important benefits for disabled children denied teaching of 'core' subjects), but it also included radical changes to bring market principles into school funding that are likely to rebound on disabled children. Certainly, the political pressure to develop performance indicators for defining success and quality has obvious consequences for schools which admit larger numbers of disabled children. Market forces have been introduced into the education system as a means of better allocating scarce resources and improving overall standards (for example in the 1993 Education Act). This has resulted in the reintroduction of compulsory testing for all children, a national curriculum, published league tables with performance indicators of educational attainment and exam results, as well as enhanced opportunities for schools to become self-governing and opt out of the state sector. In a climate of 'league tables' of performance, schools will be reluctant to take pupils thought likely to take up extra resources and lower exam results, and the stigmatization of disabled children may well be exacerbated. This is why disabled people's 'demand for change is not solely educational: it is also about the structural and social conditions of society itself' (Barton, 1995: 28).

This is captured in the calls for inclusive (rather than integrated) education. The main benefits that inclusive education might bring include: fostering friendships between disabled and non-disabled children and thus 'removing ignorance and stereotypes'; allowing children with special educational needs to experience the benefits of a broader curriculum; promoting access to more teachers; offering opportunities to develop self-esteem and confidence; and acting as an alternative to the mystique and dependency of special schools (Barton, 1995: 31). If 'integration' is about fitting the child into the school, 'inclusion' presumes a 'whole-school' policy to suit all children, and one where there is full parental and community involvement. The ethos of inclusive education is to facilitate meaningful opportunities for all children regardless of impairment. It also means the utmost flexibility in terms of teaching and learning methods and skills, resources and support (Freeman and Gray, 1989).

The 1993 and 1996 Acts promoted the merits of an inclusive policy, although doubts continue about how far this is adequately supported in practice (CSIE, 1997). For Britain to move forward along this path will also require a significant shift in professional thinking:

> Where issues of disability and special education are concerned, a whole range of professionals now earn their living by assessing, diagnosing, discovering, treating and caring for the special and disabled. Almost all of the professionals are employed as experts whose knowledge is of use to state bureaucracies. It is the professional status of those involved in assessment processes which legitimates the complex procedures which have been developed to exclude or marginalise young people from mainstream education. It is professional status which rationalises the interference with the lives of the disabled which is a routine practice. (Tomlinson, 1996: 175)

This judgement fits with a 'disabling professions' thesis (Illich et al., 1977), where different professions fight to establish their specific expertise, in a self-serving interpretation of 'benevolent humanitarianism' or acting in the 'best interest of the child'. Overall, critics charge that the British education system has failed disabled children by not providing the same educational opportunities as for non-disabled children and, moreover, through special provision, helping to reproduce their isolation and exclusion from mainstream society. Although the principle of 'integration' has been widely accepted, and the British government has adopted the rhetoric of inclusion (DfEE, 1998), educational practice lags behind. Indeed, there are significant counter-trends constraining schools to satisfy ever more demanding performance targets which threaten the presence of disabled children.

Employment

The work that we do has a crucial impact on our social and material well-being, in terms of income, class, status, influence, social relationships and personal identity. Yet the historical experience of so many disabled people is of exclusion from, or marginalization and powerlessness at, the workplace. The rise of industrial capitalism had a dramatic impact on the marginalization of people with impairments as economically unproductive. Only in times of war when shortages of labour demanded significant changes were disabled workers welcomed into the workplace on a large scale. In the 1939–45 conflict, for example, 430,000 disabled people entered mainstream employment (Humphries and Gordon, 1992). In addition, immediately following these periods of national crisis, policies were introduced to promote the continuing participation of disabled people in the labour market. Yet the results have been very disappointing, and government responses have demonstrated little conviction (Barnes, 1991; Oliver, 1995; Thornton and Lunt, 1995).

There is substantial evidence of the level of disadvantage disabled people encounter in the modern labour market. Unemployment is significantly higher. Although figures vary depending on the definitions and measures used, research from both governmental and non-governmental sources shows that disabled men and women in Britain are up to three times more likely to be without a job (Martin et al., 1989; Prescott Clarke, 1990; Berthoud et al., 1993). According to figures from the Labour Force Survey (LFS) in Britain (Sly, 1996), the unemployment rates in 1995/6 among disabled and non-disabled people were 21.2 and 7.6 per cent respectively. For men the equivalent figures are 25.2 and 8.9 per cent, and for women, 14.8 and 6 per cent (table 5.1). Both disabled women and men stay unemployed longer than their non-disabled counterparts.

Table 5.1 Economic activity and unemployment rates for disabled and non-disabled people in Britain, 1995/6

	Disabled people		Non-disabled people	
	Economic activity rate (%)	Unemployed (%)	Economic activity rate (%)	Unemployed (%)
Females (age in years)				
16–19	47.9	*	61.2	*
20–24	50.1	15.9	72.4	8.5
25–34	40.1	16.3	74.2	6.5
35–49	39.4	11.8	81.8	4.6
50–64	26.1	12.6	73.7	3.4
All	35.3	14.8	75.5	6.0
Males (age in years)				
16–19	59.2	*	64.7	*
20–24	62.5	24.6	85.7	15.0
25–34	64.2	31.8	95.4	8.8
34–49	54.3	20.5	97.2	6.4
50–64	28.8	22.6	85.9	7.2
All	43.6	25.2	90.5	8.9

* Unemployment rates calculated for 16–24 years only.

Source: adapted from Sly, 1996: tables 6 and 9.

Furthermore, these calculations do not take into account those disabled people who have given up looking for work because of repeated rejections.

All too often the only type of work available for disabled workers comprises poorly paid, low-skilled jobs which are both less rewarding and demanding – what has been called 'underemployment' (Walker, 1982). Disabled men earn about a quarter less than non-disabled counterparts (Berthoud et al., 1993). The difference between the earnings of disabled and non-disabled women workers is lower because women's underemployment is generally much higher (Lonsdale, 1990; EOC, 1991). Underemployment is also characterized by a lack of promotion opportunities, and the under-utilization of disabled people's skills and training once they are in work (RADAR, 1993; Thornton and Lunt, 1995).

The number of disabled people in employment in Britain stood at 1.2 million in 1995/6 – an activity rate of 40 per cent compared with 83 per cent for non-disabled people (Sly, 1996). Where employed, they were over-represented in less skilled, low-paid work with fewer opportunities for promotion. This includes a greater likelihood of part-time working – 29 per cent for disabled people compared to 23 per cent for non-disabled workers overall, although among female workers, 52 per cent are part-timers compared to 43 per cent of non-disabled females. Only 4.5 per cent of the disabled workforce hold professional or managerial jobs compared with 8.7 per cent of non-disabled workers. Even in organizations specializing in the employment of disabled people, such as Remploy and Outset, most management posts are held by non-disabled people. Conversely, 24 per cent of disabled workers are in unskilled or semi-skilled work compared with 17 per cent of non-disabled people. Disabled women experience particularly restricted job opportunities – with 40 per cent in unskilled or semi-skilled posts compared with 32 per cent of non-disabled women – and they have lower rates of pay and slower career progression (Lonsdale, 1990).

United States Census statistics indicate that while 82 per cent of the total American population of working age is in paid employment, this figure falls to 52 per cent for disabled people. Employment patterns also vary by ethnicity and 'race'. Thus, 72 per cent of black disabled Americans of working age are unemployed, compared with 48 per cent for all disabled Americans.

The industrial infrastructure of Western societies has developed without reference to the needs of people with impairments. Hence, inaccessible buildings, work processes and public transport systems, and poorly designed housing, prevent many from working where or when they want, or achieving their full potential if they find work. Moreover, as geographic mobility becomes increasingly important for success in the labour market, disabled people's difficulties in relocating to another part of the country to work become a further employment barrier.

Within the workplace several factors disadvantage disabled workers. The heightened emphasis upon established skills and qualifications for employment is one example. It has been estimated that the number of disabled people without 'marketable' skills is almost double that in the general population in Britain (Prescott Clarke, 1990). Critics suggest that this is due to the type of 'special' education and training many disabled people receive. At the other end of the age scale, the lower proportion of disabled people in the older age groups in the workforce can be explained by the refusal of many employers to recruit older disabled people and the higher level of 'early retirement' among disabled workers.

There is also evidence of continuing negative attitudes towards disabled people's employment potential (Honey et al., 1993; Dench et al., 1996). Employers, both in the public and private sectors, discriminate against disabled people looking for work. For example, a survey of the employment policies of twenty-six British health authorities found that a third openly discriminated against disabled job-seekers (Barnes, 1991). In general, disabled applicants are six times more likely to get a negative response to a job application than non-disabled applicants (Graham et al., 1990). Yet studies in Britain and America report that disabled employees do not have higher absentee rates or a lower-rated job performance, and that workplace adaptations cost much less than employers anticipated.

The British government has opted for a minimalist and voluntarist policy response towards encouraging the employment of disabled people. The orthodoxy in the middle of the twentieth century in Britain is enshrined in the Disabled Persons (Employment) Acts of 1944 and 1958. The 1944 Act provided for: the setting up of a disabled persons' employment register; a nationwide Disablement Resettlement Service (DRS) with assessment, rehabilitation and training facilities; a specialized employment placement service; a duty on employers of twenty or more workers to employ a 3 per cent quota of registered disabled people; designated employment; and a National Advisory Council and local Advisory Committees (Thornton and Lunt, 1995). A revealing indication of its thinking was the designated employment scheme for disabled people which was introduced in 1946 but restricted to car park and passenger lift attendants!

However, in the 1950s, British employment policy shifted dramatically in favour of initiatives focusing on labour supply, that is, on how to find jobs for individual disabled people. Demand-side considerations, such as the failure of employers to support the 3 per cent quota, have been ignored by successive governments. Indeed, the target has not been met since 1961 – falling below 2 per cent in 1975 and to 0.7 per cent in 1993. In part, these low figures are due to the unwillingness of some disabled people to register, but little pressure is put on employers – with only ten prosecutions since the quota was introduced, with the last case brought in 1975, and the maximum fine set at £100 unchanged since 1944. Despite opposition from disabled people and their organizations, the government announced the abolition of the quota in 1994. Support for work in sheltered workshops and reserved occupations gave way to 'supported placements' with mainstream employers. This form of subsidized working resurrects the problems associated with 'underemployment'. Moreover, following several organizational changes and cutbacks in funding, the DRS has evolved into a nationwide network of semi-autonomous Placing, Assessment and Counselling Teams (PACTs). Their main function is to assess and advise on the employment needs of individual disabled workers and employers.

Additionally, a range of voluntary policies has been introduced to 'persuade' employers to employ disabled individuals. With some evidence that disabled people are often more productive and have better sickness records than their non-disabled peers (RADAR, 1993), successive governments have argued that it makes 'good business sense' to employ disabled people. These initiatives include voluntary codes of practice such as Focus on Ability and the Two Ticks Symbol. The latter was introduced in 1990 as a sign of good practice, but by 1996 there were only 2,700 employers using the Disability Symbol, and most of these employed only a few disabled people (Dench et al., 1996). The impression gained is that there is relatively little employer interest in encouraging disabled employees by providing occupational training, flexible working practices, restructuring of jobs, part-time work, teleworking or flexible leave arrangements (Martin et al., 1989). Other studies noted direct discrimination in recruitment, promotion and dismissal (NACAB, 1994).

Financial incentives are also available to enhance a disabled individual's employability in Britain. For example, the Job Introduction Scheme enables employers to claim a grant towards the wages of a disabled worker during a trial period of six weeks. In the supported employment scheme, employers of those with 'severe disabilities' are compensated in cash terms for the estimated lower output of the disabled employee. The cost of making businesses and work processes accessible for particular disabled workers can be covered by the Access to Work programme, and low wages are subsidized by the Disability Working Allowance (DWA). This benefit was introduced in 1991 to encourage disabled workers into work by 'topping up' low earnings (see chapter 6). In contrast, there were no financial incentives for employers to create a generally more accessible workplace, nor a 'contract compliance' policy which would require that firms winning contracts from the public sector complied with agreed standards on the employment of disabled people.

Surveys have shown that between 40 and 60 per cent of employers in Britain do not have any disabled employees (Honey et al., 1993; Dench et al., 1996). While the lack of disabled applicants is offered as the primary reason, there is also evidence that the 'employability' of people varies with their perceived impairment. Most difficulties are linked with those with visual impairments and with learning difficulties, and are further related to their perceived inappropriateness for the jobs available, for example, not being able to move around the workplace, on safety grounds, or having communication difficulties (Dench et al., 1996).

A survey of economically active disabled people reports mixed feelings about the level and types of support offered by statutory employment services (Hyde, 1996). While a small majority expressed satisfaction, a significant minority reported negative experiences. It was argued that generally low expectations about the labour market potential of disabled people were widespread, while user choice and accountability were little recognized, and the employment services themselves were 'ghettoized' away from the mainstream. Taken together, the employment service for disabled people was described as offering a broadly 'individual rehabilitation' approach.

Under the British 1995 Disability Discrimination Act, disabled individuals in work have a statutory right to challenge unjustifiable discrimination in the workplace. The Act covers recruitment, terms of employment, promotion, transfer, training and dismissal. However, unlike the sex and race anti-discrimination legislation, discrimination is only illegal if it is 'unreasonable' (EOR, 1995) – that is, a judgement must be made of what is reasonable and affordable. This means that the employer has to make appropriate adjustments to overcome working conditions or physical features which might substantially disadvantage a disabled person such as: making existing employee facilities accessible; job restructuring; creating part-time or modified work schedules; the acquisition or modification of equipment and training materials; the provision of qualified readers and interpreters, and the like. However, the legislation operates at the individual level and employers are not required to adopt minimum standards (Gooding, 1995; Lunt and Thornton, 1993). This sets it apart from anti-discriminatory legislation policies in other countries, such as America (Quinn et al., 1993; Gooding, 1994; Doyle, 1995). Further, if a disabled worker believes that they have been unfairly discriminated against then it is their responsibility to pursue the grievance.

The new opportunities to challenge discrimination do address some of the problems, such as barriers to promotion and wage differentials, faced by disabled workers in work, but it is unlikely to transform the employment situation of the disabled population as a whole. The onus is on disabled individuals to tackle the grievances themselves, but the resort to litigation is a costly and time-consuming business. As with other recent policies, little is done to remove the environmental barriers faced by disabled people in the workplace. Thus, the offer of subsidies and financial inducements to employers to employ disabled workers reaffirms traditional assumptions that they are less capable. Furthermore, those sections of the disabled population who work in sheltered employment and supported employment schemes, the majority of whom are people with learning difficulties, are not protected under the legislation. It is also noteworthy that the British government's inertia has been matched by indifference among trade unions. The labour movement generally is 'disablist in its resistance to changing work practices to facilitate the employment of disabled people' (Oliver, 1990: 219).

Optimism has been expressed that the changing nature of work in advanced capitalist society – more flexible working hours, short-term contracts, increased reliance on information technology, home-based working, and an individualized and fragmented workforce – offers particular opportunities for some groups within the disabled population, most notably, the younger, better-educated minority. But in the absence of policies aimed at the creation of a barrier-free work environment the outlook for the majority of disabled people of working age remains bleak. However, an enduring issue is that, even with disabling barriers to the workplace significantly removed, some will remain excluded by their impairment. The spectre is raised of new divisions within the disabled population as those perceived as 'less disabled' groups advance their claim to 'economic independence' (Finkelstein, 1993a; Abberley, 1996).

Built environment, housing and transport

Social scientists have taken a particular interest in the ways in which environmental factors (broadly interpreted) affect the quality of life, measured in terms of such criteria as health, poverty, social activities and relationships, with clear evidence of variation across social groups (Giddens, 1993). Yet it is only recently that sociological interest has focused on the ways in which the environment limits the life chances of people with accredited impairments. Social exclusion is never more evident than in the restrictions placed on mobility and access by a poorly designed built environment. All too often mainstream housing, transport, and public amenities are out of bounds to disabled people.

Physical access

Over twenty years ago, Selwyn Goldsmith (1976) observed that 'buildings always have been, and always will be, geared to suit two-legged able-bodied people and not people propped on sticks or rolling about in chairs on wheels' (p. 16). For independent or integrated living to be possible disabled people need the same degree of physical access to public buildings as non-disabled people. The harsh reality is that a fully accessible physical environment is still a dream as far as most industrialized countries are concerned. Research, conducted across Europe and North America, has demonstrated that routine daily tasks like shopping, going to the bank, visiting friends, or to a restaurant for a meal are made impossible or difficult, to varying degrees, for many disabled people. The main reasons are physical barriers such as steps, heavy doors, high counters, poor lighting, and illegible signs.

Gaining access depends for many disabled people on the provision of ramps and easy-to-open doors. Once inside, inadequate signs, poor colour-contrast on doors and steps and insufficient lighting make navigation difficult for visually impaired people, while those with hearing impairments may also be confronted with problems in getting information. Wheelchair-users find that circulation areas and corridors frequently have inadequate turning space, that upper floors are 'out of bounds' due to lack of lifts or that there are no accessible toilets. Both wheelchair-users and people with low muscular strength or control encounter problems in getting through resistant internal doors, while doors installed specifically to meet fire regulations can prove a barrier to some disabled people (*Which?*, 1989).

Officially, the disabling features of public buildings and the built environment were recognized in Britain in the Chronically Sick and Disabled Persons Act 1970 (CSDP). It states that those responsible for public buildings, including schools and universities, should make provision 'in so far as it is both reasonable and practicable' for disabled people. The CSDP (Amendment) Act 1976 extended this recommendation to include places of employment (Palfreyman, 1993).

Nevertheless, two government-sponsored reports (SJAC, 1979; CORAD, 1982) concluded that local authorities, property developers and architects had largely failed to respond positively to these recommendations, or indeed to repeated government exhortations and a British Standards Institute Code of Practice for Access of the Disabled to Buildings (Imrie and Wells, 1993). A similar disdain has been shown for the stream of Planning Policy Guidance notes from the Department of the Environment intended to inform local planning authorities of their responsibilities with respect to disabled access (MacDonald, 1995). This prompted the introduction in 1985 of building regulations, part M, which stipulated that, in their design and construction, all new buildings including shops, offices, factories, and schools should be made accessible to disabled people (Imrie and Wells, 1993; MacDonald, 1995). However, the access requirement was limited to the level of entry, even in 'new' public buildings.

In addition, the amended building regulations do not cover all new extensions, nor do they apply to the growing number of 'listed' buildings and, most significantly, there is no obligation on the owners of existing properties to make them more accessible. The government argued that such a policy would 'impose unrealistic burdens on business' (DSS, 1994: 36). The long-term prospect is that physical barriers will remain the rule rather than the exception, and disabled people will still not be able to go where non-disabled people go.

However, the heterogeneity of the disabled population bedevils easy architectural answers (Goldsmith, 1976). Moreover, the needs of different groups may conflict with one another. Dropped kerbs favoured by wheelchair-users can be a hazard for people with visual impairments (DoT, 1992). Ambulant disabled people may require a narrow toilet compartment with rails securely fixed at either side and side walls to lean against for support, whereas wheelchair-users typically need space to manoeuvre and transfer. The two groups also have different preferences for the location of entry phones.

Housing

There are over 4.25 million disabled people with 'mobility related impairments' (Martin et al., 1988). Although there is general agreement that there are insufficient accessible dwellings to meet this level of demand (that is, houses where people can live with a minimum of assistance), the exact extent of the shortfall is disputed (Harris et al., 1997). This also has to be set against the policy concern about the lack of 'special needs' housing – including that for disabled people – as expressed in the British NHS and Community Care Act 1990.

Housing Investment Programme statistics for 1995 give a figure of around 44,000 dwellings suitable for wheelchair-users, plus another 96,000 for other disabled people – largely mental health survivors and people with learning difficulties. Over the last twenty-five years, local authority 'completions' (or approvals to build) of wheelchair-adapted dwellings in England rose to around 650 per year in the late 1970s, but thereafter declined dramatically to only a handful in the early 1990s. This is a result of the reduction in stock because of the 'right to buy' policy on council housing and transfers to housing associations. In contrast, there was a modest, if uneven, expansion in approvals to build by housing associations, to an average of 150 per year in the early 1990s. As a consequence, the housing association movement has become a lead player in the provision of special needs housing, although recent changes in the Housing Association Grant threaten its recent expansion (Harris et al., 1997). There is also evidence of mismatch between tenants and housing association accommodation: with only a quarter of wheelchair-adapted dwellings occupied by a wheelchair-user, and over half of wheelchair-user tenants living in non-wheelchair-adapted dwellings! (Harris et al., 1997: 7).

Although the British government acknowledged this problem (DSS, 1994), it did little to encourage either public or private housebuilders to build to accessible standards. Moreover, an 'accessible' unit may not meet other requirements of disabled people, such as having more than one bedroom. Yet most disabled people live as part of a larger family unit/household and even some single disabled people need two-bedded accommodation to allow enough space for their personal assistant. As a result, homelessness among disabled people – particularly those moved from residential institutions into the community – escalated dramatically: by 92 per cent between 1980 and 1988, compared with a

57 per cent rise among the general population (Morris, 1990b). Moreover, this estimate takes no account of those disabled people who live in institutions, hospitals, or with their parents because of the lack of accessible homes (Kestenbaum, 1995).

Nevertheless, in the early 1990s, British disabled people and their families were twice as likely to live in property owned by local authorities as their non-disabled peers. This is because, first, they are on average poorer than non-disabled people and less able to buy or rent houses in the private sector; and second, local authorities have been the main providers of accessible homes because of their statutory duty under the 1970 Chronically Sick and Disabled Persons Act. Private sector landlords rarely offer accessible homes and the deregulation of rents makes this even less likely.

In view of this shortage, adapting existing properties has assumed a higher priority as a way of meeting disabled people's housing needs. However, this solution is not the most cost-effective since the price of building accessible homes is about a third of the amount needed to adapt non-accessible ones. It is also inhibited by the complex procedures which apply to making adaptations to inaccessible accommodation. As a result, the number of house adaptations being funded is generally very small and many disabled people have to invest their own limited resources. This also means that many live in homes which have been only partially adapted. According to a national survey, only 29 per cent of disabled people living in private households thought that they had all the house adaptations they required and tenants in private rented accommodation fared even worse (Lamb and Layzell, 1994).

Transport

The government-sponsored Disabled Persons Transport Advisory Committee (DPTAC) estimated that between 10 and 12 per cent of Britain's population experience difficulties with the 'unfriendly features of the transport environment' (DPTAC, 1989: 1). Furthermore, special needs transport is limited in scope, poorly funded, and fails to give disabled people full control over their transportation needs.

Although the private car is the most popular form of transport in Britain, households with a disabled member are only about half as likely to own such a vehicle. This is because many are too poor to buy and run a car, but motoring is also more costly for disabled people. Cars are built for non-disabled people: to have one adapted for a disabled driver adds significantly to the original price. The maintenance and running expenses mount accordingly and disabled motorists usually have to pay more for car insurance. 'One option available to the disabled person in receipt of the higher rate of the mobility component of Disability Living Allowance is to seek financial backing from the charity Motability to buy or lease a new car. Motability now claims to help 140,000 disabled people a year get a new car (making it Britain's largest car fleet operator). However, those people with a severe impairment are disadvantaged because they must pay for any adaptations to the vehicle. Political pressure has been exerted on Motability to reduce these and other restrictions on eligibility and usage.'

Since running a car is not possible for many disabled people, access to public transport is particularly important. Unfortunately, like mainstream housing, most of it is not constructed with disabled travellers in mind. This applies particularly to the most commonly used forms of public transport: buses and trains. For instance, because of high steps and similar design features, using Britain's buses presents major problems for those with mobility impairments (Heiser, 1995). Similar criticisms are made of Britain's railway system. Although recent improvements mean that most Inter-City services are accessible, this is not the case for local and urban services, and it has been predicted that it will be well into the twenty-first century before regional services reach a similar standard (Barnes, 1991).

This leaves the main forms of accessible public transport as Dial a Ride systems, and subsidized Taxicard services. The former offer flexible door-to-door services using accessible minibuses. Users book their journey in advance, by telephone or post. Taxicard offers locally subsidized taxi services. In practice, funding is grossly inadequate and therefore the service is very limited. For example, in London – which boasts the most developed network in Britain – approximately 90,000 people are eligible to use these schemes, but there are so few vehicles that potential travellers cannot expect to make more than one trip per week (Heiser, 1995). It is also likely that the extent of transport availability is even worse in rural areas. Although the government has recognized that inaccessible transport is a major contributor to the discrimination encountered by disabled people (DSS, 1994), unlike many other Western countries, Britain has yet to produce a meaningful and coherent policy for tackling the problem.

The argument against making transport more accessible is usually that it will cost too much to transform existing transport systems. Yet a recent report suggests that dismantling barriers to the use of public transport may cost society less than keeping those barriers in place. It would release significant resources currently spent, *inter alia*, on domiciliary care services, residential care and hospital out-patient transport (Fowkes et al., 1993: 1). That said, transport systems were designed up to a century ago, railway rolling stock can last for three or four decades, and massive capital investment will be needed to make all London underground stations accessible to wheelchair-users.

Nevertheless, changes are slowly taking place. For example, all inter-city train services are now wheelchair accessible (at least in terms of door widths and provision of wheelchair standing spaces) although extension of this rolling stock throughout the rail system remains a distant objective. Recent light rapid transit systems such as those in Manchester, Sheffield, Tyneside and London Docklands and the London underground's Jubilee Line have been designed with improved accessibility in mind. Bus design has advanced noticeably over the last ten years, with more attention to: entrance/exit step heights, doorway widths, handrails, seating, bell-pushes and signage. Wheelchair-accessible low-floor buses have been introduced in various cities. New technologies (such as digitized speech announcements/information) have been developed to give information to people with hearing and sight impairments on bus times, routes, numbers and destinations. Long-distance coach facilities have been extended – with buffet, entertainment and toilet facilities – but high-level seating and high, narrow steps make difficulties for many disabled people.

In summary, disabled people's right to an independent lifestyle remains significantly inhibited by inaccessible transport, housing and the built environment. Moreover, like other Western societies, Britain has an ageing population, which indicates that, over the coming decades, the number of people with restricted mobility will increase as the proportion of all older people – and especially of those aged over 75 years – in the population rises. Yet despite the manifest shortfall in accessible homes, recent governments have had no major plans to remedy this situation by encouraging developments in either the public or the private sectors. Segregated special needs housing remains central to the current community care plans. Even though the Department of Transport supports in principle fully accessible buses, taxis and trains, it will be well into the next century before these are the norm rather than the exception. While recent amendments to the building regulations acknowledge disabled people's rights of access to public buildings, the inaccessible built environment remains a major barrier to disabled people.

Review

The evidence presented here confirms the existence of systematic inequalities between disabled and non-disabled people. This experience of discrimination spans education, employment and the built environment, including housing and transport. It extends from these 'public' domains to the more 'private' sphere of family life, and moral issues about what sorts of lives are valued and devalued. Although the amount of research on disability as it affects different groups of disabled people is limited, it presents a common picture, with the impact of gender, ethnicity, and age all mediating the experience of disability in specific ways.

Despite this consistent pattern of disadvantage, policy initiatives demonstrate a reluctance to address its social and economic causes. There is an enduring belief that it is unfortunate personal circumstances which are holding disabled people back. The dominant response is therefore geared to catering for disabled people's 'special needs' – as is fully illustrated in respect of education, employment and the built environment – with professionals and professional ideologies fully implicated in disablism. There is little appreciation of the possibility that disabled people are oppressed by a hostile social environment (Brisenden, 1986), and evidence of only minimal support to participate in the 'mainstream' of society.

This shifts the focus to the development of social policies for disabled people, which will be the subject for examination next in chapter 6, with particular reference to their impact both in terms of their exclusion as well as their inclusion of disabled people.

6

Social Policy and Disabled People

The objective of this chapter is to explore the contention of disability theorists that social policy has remained locked into an individualistic, medical approach and as such has been disabling rather than enabling in its impact on disabled people. The discussion will proceed by outlining the origins, content and impact of social policy directed at disabled people in Britain (Ginsburg, 1992). The concern with the *origins* of policy concentrates on how disability comes on to the political agenda. What are the pressures and forces – whether from 'established' political parties and pressure groups or arising out of social protest 'from below' – which have led to disabled people being constituted as a 'social problem' which requires state attention? The *substance* of policy comprises questions about its aims, objectives and content – for example, in terms of extending the rights of social citizenship, enhancing political regulation or promoting economic stability. And finally, it is important to analyse the *impact* of social policy. Disability has acquired a much higher policy profile over recent decades, but how far have policy initiatives diminished social inequalities and divisions and enhanced opportunities for social improvement?

The discussion will begin with the development of British disability policy during the twentieth century, with particular reference to the post-1945 decades. This is set within the broader struggles for citizenship rights as well as recent efforts to 'roll back' and restructure the welfare state. Criticism that the welfare state has 'failed disabled people' is based on wide-ranging evidence of social exclusion (see chapter 5). It is further confirmed by the general economic deprivation experienced by disabled people, and their reliance on state welfare benefits, which is explored in this chapter. The review of income maintenance and social security policy demonstrates how government policy has too often frustrated efforts by disabled people to achieve financial independence. The moves initiated by the right-wing Conservative government elected in 1979 towards a (more) mixed economy of welfare have posed specific dilemmas for disabled people. The same lack of enabling policies is also evident in the second case study, which examines social support in the community. This is contrasted with disabled people's own exploration of inclusionary objectives, notably in respect of 'independent' living options.

Disability and the welfare state

As already noted in chapter 2, the onset of industrialization and urbanization created new difficulties for those with perceived impairments. There was a move away from the traditional family-based system of production and exchange. Under industrial capitalism, individuals were dependent on their capacity to sell their labour in exchange for wages. The situation of those less well able to compete in this new economic system, including women and people with impairments, was made worse because of the associated decline in traditional support networks.

Through the Victorian period, the dominant classes' response was contained in the Poor Law Amendment Act of 1834. Its under-lying Utilitarian philosophy (with individuals rationally pursuing their own self-interest) explained poverty in terms of personal inadequacy or unwillingness to work. The poor had to be discouraged from seeking public assistance. Hence, only indoor relief in the workhouse was provided, and then under conditions designed to deter anyone from extending their stay any longer than absolutely necessary. The location of disabled people in institutions became the favoured policy response, often justified as an enlightened option, both by the state and voluntary organizations (Humphries and Gordon, 1992). In theory, disabled people fell into the category of the 'deserving poor' and might have anticipated less harsh conditions than the 'undeserving poor' but, in practice, this was not always the case. By such means disabled people were confirmed in a separate status as outsiders.

With growing concerns about working-class radicalism and the high levels of poverty, sickness and impairment, a series of health and welfare policy reforms was initiated in Britain at the start of the twentieth century. Yet the preferred level and form of state intervention shifted significantly. In the early decades, a 'residual' solution prevailed (Titmuss, 1958). This upheld an 'individualistic' explanation of poverty. The state should intervene only where the family or the market fail, and even then should restrict its actions to the most deserving cases. Public welfare assistance was condemned as self-defeating because it encourages individual dependence and reduces private initiative, hard work and thrift. It was also criticized for increasing the tax burden on the productive members of society. The state, in this model, ideally restricts its involvement to the provision of a residual safety net, to prevent people falling into abject poverty. State benefits are therefore targeted at particularly deprived groups, and set at a subsistence level to encourage recipients to seek paid employment.

This residual approach prevailed until the 1940s, when a 'post-war settlement' between capital and labour generated wide-ranging 'institutional' reforms (Titmuss, 1958). The rationale for much-augmented state intervention was that it alone could overcome the major social problems facing industrialized societies. The wartime government set up an inter-departmental committee chaired by William Beveridge to explore the whole field of social insurance. Its recommendations were contained in the Beveridge Report, 1942. This outlined far-reaching changes that heralded the post-war welfare state. Beveridge targeted the elimination of what he termed the 'five giants' – want, disease, ignorance, squalor and idleness. These supplied the rationale for, most notably, the development of: the National Health Service (NHS); universal and free primary and secondary education; compulsory insurance benefit for all employees and the self-employed to cover for unemployment and old age; various non-contributory benefits for those not covered by insurance; family and child-care support; and an expansion in council house building. Here, 'The term "welfare state" covers both the direct provision of welfare benefits and services by public agencies, and the subsidy and regulation of occupational, for-profit, voluntary, charitable, informal and other forms of private welfare' (Ginsburg, 1992: 3).

While state provision grew dramatically, there remained a flourishing commercial sector (with private schooling, health care, and insurance schemes). In addition, the voluntary sector had a continuing role, and informal care, within the family and by friends, remained significant in looking after people's social welfare needs. Although charities are characterized as making a major contribution to the well-being of disabled people, it has been calculated that in Britain in recent decades they have met only 6 per cent of disabled people's needs (Hevey, 1992).

While its overall portrayal as a settlement between capital and labour remains central to understanding the character of the post-war welfare state, other assumptions informed the translation of Beveridge's grand objectives into specific social policies. More specifically, the reforms represented a compromise between three overlapping 'welfare settlements': political-economic; social; and organizational (Clarke and Newman, 1997: 1–8).

At the political-economic level, the dominance of Keynesian macro-economic policy on governments in the immediate post-1945 years was crucial. At its heart was a commitment to full employment that proved crucial in winning agreement for, and maintaining, the welfare reforms: 'the maintenance of full employment was both a direct contribution to individual welfare and an essential support for other welfare services, because it simultaneously maximized revenue and minimized demand for them' (Lowe, 1993: 99). Thus, increased welfare state expenditure was regarded as a key stimulus to economic growth and employment. At the same time, the design of welfare policy promoted a national pooling of risk. This helped confirm the political and ideological bases of the welfare state. It became the litmus test of a civilized society, where all citizens were guaranteed basic social needs, irrespective of their ability to pay (Marshall, 1950). Nevertheless, in giving concrete expression to the high ideals of national solidarity, the implementation of welfare policies represented a compromise between 'market-driven' and 'state guaranteed citizenship' (Clarke and Newman, 1997: 1).

The basic structure and principles introduced in the 1940s remained broadly in place until the 1970s. At that time, a gathering global economic crisis presented ammunition for a critique of rising state expenditure and intervention. After a period of political consensus about the merits of the welfare state, the election in Britain in 1979 of a Conservative government, headed by Margaret Thatcher, heralded a shift in government thinking. It paralleled a similar political change of direction in the United States in 1980 with Ronald Reagan's election as President. The welfare state, which had become an instrument for dealing with social problems, was now identified as one of the primary causes. This led to calls to restructure or 'roll back' the state, reduce taxation, and introduce market forces or quasi-markets into the delivery of welfare services as a way of enhancing their efficiency and effectiveness. The encouragement of private health insurance, private pension schemes, home ownership and private education illustrate a general retrenchment of state-provided welfare. The emphasis reverted towards market-driven citizenship.

The 'social' settlement underpinning the welfare state incorporated notions of family, nation and work (F. Williams, 1992: 211–12). 'Family' and 'work' in this context were based on the 'norm' of a wage-earning male maintaining other family members. This, in turn, established various dependent groups, children and older people, married women, plus those who are in ill health or have impairments (Langan and Clarke, 1993: 28). In the same way, the design of a welfare state that would sustain 'the British Race and British ideals in the world' (Beveridge, 1942: 52) left no space for minority ethnic groups. Such exclusionary assumptions were at the heart of welfare state policies. Their effect was to 'naturalize' social divisions, not only of gender and 'race', but also 'the distinction between the able-bodied and the "handicapped"' (Clarke and Newman, 1997: 4).

Social protest among those excluded from the post-war arrangements, such as women, minority ethnic groups and, more recently, disabled people, gathered momentum in the late 1960s (see chapter 7). It was in this context that 'able-bodied' assumptions built into the notion of citizenship were exposed and challenged. The perception of disabled people as not 'normal' legitimated their classification as 'special cases', and the inappropriate and unwelcome state surveillance and regulation of their lives. Yet disabled people increasingly rejected their dependent status. The emphasis on the 'incapacity' or functional limitations of disabled people (in line with the individual/medical model) was overturned in favour of an emphasis on their ability to look after themselves, once given the appropriate assistance. What had been 'hidden' ideological assumptions in social policy were laid open and became subjects for political conflict and division.

The 'organizational' settlement which characterized the post-war welfare state comprised 'a commitment to two modes of co-ordination: bureaucratic administration and professionalism'

(Clarke and Newman, 1997: 4–8). Public service norms and values in administration reinforced claims that the new system would be more impartial and even-handed in the way it dealt with the different sections and interests in the population. The bureaucratic adherence to agreed rules and regulations in administering social welfare policy and programmes was complemented by claims to professional expertise and neutrality. These were accorded a special authority in identifying social problems and policy responses (Cousins, 1987). Professional inclusion therefore carried with it a significant degree of occupational autonomy or control in the day-to-day delivery of services. This was most evident in the influence of the medical profession within the NHS, but was also apparent in education and, to a lesser extent, personal social services.

Again, the initial acceptance of the merits of bureaucratic efficiency and neutrality and professional expertise and altruism came under growing criticism. The virtues of bureaucratic administration began to look very different from the perspective of welfare state clients. This was particularly evident at street level, where general guidelines had to be translated into the particular circumstances of individual claimants (Hudson, 1989). The 'system' seemed unable to respond to the material problems of disabled people. At another level, public administration precepts gave way to an emphasis on the virtues of private management – managerialism. This went hand in hand with the promotion of a mixed economy of welfare, encompassing the introduction of commercial sector management techniques and an opening up of services to (more) competition, including their privatization.

Welfare professionalism was subjected to similar criticism. Women, black and minority ethnic groups and disabled people all argued that institutional and professional power in the design and implementation of social policies replicated existing social inequalities – rooted in patriarchy, racism and a disabling society (F. Williams, 1989). In the case of disabled people, assessment of need and eligibility for benefits were typically determined by medical judgement, with others, such as social workers, making a significant but lesser input. More generally, the disenchantment with professional 'care' reinforced disabled people's determination to achieve more control over their own lives. Nevertheless, there was a growing debate within many professions about best practice in practitioner–client relations. The concepts of 'normalization' and 'empowerment', for example, entered the day-to-day professional vocabulary as confirmation of their 'enlightened' credentials. More problematic is the translation of these concepts into street-level (or consulting room) practices. In some cases, professional claims to be forging an alliance with a client group looked more like a mechanism for professional advancement.

Disabled people and their organizations have extended their demands from achieving a fair distribution of welfare benefits to seeking fundamental changes in the bases on which assistance is delivered. This amounts to an attack on traditional welfare policies and principles, as well as a rejection of professional domination of their lives. In addition, disabled people sought to exploit the new opportunities for 'consumer' choice contained in the neo-liberal critique of public monopolies. The welfare benefit system was also widely criticized as a disincentive to seek work – the 'benefit trap' – because taking a low-paid job means less income than if the individual stays on income support.

The post-war decades have therefore witnessed a remarkable shift in thinking about the welfare state in general and the role of social policy towards disabled people in particular. These changing perspectives will be illustrated by reviews of key issues and policy changes in respect of first, social security and income maintenance and, second, social support in the community.

Social security policy

The social security system in Britain between the 1950s and 1970s gave little specific recognition to the needs of people with perceived impairments. There were only a few specific schemes, notably war disablement pensions and benefits under the National Insurance (Industrial Injury) Act 1946 for those who acquired an impairment at work. These long-term benefits were based on degree of impairment, measured by functional loss in comparison with a 'non-disabled' person of the same age and sex. All others unable to work, irrespective of whether they had an impairment or not, were entitled to claim from the range of existing benefits. This presented a stark contrast with the unified social security package for disabled people envisaged by Beveridge, which did not differentiate on the basis of the cause of the impairment (Walker and Walker, 1991).

This system continued until the 1970s, when the 'compensation for injury' emphasis began to give way to a range of new measures designed to address the specific needs of people with perceived impairments, such as a general attendance allowance – a universal benefit based on evidence of severe impairment; a non-contributory invalidity pension; a mobility allowance; and an invalid care allowance (ICA).

However, the piecemeal nature of these developments produced 'an incoherent mixture of benefits':

> Rather than depending upon the impact of disablement, an individual's benefit entitlement, and the amount of benefit received, rests crucially on: how the disability occurred, the age when a claim is made, the length of time spent in the UK, ability to work, and whether national insurance contributions have been paid for the required period of time. (Walker and Walker, 1991: 25)

As part of its agenda for restructuring the welfare state, the Thatcher government in Britain embarked on a wide-ranging review of the social security system. This had twin objectives: to control the level of social security expenditure, which stood at around 10 per cent of Gross Domestic Product (GDP); and to reduce the 'welfare dependency' culture. It aimed to target resources on those in most need, while also simplifying the benefit system. In practice, the consideration of disability policies was held up while the Office of Population Censuses and Surveys completed its wide-ranging study of 'disability', including the financial circumstances and needs of disabled people.

Financial circumstances of disabled people

'Want' or poverty was one of the 'five giants' that the welfare state was designed to eliminate. This is not simply a question of material deprivation, but extends into people's sense of loss of dignity and self-worth, and of social exclusion. Poverty is also associated with higher levels of ill health, impairment and premature death (Townsend, 1993: 18). Political urgency was injected into these debates by the rediscovery of poverty at repeated intervals since the late 1960s (Townsend, 1979).

Poverty, in the 'absolute' sense of being unable to buy the basic necessities of life, such as food and shelter, is distinguished from 'relative' poverty, where the emphasis is on those who lack the financial resources to meet what are regarded minimum 'social' necessities. For Townsend this is 'when they lack the resources to obtain the types of diet, participate in the activities and have the living conditions and amenities which are customary or at least are widely encouraged or approved in the society in which we live' (Townsend, 1979: 3). Surveys of public opinion are used to determine what the majority regard as necessities in life. In a similar vein, Mack and Lansley (1985) define the 'poor' in terms of whether three or more of these necessities were lacking, taking as their base a list of fourteen, including three meals a day for children, carpets, birthday presents and a TV.

Following this 'relative' approach, Townsend's national study *Poverty in the United Kingdom* (1979) demonstrates that disabled people make up a disproportionate section of those falling on and below the (relative) poverty line. This ties in with other known risk factors: a higher proportion of disabled people are over 60 years of age, and fewer are in full-time employment, compared with the general population. There was also a significant positive relationship between 'degree of incapacity' (or severity of impairment) and a lack of 'the necessities and comforts of life' measured by a 'deprivation index' score (Townsend, 1979: 714–16). As the figures in table 6.1 illustrate, 49 per cent of those with a 'severe incapacity', compared to 13 per cent of the non-disabled population, were rated as 'highly deprived' with a deprivation score of 6 or higher.

An OPCS report on the financial circumstances of disabled adults offered further confirmation of the economic deprivation of disabled people in Britain (Martin and White, 1988). Only a minority of disabled people (31 per cent) under retirement age were in work. The average weekly earnings of disabled males in full-time employment were 81 per cent of the general population level,

Table 6.1 Level of deprivation and degree of incapacity (UK)

| | Deprivation index | | Degree of incapacity (%) | | |
	None (0)	Minor (1–2)	Some (3–6)	Appreciable (7–10)	Severe (11+)
0–1	19	11	10	6	1
2–3	40	36	31	27	15
4–5	28	32	34	29	35
6–7	11	18	21	32	32
8+	2	3	5	7	17

Source: Townsend, 1979: table 20.14.

while among females it was 88 per cent (pp. 16–18). A high proportion depended on state benefits as their main or sole source of
income (although at least two of these – child benefit and the state
retirement pension – are not 'disability-related'). Among non-
pensioner families, 35 per cent received a 'disability-related'
income maintenance benefit, compared with 6 per cent of pensioner families. A 'disability' costs allowance was received by 15
per cent of non-pensioner and 11 per cent of pensioner families
(Martin and White, 1988: 20).

In families with a disabled adult, state benefits comprised 58 per
cent of total income, with 24 per cent from earnings and 18 per
cent from other sources (most often a pension or redundancy
payment from a previous employer, or interest on savings/invest-
ments). Among pensioner families, state benefits made up 74 per
cent of total income. Three-quarters of disabled adults depended
on state benefits as their main income source, with married
couples of working age the only exception – typically because
there was a non-disabled partner (Martin and White, 1988: 26–8).
There was also considerable income variation, with 62 per cent of
disabled non-pensioners, compared with 41 per cent of non-
disabled non-pensioners, earning less than three-quarters of their
group's mean income. Conversely, only 19 per cent of non-
pensioner disabled adults received an 'above-average' income,
compared with 42 per cent in the general population (pp. 30–2).

Disabled women are more likely to be in or close to poverty,
with 21 per cent of non-disabled women at the poverty level, compared with 35 per cent with a 'minor' impairment, and 47 per cent
with the most 'severe' rating (Townsend, 1979: 733–4). The contrast
was even more accentuated among those over 60 years of age.
These surveys also agreed about the major effect on family
employment patterns, and hence on family income, of having a
disabled child (Younghusband et al., 1970; Baldwin and Glendinning, 1981). Almost a third of family units with a disabled child
also had no one in paid work (most of these were single parents)
and hence relied heavily on state benefits (Smyth and Robus, 1989:
10, 13).

The OPCS survey also examined the 'extra expenditure' that a
person with an impairment incurred (due to living in an 'able-
bodied' society) to maintain a basic standard of living. Four categories were identified: capital payments for special equipment;
capital payments for 'general' support such as a washing machine;
regular impairment-related expenditure, on items such as

medicines and domestic back-up; and regular payments for an impairment-related component of 'normal' expenditure, such as additional food or transport costs. On average, OPCS calculated that these totalled £6.10 per week, or 8 per cent of average income – comprising £2.60 on special items/services, and £4.80 on normal items. There was, however, significant variation, from £3.20 to £11.70, according to degree of severity, and further contrasts linked to the type of impairment (Martin and White, 1988: 52–4).

These figures have been widely disputed as far too low on the following grounds: the OPCS survey was conducted before benefits cuts were introduced in 1988; there was a gross underestimate of expenditure on 'one-off' special items because only purchases in the previous year were considered; not enough severely disabled people were included in the sample; and the chosen interview format restricted the time allowed to discuss these 'impairment costs' (DIG, 1988; Abberley, 1992; Berthoud et al., 1993). The Disablement Income Group's follow-up study (DIG, 1988) suggested that, using the OPCS approach, the average extra weekly expenditure amounted to £41.84, while using its own revised format produced a figure of £65.94 – a difference of 58 per cent.

Hence, disabled people are less likely to be in employment, have lower average income levels, and have to meet the 'extra costs' of impairment:

> In general, the greater poverty of disabled people is explained by their uneven or limited access to the principal resource systems of society – the labour market and wage system, national insurance and its associated schemes, and the wealth-accumulating systems, particularly home ownership, life insurance and occupational pension schemes; by the indirect limitation which disability imposes upon the capacities of relatives, pooling personal resources in full or part in the household or family, to earn incomes and accumulate wealth themselves; and by the failure of society to recognise, or to recognise only unevenly or fitfully, the additional resources that are required in disablement to obtain standards of living equivalent to those of the non-disabled. (Townsend, 1979: 734–5).

A comprehensive disability income?

In considering new ways forward in social security policy, one of the first radical proposals advanced by disabled people in Britain was for a national, and comprehensive, disability income (Walker and Townsend, 1981). The campaign for a National Disability

Income had taken off in 1965 with the formation of the Disablement Income Group (DIG) by two disabled women – Megan du Boisson and Berit Moore. In 1974, new momentum was given to the campaign by the formation of the Disability Alliance (DA), which comprised a group of experts and representatives from disabled people's organizations. Despite their differences, both shared a commitment to a comprehensive state-funded scheme which would offer full coverage of all physical and 'mental' impairments, no discrimination on grounds of cause, recognition of the greater financial needs of the most 'severely' impaired people, and the necessity of an adequate income to enable disabled people to participate fully in everyday life.

DIG (1987) proposals comprised a disablement costs allowance and an income maintenance element for all those with an accredited impairment and unable to work. The tax-free disablement costs allowance would depend on the nature and severity of the impairment. Benefits would be paid at all ages but not necessarily at the same rates, given that financial need varies over the life course. Assessment would reflect the impairment's restriction in everyday activities, and the cost and quality of life. In addition, there would be allowances for large identifiable expenses. An additional rate of Attendance Allowance would be introduced to enable people to buy the help they need to live outside residential institutions. A 'carer's allowance' would also be paid to supply full-time assistance to a person with a severe impairment. The aim was to move away from means-tested benefits and ensure that the disability income was available as of right.

However, critics within the disabled people's movement, such as the Union of Physically Impaired Against Segregation (UPIAS), argued that these proposals failed to make a clear break with the traditional individual approach to disability and did not address the systematic exclusion of disabled people from mainstream society: 'Benefits which are not carefully related to the struggle for integrated employment and active social participation will constantly be used to justify our dependence and exclusion from the mainstream of life – the very opposite of what is intended' (UPIAS, 1976: 15).

New benefits, old ways?

The OPCS surveys confirmed that social security provision was central to the well-being of so many disabled people. Disabled people were assured that they were among the most 'deserving' of government assistance (Glendinning, 1992). Nevertheless, the British Conservative government persisted with a policy of pruning disability benefits and applying them more selectively. For example, the non-contributory invalidity pension was replaced in 1984 by the severe disablement allowance (SDA), and eligibility was restricted to 'incapacity to work', and paid at 60 per cent of full invalidity pension. One of the main routes of entitlement to SDA now involves claimants undergoing a 'disablement test' in order to demonstrate functional limitations that add up to a legal (rather than functional) '80 per cent disability' (box 6.1). This closely follows the *International Classification of Impairments, Disabilities and Handicaps* (WHO, 1980), with a medical assessment of how far 'loss of faculty' and 'disability' restrict individual performance over everyday activities (DA, 1998). The applicant's 'capabilities' are compared with a 'normal' person of the same age and sex.

In 1988, major revisions were introduced to means-tested supplementary and housing benefits which hit disabled people particularly hard. For example, ten of the fourteen 'additional requirements' payable under the previous supplementary benefit scheme were related to the extra costs of impairment. Estimates in 1986 suggested that around 300,000 people received payments for such items as extra heating, laundry, special diets and the costs of personal assistance – yet these were lost in the new income support scheme (Andrews and Jacobs, 1990).

The Conservative government finally published its proposals for reforming benefits directed at disabled people in 1990 in its White Paper *The Way Ahead: Benefits for Disabled People* (DSS, 1990). The overall objectives remained: to focus more specifically on disabled people's needs, help those who wanted into work, give more help to those in most need, and avoid duplication of benefits (p. 5). The White Paper proposed further changes to existing benefits, as well as the introduction of new ones (Dalley, 1991a: 11–12). However, a comprehensive disability income benefit was rejected, and the much-discussed simplification of the social security system left as many measures in place as previously. It also ignored OPCS findings of the relatively low take-up of existing allowances and lack of information of available benefits (Martin and White, 1988; Walker and Walker, 1991).

The new disability benefits comprised the Disability Working Allowance (DWA), a means-tested benefit intended to aid people with impairments in low-paid employment, and the Disability

Living Allowance (DLA), a non-contributory, non-means-tested benefit, designed to cover some of the 'extra' costs of disability. It established two new, lower rates designed for those who did not qualify for the existing Attendance and Mobility Allowances, but who were severely impaired and unlikely to enter paid employment. However, the DLA was only available to those under 65 years, who had a severe impairment, and required constant attention during the day and/or night and were unable to go out of the house unaided.

Both benefits illustrate the continuing dominance of medical assessment. To claim the Attendance Allowance component of DLA, for example, a disabled person has to prepare detailed information about the problems they encounter undertaking personal tasks such as washing, eating and using the toilet. Although the initial claim is based on self-assessment, claimants are expected to give supporting medical evidence. Those whose claims have been rejected must undergo a medical test if they reapply. Given that the DLA is paid at three different rates, a confrontational atmosphere is encouraged, with claimants expected to emphasize their impairments and functional limitations in order to receive what they regard as a 'fair' level of benefit. In addition, new claimants for DWA can only apply when they have a job; and they cannot be sure that they will be allowed to return to long-term incapacity benefit if they become unemployed again.

In response to concerns about the disincentive to work under the former system, the DWA allows for the 'topping up' of earnings to encourage disabled workers into otherwise low-paid employment. However, the DWA is means-tested and, therefore, rising income has to be balanced against diminished cash benefits. It was predicted that DWA would help around 50,000 of the 2 million disabled people of working age, yet in 1995 there were merely 4,000 recipients, and it was estimated that only 200 of these had entered employment because of the benefit incentives (Berthoud, 1995). Evidence on whether the target group for the take-up of the newer, lower rates of DLA has been reached has been mixed, although Noble et al. (1997) report that DLA has brought in large amounts of money to low-income areas. Daly and Noble (1996) outline a similarly uneven picture in the receipt of the mobility component of DLA, with the new benefit/rate not being taken up by significant numbers of those with the most severe impairments.

The failure of DWA to facilitate the entry of disabled people into

Box 6.1 Criteria for the 'all work' test (selected examples only)
To pass the 'all work' test, it is necessary to score 15 or more points under one or more activities.

Physical impairments (fits excluded)
Selected examples of conditions and points score in brackets (passing the test requires 15 points):

Walking cannot walk more than 50 yards without stopping or discomfort (15); cannot walk more than 200 metres without stopping or severe discomfort (7).

Sitting cannot sit comfortably for more than 10 minutes without having to move from the chair because the degree of discomfort makes it impossible to continue sitting (15); cannot sit comfortably for more than 30 minutes without having to move from the chair because the degree of discomfort makes it impossible to continue sitting (7).

Standing cannot stand for more than 10 minutes before needing to sit down (15); cannot stand for more than 30 minutes before needing to sit down (7).

Manual dexterity cannot turn the pages of a book with either hand (15); cannot turn a sink tap or the control knobs on a cooker with one hand, but can with the other (6).

Lifting cannot pick up and pour from a full saucepan or a kettle of 1.7-litre capacity with either hand (15); cannot pick up and carry a 2.5 kg bag of potatoes with either hand (8).

Speech speech cannot be understood by family or friends (15); strangers have some difficulty understanding speech (8).

Hearing cannot hear well enough to understand someone talking in a loud voice in a quiet room (15); cannot hear well enough to understand someone talking in a normal voice on a busy street (8).

Sight cannot see well enough to read 16-point print at a distance greater than 20 cm (15); cannot see well enough to recognize a friend across the road at a distance of at least 15 metres (8).

Continence loses control of bowels at least once a week (15); loses control of bowels occasionally (9).

'Mental' impairments
Selected examples of conditions awarded 2 or 1 points:

Task completion cannot answer the telephone and reliably take a message (2); overlooks or forgets the risks posed by domestic appliances or other common hazards due to poor concentration (1).

Daily living needs encouragement to get up and dress (2); is frequently distressed at some time of the day due to fluctuation of mood (1).

Coping with pressure frequently feels scared or panicky for no obvious reason (2); is unable to cope with changes in daily routine (1).

Interaction with other people cannot look after self without help from others (2); gets irritated by things that would not have been a bother before becoming ill (1).

Source: adapted from DA, 1998: 70–2.

work at the anticipated rate has added fuel to the debate about how government funds to support those with perceived impairments are best allocated (Noble et al., 1997). Should these be targeted at individuals or directed to environmental improvements? Berthoud et al. (1993) estimate that in the second half of the 1980s for every £19 spent on benefits, £1 was spent on employment policies. The introduction of the DLA and DWA does not address this gap. Their emphasis remains firmly tied to an individualized approach to disability. Similarly, enthusiasm for a non-means-tested income addition to meet the 'extra costs' of disability must be tempered with what actually happens to that money. For some, if not most, the extra income simply pays for increased living costs.

The post-war history of income maintenance for disabled people in Britain has not broken the underlying link between disability and poverty. Means-tested benefits still play a major role in the lives of disabled people (table 6.2). There has been no significant movement towards a comprehensive disability income. Moreover, by focusing on physical impairment, policy-makers have concentrated provision on one section of the disabled community, leaving the remainder, including older people, the 'mentally ill', and those

Table 6.2 Examples of British social security benefits in the 1990s

Contributory (paid only to those who have paid insurance contributions)	Non-contributory (and not means-tested)	Means-tested (paid only to those on limited means)
Statutory Maternity Benefit	Children's Allowance	Income Support
Retirement pension	Mobility Allowance	Income Maintenance
Unemployment Benefit	Attendance Allowance	Social Fund
Widows' pension	Disabled Living	Disability Working
Widowed Mothers'	Allowance	Allowance
Allowance	Invalid Care Allowance	Supplementary
Incapacity Benefit	War pensions	pension
		Death Benefit
		Family Credit
		Housing Benefit
		Council Tax Benefit

Disability related benefits are underlined.

Source: adapted from Ackers and Abbott, 1996: 100, box 5.1.

with learning difficulties, relatively more disadvantaged (Walker, 1981a: 15).

> In addition to its failure to combat poverty, the social security system has been used to create important divisions in financial status between different groups of people with disabilities based not on need, but on the place where the disablement occurred, type of disability, and the age of onset of disability. (Walker and Walker, 1991: 20)

The 'way ahead' charted by government policy demonstrates moves towards more selectivity by targeting resources on those in most need, with the highest costs or the severest impairment. The 'New Labour' government elected in Britain in May 1997 outlined its own version of a social security system that is less complex and more coherent. However, as far as disabled people are concerned, the growing emphasis on 'residualism' reinforces the perception of the social security system as a form of social control, discouraging take-up because the benefits are stigmatizing, set at inadequate levels and, moreover, extremely difficult to work out.

Social support in the community

Throughout the post-1945 period, the organization and delivery of social services for disabled people in Britain have been shaped by inadequate funding and traditional assumptions that people with impairments needed to be 'cared for' (Oliver, 1990; Morris, 1993). Nevertheless, it was also a period when a broad consensus emerged on the importance of moving disabled people out of residential institutions and into the community, where much more appropriate services could be delivered.

Service development for those with physical impairments was highlighted in the 1970 Chronically Sick and Disabled Persons (CSDP) Act. This laid emphasis on the enhancement of services, and the participation of disabled people in service delivery. It came at a propitious time for social policy innovation: slow but consistent economic growth since the 1950s; a rise in the disabled population due to medical advances and increased life expectancy (Harris et al., 1971); rising expectations – fuelled by publication of the Seebohm Report in 1968 – that existing provision, established under the 1948 National Assistance Act, was inadequate. In addition, a succession of government discussion papers through the 1970s promoted the importance of social and community care for disabled people – *Better Services for the Mentally Handicapped* (DHSS, 1971), *Better Services for the Mentally Ill* (DHSS, 1975), and *Priorities for Health and Personal Social Services in England* (DHSS, 1976).

Evaluation of the CSDP Act was mixed. Topliss and Gould (1981) saw it as a significant recognition of the social rights of disabled people, while admitting that it failed to deliver the services required by disabled people. Ann Shearer took a contrary line, arguing that the 1970 CSDP Act actually reinforced the notion that people with impairments 'are "helpless"; unable to choose for themselves the aids to opportunity they need. What this effectively does is to lock them into the service providers' perceptions of what is good for them, and so limit rather than expand their areas of effective choice' (Shearer, 1981a: 82–3).

Such criticism spread out into a wider attack on institutional care and demands by disabled people to be relocated within the mainstream of community life (Campling, 1981; Davis, 1981; Hunt, 1981; Sutherland, 1981). There was ample research evidence of the harmful consequences of long-stay institutions. Institutional life was criticized as a degrading and dehumanizing experience for residents, with scant evidence of its long-term therapeutic benefit (Goffman, 1968; Jones and Fowles, 1984). Disabled people contributed their own attack (Hunt, 1966, 1981). Policy-makers were particularly persuaded by arguments that institutional services were a relatively more expensive option than community assistance. Grand plans were prepared to drastically reduce the numbers in long-stay psychiatric and 'mental handicap' hospitals and institutions.

Community care

Arguments favouring community care for disabled people intensified in the 1970s and early 1980s, although its attraction varied:

> To the politician 'community care' is a useful piece of rhetoric, to the sociologist, it is a stick to beat institutional care with; to the civil servant, it is a cheap alternative to institutional care which can be passed to the local authorities for action – or inaction; to the visionary, it is a dream of the new society in which people really do care; to social services departments, it is a nightmare of heightened public

expectations and inadequate resources to meet them. (Jones et al., 1978: 114)

Clarification of what community care should be delivered, and by whom, remained unresolved (Bayley, 1973). In practice, it typically entailed dependence upon family and friends – the majority of whom were women (Parker, 1990). Hence, community services are geared to help these 'informal carers'. Services are supplied directly to the disabled person only when they live alone. Even then the services are not delivered in a way which enables people to have control over their daily living activities nor are they enabled to play a role in the wider society. Such community care is attacked as 'the most exploitative of all forms of so called care delivered in our society today for it exploits both the carer and the person receiving care. It ruins relationships between people and results in thwarted life opportunities on both sides of the caring equation' (Brisenden, 1989: 10).

To make matters worse, the complexity of the social security system was matched by a bewildering array of provider agencies and organizations, including health authorities, local authority social service departments, as well as those in the voluntary and private sectors. This encouraged little sense of coherence in service provision, which also varied considerably around Britain (Beardshaw, 1988). On top of all this, there was an extraordinary growth in the numbers of older people moving into private sector residential homes because those receiving supplementary benefit were allowed to claim back their costs.

At the same time, significant numbers of people with severe impairments, particularly older people, have had little choice but to live in residential institutions. According to the OPCS survey, 80 per cent of the 422,000 disabled adults living in institutions were above retirement age in the mid-1980s (Martin et al., 1988). However, the average length of time spent in institutions has diminished significantly for some (younger) groups, notably those with a 'mental' illness (although a significant minority now experience a 'revolving door' philosophy, with shorter but repeated stays). There has also been a significant transfer of people with learning difficulties from 'old-style' large, institutions into much smaller units of supervised or sheltered accommodation. Conversely, for other groups such as older people, once taken into residential care it is very difficult to return home.

Amidst mounting criticism, spearheaded by reports from the

Audit Commission (1986) and Sir Roy Griffiths (1988), the government announced plans for a shake-up in community services in the White Paper *Caring for People* (DoH, 1989). The aim was to promote a 'mixed economy of welfare', by integrating public, private and voluntary sectors, end the confusion over services so that there was a clearer division between social and medical/health services, remove the social security incentives to increase residential care, extend consumer choice, and make services more accountable. These proposals were largely incorporated into the NHS and Community Care Act 1990 which came into force in April 1993.

Local authority social service departments were given overall responsibility for the administration of 'social care' services, along with other local authority services, which created uncertainties about the level of funding. Social service departments were also instructed to engage in compulsory tendering for services, with the private and voluntary sectors competing with the public sector. However, with most disabled people on low incomes or reliant on welfare payments, their 'choice' is effectively limited to services chosen for them by the local authority social service department.

Crucially, the 1990 Act requires local authorities to organize 'packages of care' for disabled people. Individual needs and circumstances (involving assessment of impairment-related functional limitations, family situation and financial resources) are subject to detailed assessment by social workers and other professionals. Case or care managers are then appointed to co-ordinate services and be responsible for budgeting. However, disabled people have little opportunity to challenge professional assessments of need or decisions by social service staff (GMCDP, 1995: 3). To this extent, the Act represents a potential step backwards in the power balance between the professionals and the service users. Although care management is supposed to be an empowering experience, most disabled people disagree (Evans, 1995: 118). Accountability and consumer choice carry far less weight than promised, and the emphasis on 'care' reiterated previous dependency-creating service provision: ' "Care in the community", "caring for people", providing services through "care managers" . . . all these phrases structure the welfare discourse and imply a particular view of disabled people' (Oliver and Barnes, 1991: 9–10).

These concerns were also directed at organizations campaigning for the rights of 'carers' which seemed to reaffirm the dependency of those with impairments. There have been few signs of the two groups uniting around the common grievance that inadequate income and inappropriate services create the demand for unpaid assistance. For the government, backing 'informal carers' makes sound economic sense, since it requires lower funding, and it has therefore been placed at the heart of its community care policy.

As the 1980s progressed, professionals and policy-makers began to respond more positively to arguments for greater user input to service delivery. The notion of user involvement was incorporated into the 1986 Disabled Persons (Services Consultation and Representation) Act, and later into the 1990 NHS and Community Care Act. However, as far as disabled people are concerned, there was little meaningful consultation with user groups (Evans and Hughes, 1993; Evans, 1995). Local authorities continued to rely heavily on established networks of voluntary organizations, many of which are organizations *for*, rather than organizations *of*, disabled people (Croft and Beresford, 1990; Bewley and Glendinning, 1994; Lindoe and Morris, 1995). This is not altogether surprising given that the majority of organizations controlled and run by disabled people have been drastically under-resourced.

A vivid illustration of disabled people's experiences is contained in Barrie Fielder's (1988) review of the Living Options Project set up in 1984. This entailed an action-research study involving some thirty voluntary organizations who were concerned about the lack of housing and support services for people with severe physical impairments. Although identified as a 'priority group' (DHSS, 1981a), their ambitions for 'independent and ordinary lifestyles' (Fielder, 1991: 86) were widely denied in practice. The report concludes that 'provision was largely ineffective, uncoordinated and patchy and was meeting the needs of very few disabled individuals' (Fielder, 1991: 86). The majority were assisted at home by relatives or friends with little or no backing from statutory services. Others were in hospitals or residential homes. To achieve greater autonomy required personal determination and hard work in the face of overwhelming obstacles. Nevertheless, the report remains optimistic that:

> There is no degree of physical disability that cannot be supported in the community (non-institutional, non-medical setting). Even the most severely disabled people can and do live independently with appropriate help . . . An apparent demand for residential care, and for short stay respite care, results from the lack of home based alternatives. (Fielder, 1988: 71)

A parallel picture of the demand for user-led services which facilitate integration into the wider community is illustrated in *Walking into Darkness: The Experience of Spinal Cord Injury* (1988) by Mike Oliver and his colleagues, and in Jenny Morris' (1989) collection *Able Lives: Women's Experience of Paralysis*. Living full lives in the community means that disabled people should have access to a comprehensive range of services which enable them to pursue an 'ordinary' (not 'special') lifestyle. The notion of independent living espoused by the disabled people's movement around the world is diametrically opposed to orthodox approaches – the equivalent of community care in the UK (Davis, 1981; Crewe and Zola, 1983; HCIL, 1986). While the former is concerned with basic civil and human rights, community care is regarded as professionally controlled:

> In many areas of their lives, disabled people's experiences do not accord with the lifestyle expectations of their contemporaries: for example, many disabled adults do not have the right to decide what time to get up or go to bed or indeed who to go to bed with, when and what to eat, how often to bath or even be in control of the times when they can empty their bladders or open their bowels. (Oliver, 1996a: 48)

DCDP's 'seven needs'

The Derbyshire Coalition of Disabled People (DCDP) was in the forefront of those arguing that existing policies have been dependency-creating because they have denied disabled people's own view of their social needs. Instead, non-disabled professionals have been left to decide the appropriate type and level of service provision. As a result, service provision has been dominated by a 'rehabilitation' approach. To counter this, DCDP developed a comprehensive strategy to enhance community provision, based on seven key needs and priorities formulated by disabled people. These were: information, access, housing, technical aids, personal assistance, counselling and transport (Davis and Mullender, 1993). (Social barriers in access, housing and transport are not dealt with here as they have already been examined in chapter 5.) The importance of other 'needs', such as education, work and leisure, was recognized, but it was argued that these could be offered by mainstream services once the seven 'primary' needs had been met.

Access to information is fundamental to meaningful participation in contemporary society. Yet disabled people have traditionally been denied adequate information relevant to their circumstances, whether accessible schools, employment opportunities, or social benefits. This highlighted a need for a national network of disablement information services. This was formally recognized to some extent in both the 1948 National Assistance Act and the 1970 CSDP Act – and restated in the 1986 Disabled Persons (Services, Consultation and Representation) Act. Ken Davis, a disabled activist, took the lead in creating one such user-led service – Disablement Information and Advice Line (DIAL) – in 1976; which was followed by the National Information Forum, established in 1986, and the three-year National Disability Information Project (NDIP) which concluded in October 1994. However, concerns have been expressed within the disabled people's movement that DIAL has been 'colonized' by 'non-disabled' experts, following much the same trajectory as DIG and the Disability Alliance (Oliver and Barnes, 1998). Notwithstanding this criticism, disability information services are still characterized by uneven provision, lack of resources, and a paucity of services in key areas, notably the information needs of minority ethnic and other marginalized groups (Barnes, 1995; Moore, 1995).

A further social need of disabled people is *personal assistance*. Official figures show that 60 per cent of all disabled adults require some form of personal and/or domestic back-up (Martin et al., 1988), such as using the toilet, dressing, cooking, and cleaning the house. The majority of these people rely on unpaid, informal 'carers'. A combination of statutory and voluntary supplementary services are available, but delivery is far from guaranteed (and under continuing threat of financial cutbacks). This creates problems for disabled people in organizing their daily lives as they want. Statutory provision is increasingly limited to home-based assistance for the most basic personal care tasks (Kestenbaum, 1995: 21).

Many of these difficulties can be resolved by disabled individuals employing their own personal assistant. However, this is not welcomed by the entire disabled population, particularly where partners or close family relations are involved (Parker, 1993), and in certain circumstances has particular disadvantages for disabled women with a partner, who may feel that employing a younger, 'non-disabled' female 'threatens' her domestic role and relationships (Rae, 1993). Nevertheless, research studies report that it is how large numbers of disabled people want to manage their lives (Kestenbaum, 1995), and it is now closer to becoming a real possibility as a result of the legalization of direct payments to disabled people to purchase personal assistance (see next section). Nevertheless, the arrangement of a personal 'care' package is a time-consuming matter, and potentially conflictual as disabled people become 'employers'. With such issues in mind, the British Council of Disabled People (BCODP) recently launched the National Centre for Independent Living to advise local groups of disabled people and supply training for social service departments.

Counselling and peer support is also much in demand. Information by itself is not necessarily empowering unless it is linked to knowledge about how it can be used. Hence the significance of advice and counselling. Peer-provided services, by disabled people with similar experiences, are much preferred to specialized, professional services run by hospitals, local authority social service departments, and national charities (Davis, 1990). However, there is a lack of peer support services and, as with information and advice services, there are specific concerns about the absence of support for minorities within the disabled population (Barnes, 1995).

A further need is *technical aids and equipment*. The OPCS survey concluded that 69 per cent of all disabled adults in Britain use some form of special equipment, including wheelchairs, surgical braces, artificial limbs, and aids to help vision (in addition to glasses), hearing, and to control incontinence (Martin et al., 1989). However, there are also clear gaps in provision, with a lack of appropriate equipment among 7 per cent of those with mobility impairments; 13 per cent with visual impairments; 29 per cent with a hearing impairment; 17 per cent with continence impairments; and 25 per cent with impairments which affect their arms and hands (Martin et al., 1989).

There are a number of reasons for this under- or uneven provision. First, identifying what disability aids and equipment are available can be confusing because they are supplied by a variety of state agencies, voluntary groups and charities, with further local variation. Second, many disabled people encounter long delays before they get items. Third, much of the new equipment supplied by the state sector is simply not good enough. One study found that over a quarter of all disabled young adults under 30 in London were using unsatisfactory or worn-out equipment (Thomas et al., 1989). This was particularly the case with wheelchairs because funding of high-quality chairs has been extremely limited. Provision of essential accessories such as special seating has also been very inadequate. As a consequence many people have to look to charities or the secondhand market for suitable equipment (Smith and Goddard, 1994; Lecouturier and Jacoby, 1995).

Independent and integrated living options

For many, alternative service development for disabled people starts with the American Independent Living Movement (ILM), and its emphasis on a radical move towards 'self-empowerment' (DeJong, 1983; Hahn, 1986). Out of these developments, the first Centre for Independent Living (CIL) was set up in 1972 in Berkeley, California as a self-help group managed by disabled people. Throughout the late 1960s and early 1970s the number of disabled students at Berkeley had risen dramatically because of the increasing accessibility of the campus and generally supportive culture. Their experience of the university support programme inspired disabled students to develop a CIL in the local community (Zola, 1994). It established such a reputation that other CILs soon followed. The emphasis was on providing a range of services including wheelchair repair, ramp construction, screening and training personal assistants, information and referral on accessible housing, peer counselling, and political and legal advocacy.

Federal government funding played a crucial role in developing CILs both in Berkeley and more generally around the country. Congress amended the Rehabilitation Act in 1978 to establish 'a programme of Comprehensive Services for Independent Living'. This allowed funds previously designated for use in employment-related training to be utilized to promote independent living for people with 'severe disabilities' unable to find work. A condition of receiving funding was that disabled people were involved in the CIL's policy direction and management. By the late 1980s, over 300 CILs had been established across America. Besides providing essential services, they became a site for consciousness-raising and political organizing 'although not all have been unambiguously controlled by disabled people' (Scotch, 1989: 394).

Britain's first CILs were set up in the mid-1980s by two pioneering disabled people's organizations: the Derbyshire Coalition of Disabled People and the Hampshire Coalition of Disabled People (HCODP). These are both community-based organizations controlled by disabled people, although Derbyshire CIL (DCIL) opted to deliver a more comprehensive range of services – following the 'seven needs' (discussed above) – while Hampshire CIL (HCIL) has concentrated more on personal assistance and training in 'independent living skills'. As organizations led by disabled people, they give life to the social model, and contradict traditional assumptions that disabled people are a burden on the state, and 'charity cases'.

In Hampshire, disabled people living in the Le Court residential home developed Project 81: Consumer-Directed Housing and Care in 1979. Drawing extensively on the experience of disabled people in other parts of the country and overseas – the Project 81 management team persuaded the local authority that the resources used to finance 'residential care' for disabled people could be used to establish more appropriate assistance in the community. Funding was then reallocated to adapt houses for use by disabled individuals and to enable them to employ their own personal assistant. In stark contrast to conventional policy and practice, the Project 81 group asserted that disabled people must be responsible for assessing and controlling their own support needs. These spanned 'personal care needs', such as getting up, washing, and using the toilet; 'domestic matters', which covered laundry, shopping, cooking and 'social care'; plus aid with employment, and leisure activities.

The Project 81 group was also responsible for establishing the HCIL in 1985. From the start, it offered a community-based resource, both for people with impairments wishing to leave institutions, and also for those already living in the community and under threat of being forced (back) into 'residential care'. HCIL's primary functions revolved around personal assistance, information and advocacy, although it also provided training in 'independent living skills'. These are necessary to access essential community-based services, and organize and manage personal assistant schemes, and generally maintain an independent and autonomous lifestyle (HCIL, 1990, 1991; Evans, 1993). Evidence of the attraction of these initiatives to disabled people is that, by 1997, there were 530 personal assistance users in Hampshire alone, while nationally, despite considerable resistance from professionals and their organizations, there were twelve CILs (BCODP, 1997).

If independent living is to become a reality, disabled people have to be freed from their reliance on welfare professionals and unpaid carers. A major stumbling-block was the prohibition, by the National Assistance Act 1948, of direct funding to disabled individuals for the employment of a personal assistant. The Hampshire group found a way round this by agreeing with the local authority for funding to be made available through a third party – the Le Court residential home – in 1982 (Evans, 1993). This encouraged several other similar initiatives around Britain. A further, if unintended, stimulus arrived with the Independent Living Fund (ILF), set up in 1988 with a budget of £5 million. Although intended as a temporary measure, it proved extraordinarily successful among those people wanting aid with self-care and domestic tasks. Applications far outstripped government expectations of 300 per year, and the 1990/1 budget rose to £32 million. When the scheme ended in April 1993, around 22,000 disabled people were receiving payments (Lakey, 1994; Zarb and Nadash, 1994).

Since 1993, payments have continued to existing recipients, while an Independent Living (1993) Fund was set up to run alongside services included under the 1990 NHS and Community Care Act reforms. The replacement scheme restricted new claimants to those of working age, who were in receipt of services from the local authority social service department to the value of £200 per week. A cash limit of £500 per week was enforced, and people whose service needs exceeded this figure were expected to move into residential institutions (Kestenbaum, 1995). Once their expectations had been raised in this way, disabled people and their organizations campaigned vigorously for the legalization of such a scheme. This resulted in the Community Care (Direct Payments) Act 1996, which came into effect in April 1997, allowing local authorities to make direct payments to disabled people under 65 years of age in order to purchase their own support services. By the end of 1997, eighty personal assistance schemes had been established across the country.

Research evidence suggests that giving disabled people control over purchasing packages of care is welcomed as 'empowering' (Kestenbaum, 1993a, 1993b; Morris, 1993). The system of 'direct payments' enables disabled people to have a greater say in developing their own support system, and leading their lives, including work and social activities, as they choose. It lifts the weight of dependency, including that on family and friends. Moreover, people with learning difficulties were eligible for such payments. From the funder's perspective, it has been presented most significantly as a less costly option than community-based or residential services (Lakey, 1994; Zarb and Nadash, 1994).

In Britain, there is a continuum of user involvement stretching from the provision of information at one end, through consultation (listening to the consumers or users of services and trying to base decisions upon the opinions expressed), joint working, to delegated control (over budgets and service provision). For the disabled people's movement, the 'direct payments' route represents an important, but as yet isolated, example of how innovative service backing enables them to lead more 'ordinary' lives.

Amidst the changing legislative arrangements, management structures, and concerns over funding, there has been a growing stream of initiatives from disabled people's organizations to develop user-led and controlled services. For many professionals and those working in the personal social services, the concept of independent living has entailed little more than what used to be called social and life skills such as dressing, washing, cooking and shopping (Bracking, 1993: 13). Disabled people have generated a radical reformulation of their needs and priorities, and explored various independent or integrated living options, including housing schemes and personal assistance.

Review

The development of social policy through the twentieth century has done little to overturn the maginalization of disabled people. State guaranteed citizenship has far less meaning for a group whose members experience high levels of exclusion from the labour market and low standards of living, where disability is 'naturalized' as a social division and unequal treatment justified on grounds of biological deficiency, and where the dominant organizational 'modes of co-ordination' regard disabled people as having 'special needs' which render them dependent, and their lives controlled by professional experts.

In the case of social security and income maintenance, there has been little advancement towards a comprehensive or coherent set of policies for disabled people. The British welfare system still discriminates against specific sections within the disabled population, notably older people and people with learning difficulties. Similarly, community care and support for disabled people has flattered to deceive. All too often a rhetoric of enabling services is followed by variations on traditional dependency-creating practice. However, the exploration of innovative practices in independent and integrated living options by disabled people and organizations controlled by them presents another way forward, which offers more empowering and inclusionary possibilities. This in turn raises important sociological questions about the involvement of disabled people and their organizations in the political process which will be explored in the next chapter.

7

Politics and Disability Politics

The discussion in previous chapters has documented wide-ranging inequalities between disabled and non-disabled people. A striking feature of the latter part of the twentieth century has been the way in which these have provoked considerable political activity and protest by disabled people around the world. This has also transformed disability into a major area of concern for both politicians and policy-makers. One tangible sign has been the recent introduction in many liberal democratic societies of some form of anti-discrimination legislation to protect disabled people from unjustifiable treatment and overt discrimination (Quinn et al., 1993; Gooding, 1994; Pfeiffer, 1994; Doyle, 1995, 1996). A sociological approach brings together two dimensions of 'politics': disabled people's relationship to 'conventional' political institutions and processes, and the emergence of a 'politics of disability'.

The traditional focus for the study of politics comprises the formal institutions and office-holders responsible for the organization and regulation of society. In Western-style liberal democracies, such as Britain and the United States, these include Parliament and Congress, Prime Minister and President, local and state governments, the civil service and sponsored bureaucracies, political parties and pressure groups and the courts. These exercise varying degrees of power and influence in passing, implementing and interpreting laws and regulations which affect every aspect of our daily lives. In contrast, sociological approaches to politics concentrate on those aspects of social life where there is an imbalance of power between individuals and groups, and where attempts are made to bring about a change in that relationship. This extends the focus way beyond the 'official' institutions of political activity, or a definition of politics as 'what politicians do'. As the contemporary women's movement has argued, the 'personal is political' – in that even the closest personal interactions involve inequalities of power and a struggle for change.

In this chapter, both interpretations of politics will be examined. The first part examines the formal political structures and processes and the diverse barriers to the participation of disabled people. The existence of such restrictions has unintentionally precipitated the growth of a disabled people's movement. Claims that this exemplifies a 'new social movement' (Oliver, 1990, 1996a) will be explored in the second part of this chapter. The final section will evaluate these arguments with particular reference to the politicization of a disabled identity and its potential as a catalyst for meaningful social change.

Politics and disabled people

According to T. H. Marshall (1950), political, along with civil and social, rights constitute the basis of modern citizenship. In his account, a distinguishing feature of a liberal democratic society is the right to participate in the political process, and gaining the vote is at the heart of these struggles. These were a feature of the political campaigns in the latter half of the nineteenth and second half of the twentieth centuries. However, full adult suffrage was still denied to some groups within the disabled population, and the formal entitlement to vote, and be involved in politics, is not always sustained by appropriate practical measures, as disabled people around the world have also found to their cost.

Barriers to voting in the UK

In practice, there are several obstacles which may inhibit many disabled people from exercising their right to vote. Most basically, some disabled people are excluded from the electoral register (Fry, 1987; Ward, 1987; MIND, 1989; Enticott et al., 1992). There are a number of reasons for this, including traditional assumptions about disabled people's inability to exercise an independent judgement. For example, Section 4(3) of the British Representation of the People Act 1949 prohibited people resident in institutions for those with a 'mental illness' or 'learning difficulties' from joining the electoral roll. The Representation of the People Act 1983 subsequently allowed 'patients' to vote, but 'only under certain narrowly defined conditions'. Thus, those in institutions for people with intellectual impairments have to prove themselves capable of voting by annually completing a 'Patient's Declaration Form' which must then be countersigned by a staff member. A similar situation applies to those in residential homes (Fry, 1987). The right to be entered on the electoral register, and subsequently to vote, is basically determined by the awareness and integrity of those in charge.

However, not all disabled people living at home with their families are entered on the electoral register by the head of the household. A significant minority are unaware whether they have been registered or not (Ward, 1987; Lamb and Layzell, 1994). It is likely that part of the problem, particularly for people categorized as having 'learning difficulties', stems from low expectations on the part of other family members or from a mistaken belief that those so labelled are not entitled to vote.

Even if registered to vote, other major problems may arise, particularly of physical access. Studies have documented the negative voting experiences of disabled people (Fry, 1987; Ward, 1987). These include: transport difficulties in getting to the polling station, access to the polling station itself and to the polling booth, as well as problems for some disabled people in marking the ballot slip without assistance. A study of twenty-six British parliamentary constituencies in the 1992 General Election found that 88 per cent had one or more access problems. Some disabled people were unable to vote, others were forced to complete the process outside the polling station, and a few were even 'injured negotiating obstacles at polling stations' (Enticott et al., 1992: 1–2). As a direct result, disabled people are more reliant on others, such as relatives, friends and/or professional helpers, if they want to vote, which may prove a further deterrent to their participation. Conversely, some disabled people do not vote simply because they have no one to help them.

Some of these problems can be overcome by disabled people voting by post or by proxy, where someone else casts their vote for them. However, those wishing to take either of these options must, first, obtain the appropriate form from their local Electoral Service

Office, secondly, fill it in, thirdly, get it signed by at least one other person and, finally, return it two and a half weeks before polling day. This process must be repeated at each election, national and local. Some find the application process a daunting prospect (Fry, 1987). In addition, little political information is produced in accessible formats such as Braille, tape, video, or symbols, for different sections of the disabled community (Fry, 1987; Ward, 1987; Enticott et al., 1992). Others object to using a postal vote because it necessitates voting before the election campaign is over. Hence, postal and proxy voting are often regarded as poor substitutes for proper access facilities.

Political parties and pressure groups

Disabled people experience further constraints in becoming active in party politics. First, many local constituency meeting-places and party headquarters are physically inaccessible to people with mobility-related impairments so that it is hard for them to attend meetings or become party activists. Second, local parties may be reluctant to choose a disabled candidate because of the environmental and social barriers to being fully involved in campaigning and door-to-door canvassing (Oliver and Zarb, 1989). Third, disabled people are not encouraged to seek selection as party candidates. This stands in stark contrast to recent initiatives to expand the number of women candidates, especially in constituencies which the party has a good chance of winning. The number of disabled MPs in Britain rose slightly following the 1997 General Election, but these remain exceptions to the general rule, and not all particularly identify with disabled people. In this, as in other respects, the political party system reflects the wider ignorance of, and lack of interest in, the concerns of disabled people and their organizations.

A further avenue for political action by disabled people has been single-issue pressure group activity or campaign. This form of political participation has increased dramatically over the last couple of decades (House of Commons Commission on Citizenship, 1990; Patten, 1990). There are now hundreds of such organizations, varying widely in membership, operating at both local and national levels.

Pressure groups vary significantly in their access to, and influence on, the policy-making process. The more established interest groups within industrial capitalist society, such as employers' organizations and trade unions, owe their existence to their central position in relation to capital and the division of labour. This provides them with economic power and influence, although in contrasting degrees. In addition, there is another, more pluralistic world of competing interest groups, which are formed by voluntary interaction (Cawson, 1982). Since they have a less crucial socio-economic location, they tend to exert less influence, although this varies across campaigns. Notwithstanding the 'competitive' label, there are significant differences between disability and disabled people's organizations, for example, in their objectives, membership, and control by disabled people (see box 7.1).

The charitable status of many disability groups in Britain means that, if they are to retain their status, they cannot engage in direct

---

Box 7.1 A typology of disability organizations

1 Partnership/patronage
Organizations *for* disabled people; charitable bodies; provision of services (often in conjunction with statutory agencies); consultative and advisory role for professional agencies – e.g. Royal Association for Disablement and Rehabilitation, Royal National Institute for the Blind, SCOPE, Rehabilitation International.

2 Economic/parliamentarian
Primarily organizations *for* disabled people; single issue; parliamentary lobbying and research; legalistic bodies – e.g. Disablement Income Group, Disability Alliance, American Foundation for the Blind.

3 Consumerist/self-help
Organizations *of* disabled people; self-help projects; sometimes campaigning groups, or working in collaboration with local or voluntary agencies – e.g. Spinal Injuries Association, Derbyshire Centre for Integrated Living, Berkeley Centre for Independent Living.

4 Populist/activist
Organizations *of* disabled people; politically active groups, often antagonistic to partnership approach; primary activities focused on 'empowerment', personal and/or political; collective action and consciousness-raising – e.g. Union of the Physically Impaired Against Segregation, British Deaf Association, Americans Disabled for Accessible Public Transport (subsequently renamed Americans Disabled for Attendant Programs Today).

Source: adapted from Oliver, 1990: 117–18.

and overt political activity. Furthermore, it is illegal for the 'benefi-ciaries' of charities to be members of their management councils, so it is often difficult for disabled people to control these organiza-tions, or for charities to openly engage in politics (I. Williams, 1989). In addition, 'many of these organisations, which for many years have acted as both charities and disability pressure-groups, have built up close working relationships with official policy-makers, which gives them a degree of credibility but relatively little power' (Barnes, 1991: 218).

Hitherto, traditional voluntary and 'self-help' groups have dom-inated the health and social welfare area (Robinson and Henry, 1977). These are usually organized on the basis of medical classi-fications of impairment. Often parents or professionals predomin-ate, despite the avowed stress on self-help and self-advocacy. Activities include exchange of information, mutual support and social events, but with little emphasis on political campaigning, beyond minor lobbying and letter-writing activity, and with a greater emphasis on charitable activities.

This emphasis on voluntary organization has been reinforced by the efforts of policy-makers to marginalize other forms of disability organization by giving greater encouragement and succour to organizations *for* disabled people, such as the Royal Association for Disablement and Rehabilitation (RADAR) and traditional charity organizations, in comparison with activist organizations *of* disabled people, such as the British Council of Disabled People (BCODP), whose demands are thought too 'extreme': 'The estab-lished groups seek to perpetuate their monopolies by co-opting or vigorously opposing new groups claiming to represent the same interests . . . The government often subsidises the privileged groups and denies such funding to unofficial bodies' (Wilson, 1997: 69).

Until recently, it was not thought important that disability organ-izations should 'represent' as much as 'look after' disabled people's interests. Historically, organizations *for* disabled people have lacked direct input from their disabled members. Instead, the key decision-makers have been salaried professionals who put forward their own ('expert') views about the needs of disabled people (Drake, 1994, 1996). This failure to represent disabled people's views is in addition to their fund-raising strategies and dependency-creating services which continue to undermine the efforts of disabled people to empower themselves.

Nevertheless, several notable examples of collective action

occurred earlier this century. In 1920 the National League of the Blind and the Disabled (NLBD) organized marches of blind workers from all over Britain to London in the pursuit of higher pay and better working conditions for blind workers in sheltered workshops. The League also campaigned against charities for blind people, which were seen as being staffed by inefficient, self-serving bureaucrats rather than blind people themselves. This led to the introduction of the 1920 Blind (Education, Employment and Maintenance) Act, but little else (Pagel, 1988). It was still felt necessary to repeat the marches in 1933, 1936 and 1947 (Humphries and Gordon, 1992). Despite all this activity, throughout the post-1945 period wages in workshops for blind and other disabled workers remained disproportionately low when compared to wage levels generally, and unemployment is especially high among blind people (RNIB, 1996).

The British campaign for a national disability income provides another illustration of pressure-group activity. It began in 1965 with the formation of the Disablement Income Group (DIG) which became a major focus for pressure-group activity in the subsequent decade (see chapter 6). A decade later, fifty voluntary groups came together to form a larger umbrella organization known as the Disability Alliance (DA). Both DIG and DA have produced a number of reports documenting the link between impairment and poverty, and the case for a national disability income, and have lobbied extensively for its introduction.

The British focus on single-issue groups and campaigns working through conventional political institutions and parties contrasts with other political actions being developed at this period, notably by disabled people in the United States, which differed both in terms of their character and objectives.

Campaigns for civil rights and anti-discrimination legislation

It is the campaign for civil rights, and more specifically for anti-discrimination legislation (ADL), which has become one of the most widely favoured routes for political activism by disabled people around the world. The struggles in America for black civil rights, particularly in the 1960s, served as the model for others to emulate (Hahn, 1985, 1986). In the case of disabled people, the pursuit of civil rights acted as a stimulus to their introduction into 'mass' political action, alongside more traditional political lobbying tactics.

Until the mid-1970s, the American disabled people's movement was a loosely structured grass-roots movement, comprising groups such as Disabled in Action (DIA), which was formed specifically to mount protest campaigns against the social barriers experienced by disabled people (Scotch, 1989). Although their actions did not bring the political recognition achieved by other minority groups, governments were persuaded to introduce legislative changes. In line with President Johnson's promotion of 'the Great Society' and a 'War on Poverty', the federal government assumed a greater proportion of the costs of rehabilitation programmes, extended eligibility and instituted various measures to extend information and support for disabled people (Albrecht, 1992).

However, demonstrations continued into the 1970s, with a number of disabled Vietnam War veterans playing a prominent role. Lobbying within Congress also continued apace, with sympathetic and strategically placed members instrumental in inserting disability-related provisions into the 1973 Rehabilitation Act, although its enactment was delayed because it was twice vetoed by President Nixon. For disabled people, attention was focused on section 504 – a historic clause which prohibited discrimination against disabled people in any federally funded programme. The Act also enhanced environmental access, and encouraged more comprehensive services, employment opportunities, and Centres for Independent Living (Albrecht, 1992). It promised a new relationship with disabled people. Moreover, it proved an important vehicle for entrenching the disability rights cause and approach within the political process. 'The enactment of section 504 was brought about largely by the activism of disabled people themselves. A number of sit-ins took place before the appropriate regulations were finally issued. The militancy of these sit-ins . . . vividly contradicted the stereotype of the disabled person as powerless' (Zola, 1983b: 56).

However, it took several years and vigorous campaigning by disability groups to translate section 504 into the necessary array of policy regulations required for its implementation. One of the leading groups in these activities was the American Coalition of Citizens with Disabilities (ACCD). It was formed in 1974, from an existing network of self-help groups, as an organization with over sixty local and national affiliated organizations. It was also at this time that a tension emerged between those involved in advocacy within the federal or state-level political institutions and processes, and those 'outsiders' engaged in grass-roots campaigns (Scotch, 1989; Zola, 1994). Through the 1980s, the emphasis on 'mass' political action gave way to a rising tide of judicial battles, which attracted considerable media attention, involving individuals seeking legal redress for the denial of their constitutional rights.

The continuing pressure by disabled people's groups over the previous two decades to establish disability as a civil rights issue within the American political process achieved its most notable success with the passing of the 1990 Americans with Disabilities Act (ADA). Although it did not achieve all that disabled people's groups had argued for, ADA importantly outlawed discrimination against disabled people in respect of employment, public accommodations (access), transportation, state and local government, and telecommunications. Its formal objective was to achieve 'mainstreaming', or the integration of disabled individuals into American society as fully as was practicable. The passage and enforcement of this act symbolized a significant shift in the perception of disabled people (Albrecht, 1992).

As with previous legislation, concerns were expressed about its implementation and how far its original goals would be achieved. Attempts to evaluate the costs of changing existing practices suggest that employers generally have been surprised at the relatively low financial outlay on 'accommodations' or making access a reality. In addition, these costs are spread across different levels of government, private businesses and consumers. ADA's most conspicuous successes have been in improving the accessibility of the built environment, and so facilitating disabled people's greater involvement in 'public' activities. Moves towards more integrated employment are less well documented. There have also been concerns about ADA's monitoring and enforcement provisions, and whether it is adequately reaching minority groups within the disabled population (Johnson, 1997).

To date, ADA is the most extensive piece of anti-discrimination legislation anywhere in the world (Gooding, 1994; Doyle, 1995). Subsequently several other countries, including Australia, New Zealand and France, introduced some form of this civil rights legislation.

In Britain, since the mid-1970s, organizations controlled and run by disabled people, such as the Union of the Physically Impaired Against Segregation (UPIAS), the Liberation Network, and Sisters

Against Disability (SAD), have shared the same basic goals to secure equal rights for disabled people, and remove negative discrimination in all its forms. These were adopted by BCODP following its inception in 1981. However, the first steps to getting anti-discrimination legislation on to the parliamentary agenda were taken by the Committee on Restrictions Against Disabled People (CORAD). It located the problem of discrimination within a structural or institutional context, by focusing on a range of issues including access to public buildings, transport systems, education, employment and entertainment. It made a number of recommendations, including the call for legislation to secure disabled people's rights (CORAD, 1982). In contrast, the Thatcher government was less than sympathetic. Jack Ashley, a deaf Labour MP, introduced a private member's anti-discrimination bill in July 1982, but this was rejected. It was only after fourteen subsequent attempts, and thirteen years later, that the 1995 Disability Discrimination Act was passed.

The campaign gathered momentum in 1985 with the setting up of the Voluntary Organisations for Anti-Discrimination Legislation committee. This heralded an alliance between organizations controlled and run by disabled people, such as the BCODP, along with the more traditional organizations for disabled people. The latter, such as RADAR, had been reluctant to support, if not actually opposed to, civil rights legislation for disabled people. For its part, the government denied that discrimination was a problem. However, its claim was undermined by the publication of the BCODP-sponsored *Disabled People in Britain and Discrimination* (Barnes, 1991). This contained the most extensive documentation yet produced of the discrimination against disabled people. Five days after its official launch, Nicholas Scott, the Minister for Disabled People, acknowledged for the first time that 'discrimination against disabled people is widespread' (*Hansard*, 1992).

This was also a period when the influence of a radical new method of consciousness-raising, based on the social model of disability and known as Disability Equality Training (DET) became evident. It promoted 'the politicisation and subsequent radicalisation of increasingly large sections of the disabled population. These and other initiatives intensified the pressure for nothing less than the full inclusion of disabled people with comprehensive civil rights legislation as the main vehicle for its achievement' (Oliver and Barnes, 1998: 90).

By the mid-1990s, the major political parties acknowledged the force of the campaign. The Conservative government's response came in 1994 with the introduction of the bill which was the basis for the 1995 Disability Discrimination Act. However, it did not receive uncritical approval in the disabled people's movement. The Act is founded on the individualistic, medical view of disability, with scant admission of the ways in which society 'disables' people with impairments. Moreover, the Act gives only limited protection from direct discrimination in employment, the provision of goods and services, and in the selling or letting of land. In addition, not all disabled people are covered by the Act and, most importantly, employers and service-providers are exempt if they can show that compliance would damage their business.

Furthermore, there is no enforcement mechanism. Those disabled individuals with a grievance must challenge unfair discrimination themselves. There is a National Disability Council (NDC), but its role is simply to 'advise' government on the implementation of the Act, and even then not in the area of employment. This responsibility fell to the existing National Advisory Council on Employment of People with Disabilities (NACEPD). The chair of the NDC works on disability issues one day a week; the other sixteen members one day a month (Barnes, 1996c). However, the incoming New Labour government of 1997 quickly established a Disability Task Force to assess the 1995 Act. The Task Force includes representatives from both organizations *for* and *of* disabled people, including BCODP. It agreed to establish a Disability Commission by June 1999 to orchestrate future disability discrimination policy. Hence the continuing campaign for the introduction of an effective civil rights policy by organizations such as BCODP (Oliver and Barnes, 1998).

The 1995 Disability Discrimination Act reopened internal divisions and brought to an end the uneasy coalition between organizations *of* and organizations *for* disabled people. The former opposed the legislation as too weak and unenforceable. In contrast, after NDC was established, six of the main organizations *for* disabled people – RADAR, the Royal National Institute for the Blind, the Royal National Institute for the Deaf, Mencap, MIND, and SCOPE – agreed to work with the government to implement the new law. This mirrors divisions in other campaigns for political rights, between those from more 'reformist' organizations wanting to change the system from within, and another more 'radical', tendency which argues that members' interests will be diluted as organizations are co-opted into the 'system'. It also parallels the tendency for American disability rights leaders to be incorporated into formal and informal associations of civil rights lobbyists (Scotch, 1989).

On a final comparative note: as Mike Oliver (1990: 120–1) stresses, the situation in America, which witnessed the development of the Independent Living Movement and civil rights struggles, is very different from that in Britain in at least three respects. First, America has a long and well-established tradition of viewing 'social problems' as human rights issues, both because of its constitutional history and the influence of the civil rights movement. Britain, unlike America, has no formal written constitution establishing citizenship rights in law. Second, the USA has relatively few statutory services available to disabled people compared to Britain. For instance, America has no national health service providing free health care at the point of delivery to all regardless of the individual's ability to pay. It was estimated in the late 1980s that more than 35 million Americans had no health care insurance (Albrecht, 1992). Third, in comparison with Britain, America has no large organized voluntary sector catering specifically for disabled people. Hence, CILs in the British context were as much concerned to control existing services, as to create new ones. Hence, also, the preference for the term 'integrated' rather than 'independent' living, and the focus on 'political' tactics rather than following a legal or civil rights course.

Disability protest: a new social movement?

From the perspective of a growing number of disabled people, conventional politics had failed to address disability-related issues. One reaction was the emergence of a socio-political movement advocating disabled people's rights in the late 1960s and early 1970s. There was a trend away from pressure-group activity and support for traditional organizations *for* disabled people to 'self-help/populist' organizations and groups, and a more overt and direct form of political action and participation. For some, this constitutes a 'new social movement' (Oliver, 1990, 1996a), for others, a 'liberation struggle' (Shakespeare, 1993).

The polarization of 'old' and 'new' forms of social protest runs parallel to claims that there have been significant changes in the late twentieth-century social and economic order which herald the emergence of what has been variously termed 'post-industrial', 'post-capitalist', or 'post-modern' society. A shift towards consumption rather than production, consequential changes in the division of labour and social structure, with deepening social and cultural disorganization and crises in the (welfare) state have all been identified as key features. In turn, novel social divisions and conflicts have given rise to new forms of social protest.

One of the first exponents of new social movement theory was the French theorist Alain Touraine (1977, 1981). He referenced a new core conflict within western European societies. This was linked to the breakdown of traditional work patterns and class boundaries and the decline of traditional forms of class struggle. Similarly, Melluci (1980) argued that new or 'contemporary social movements' were indicative of an unprecedented structural transformation which entailed a major realignment between society, the state and the economy. More recently, these themes have been developed with reference to what are seen as the harsh social and economic conditions during the 1980s, and their effects on welfare provision and delivery (Williams, 1992; Hewitt, 1993; Taylor-Gooby, 1994).

For Touraine (1981), these 'new' social movements have the potential to transform society as they centre on the very meanings and values that predominate within 'post-industrial' society. Claus Offe (1985) regarded the new forms of social protest as representative of minorities hitherto marginalized by governmental structures and powerful interest groups. These movements are not class-based, and celebrate alternative political agendas, such as the mélange of community action and self-help groups which flourished in urban areas, as well as the national and international civil rights, student action, women's, environmental and peace movements. Sociological interest also concentrated on emergent and divergent subcultural lifestyles and 'alternative' cultural values and meanings.

Several disability theorists have argued that the disabled people's movement fits the criteria of a new social movement:

> These movements have been seen as constituting the social basis for new forms of transformative political action or change. These social movements are 'new' in the sense that they are not grounded in traditional forms of political participation through the party system or single-issue pressure group activity targeted at political decision-makers. (Oliver, 1990: 113)

However, the distinguishing criteria of a new social movement are the subject of continuing debate. Hence, determining whether the disabled people's movement belongs to the 'new' or 'old' category, or something in between, is far from straightforward. For his part, Mike Oliver (1990: 118) stresses the following features:

- marginalization from traditional politics;
- critical evaluation of society;
- (qualified) 'post-materialist' or 'post-acquisitive' values; and
- concern with issues that cross national boundaries.

These are in addition to the standards which might be used to evaluate any social movement (whether old or new). These revolve around the impact of the movement on society, whether in terms of general political or economic changes, specific policies, effecting a shift in public opinion, or sponsoring new organizations (Campbell and Oliver, 1996).

On the margins?

With regard to the first criterion, the disabled people's movement felt that traditional party politics and lobbying had failed disabled people. Hence the significance attached to a shift to self-organization, with disabled people themselves taking control of organizations representing their interests. Traditionally, voluntary bodies and charities have prevailed – dating back to the establishment of the Royal National Institute for the Blind (RNIB) in 1868. In Britain the dominance of impairment-specific organizations continued through into the early decades of the welfare state after the Second World War, while some voluntary provision continued to run alongside the new state services.

However, in the 1960s, more and more disabled people became disenchanted with the lack of impact of existing voluntary organizations. This led to a growth in campaigning, self-help and activist organizations (see box 7.1). The pre-eminence of the traditional voluntary body was challenged on two fronts, by a new campaigning form of single-issue group, such as DIG, and by initiatives from disability activists to set up organizations which were controlled by disabled people themselves and adhered to the social model of disability.

While the emerging activist groups borrowed from self-help groups, they emphasize indigenous organization and self-reliance, and a political, rather than therapeutic, orientation. The central aim is not to modify their own behaviour in conformity with traditional expectations of disabled people, but rather to influence the behaviour of groups, organizations and institutions (Anspach, 1979: 766). As far as the British experience is concerned, the demand for anti-discrimination legislation was stimulated by the Sex Discrimination Act 1975, and the Race Relations Act 1976. Again, the approach of disabled people's organizations has been influenced by the experience of other oppressed groups, but it has also been reinforced by the adoption of the social model and the espousal of a disabled identity: 'Clearly the purpose of disabled people's self-organisation is to promote change: to improve the quality of our lives and promote our full inclusion into society. It does this both through involvement in the formal political system and through promotion of other kinds of political activity' (Campbell and Oliver, 1996: 22).

In response to the apparent failure of the incomes approach of the DIG and the Disability Alliance and their colonization by 'non-disabled experts', overtly political self-organization began in earnest in 1974 with the formation of UPIAS by a small but influential group of disabled activists including Vic Finkelstein, Ken Davis, Maggie Hines, Paul Hunt and Brenda Robbins. Although such populist self-help groups were slow to develop, they have subsequently flourished and represent a 'powerful source of mutual support, education and action' for disabled people (Crewe and Zola, 1983). There was a surge in user-led groups within the disabled community during the 1960s and 1970s. Notable examples include Disablement Information and Advice Line (DIAL) and the Spinal Injuries Association (SIA). They were motivated to enable members to define and solve their own problems rather than rely on non-disabled 'experts'. Their aim was to articulate the needs of the membership as a whole, both to statutory agencies and political parties, at both local and national levels (Oliver and Hasler, 1987).

A further significant development was the emergence of BCODP as a credible national umbrella body of organizations of disabled people. Initiated by members of UPIAS, it had representatives from only seven national groups at its first meeting in 1981. However, it quickly became a national voice of disabled people in the campaign for political rights (Campbell and Oliver, 1996). By

June 1997, BCODP had grown to a membership of 120 organizations of disabled people representing over 300,000 individuals (BCODP, 1997).

This new-found climate of confidence, generated by the enhanced public profile of disabled writers, activists and organizations controlled and run by disabled people themselves, has encouraged more and more people with accredited impairments to speak openly of their experiences of disability, and seek acceptance on their own terms, that is, 'the personal and public affirmation of disabled identities and the demands that disabled people be accepted by and integrated into society as they are; that is, as disabled people' (Oliver and Zarb, 1989: 225).

These contributions have bridged the personal and the political by including: physicality and the limitations of impairment (Campling, 1981; Morris, 1991; Crow, 1996); sexuality and personal relationships (Gillespie-Sells, 1993; Shakespeare et al., 1996); marital relations (Parker, 1993); parenting (Mason, 1992; Campion, 1995); and physical and emotional abuse (Cross, 1994; Roeher Institute, 1995; Westcott and Cross, 1996). This growing exploration of the personal and emotional politics of disability adds 'a vital dimension to our understanding of the social model and of the experiences of disabled people' (Shakespeare et al., 1996: 9).

The rights road

The defining feature of disability theory has been its focus on the social exclusion and oppression of disabled people. The barriers are embedded in policies and practices based on the individualistic, medicalized approach to disability. Consequently, the removal of such obstacles involves far more than gaining control over material resources and the range and quality of services. It requires a fundamental reappraisal of the meaning and hence medicalization of disability, and recognition that the multiple deprivations experienced by people with accredited impairments are the outcome of hostile physical and social environments: in other words, the way society is organized (Barton, 1993).

This was given immediate urgency in Britain and elsewhere by the looming crises in the economy and the state which led to policies to control welfare expenditure. This left disabled people among the early casualties. The response by organizations of disabled people was to advance a 'discourse of alternative rights which can only be met by radical change in the existing structure of society and which involve the construction of new political and social institutions' (Fagan and Lee, 1997: 151). A further dimension to the confrontation with the political establishment lay in the choice of political tactics. Disabled people emulated the street demonstrations and sit-ins that became a feature of social protest in the late 1960s and 1970s. This embrace of 'unconventional' political activity was much in evidence in civil rights campaigns by American disabled people: 'The civil rights movement has had an effect not only on the securing of certain rights but also on the manner to which those rights had been secured. When traditional legal channels have been exhausted, disabled people have learned to employ other techniques of social protest' (DeJong, 1983: 12).

In Britain, early initiatives included the Campaign for Accessible Transport (CAT) and the Campaign Against Patronage and the 'Rights not Charity' march of July 1988. Since then there has been a growing resort to demonstrations and civil disobedience against a range of disabling barriers and activities. A major demonstration against Independent Television's charity show Telethon was held in 1990 (emulating a similar protest in America). The next Telethon, two years later, drew over 2,000 disabled demonstrators. It proved the last such event. This and other successes precipitated the formation in 1993 of the Disability Direct Action Network (DAN). With a voluntary membership of over 1,000 disabled individuals, and reliant on member's contributions, DAN has organized more than 200 local and national demonstrations.

Post-material values

What has been termed the commitment by new social movements to 'post-materialist' or 'post-acquisitive' values – over those that have to do with income, satisfaction of material needs and social security – is based on an opposition to the traditional political claim for more resources. Indeed, it is identified as a primary orientation among members of new social movements: 'The presence of materialist or post-materialist values proves to be the most important single influence on whether a given individual will support new social movements' (Inglehart, 1990: 64). In fact, the evidence for this 'value switch' is overstated. Most new movements are about resource allocation: women, black and minority ethnic groups, and disabled people are crucially concerned with their economic exploitation and poverty. Within feminism there is a central concern with equal pay, with gender inequality in the marketplace, with discriminatory benefit systems, and so on. The whole thrust of the British disabled people's movement has been to channel more resources to disabled people. Whilst some contemporary movements, such as environmentalists and the peace movement, may be clustered around selected post-acquisitive values, women, minority ethnic groups and disabled people cannot afford to ignore or downgrade pressing material concerns.

In response to these arguments, Oliver (1996a: 157) extends the interpretation of 'post-materialism' to include counter-cultural shifts, such as are identified in a disability culture (see chapter 8), which has confronted the 'stigmatisation of difference', and presented an altogether more positive disabled identity.

Internationalization of disability politics

A remarkable feature of disability campaigns has been the globalization of the disabled people's movement (Driedger, 1989). Disabled People's International (DPI), the international equivalent of the BCODP, was formed by disabled activists in 1981. Its first world congress was held in Singapore and attracted 400 disabled delegates with all types of impairment, and cultural backgrounds from rich and poor countries. They united around a common purpose: the empowerment of disabled people through collective political action (DPI, 1982). For DPI delegates, the prerequisite for change lay in the active, grass-roots organizations, and the development of a high level of public awareness of disability issues among the population as a whole.

This is demonstrated in the part played by DPI in acting as a catalyst for advancing debates on 'global issues such as war, poverty and industrial exploitation and the role they play in creating impairments and sustaining disability' (Oliver, 1996a: 157). Disabled people have drawn inspiration from the experiences of political action in other countries – with the American civil rights movement a major catalyst, both in its objectives and in its campaigning methods. Disabled people have also drawn inspiration from developments in other countries to explore new forms of self-organization. The British disabled people's movement was significantly influenced by innovative practice in the USA, and most particularly in the promotion of 'independent living' options. Indeed, there are now CILs or similar organizations in most 'developed' countries such as Australia, Canada, Japan, and Europe, and in several 'developing' nations of the majority world,

such as Brazil and Zimbabwe (Ratska, 1992). Further confirmation
of the widening impact of the disabled people's movement has
been its increasing international presence, with a new awareness
around the world in organizations such as the United Nations and
the International Labour Organisation of the need to consult disabled people (Driedger, 1989).

The challenge for the disabled people's movement has been to
encourage national movements to learn from the experience of disabled people in other countries, without presuming that there is a
single 'royal road' to 'independent living' or 'empowerment', or
that there is one set of political tactics or form of self-organization
which will suit disabled people living in very different societies
and political contexts. Even within Europe, the approach taken by
the disabled people's movement in individual countries demonstrates considerable variation, with some barely attached to a
social model approach. There are instances where movements are
organized on the basis of confederated mono-impairment groups,
implicitly adopting the medical model and self-help format. The
existence of considerable social disadvantage and poverty in
central and eastern Europe has inhibited the growth of disabled
people's organizations there; this is due also in part to the central-
izing and paternalistic tendencies of the former socialist regimes.
Conversely, the disabled people's movement is generally more
politicized and committed to a social model-type approach in the
more industrialized societies of western Europe.

What's in a name?

There are various counter-arguments to the proposition that the
disabled people's movement constitutes a new social movement.
One position is that the claims surrounding new social movements
overstate the contrast with earlier protest movements (Shakespeare, 1993). A second area of doubt concentrates on the transformative potential of contemporary movements. A third bone of
contention centres on the claims of the disabled people's movement to properly represent the general population of people with
accredited impairments.

The emphasis on discontinuity with earlier forms of political
action is typically illustrated by a comparison of the labour and
socialist movements in the mid-twentieth century with their counterparts from the 1960s onwards. The 'break with the past' in other
areas is far less apparent. For example, clear links have been

drawn between the women's suffrage movement and the present-day women's movement. Nevertheless, in the case of disability organizations there is a veritable chasm between traditional voluntary organizations and contemporary democratic and representative organizations of disabled people, committed to the social model.

It has also been suggested that 'unconventional' tactics and civil disobedience, such as the march, the sit-in and the public demonstration, have a long political pedigree – involving many different groups and issues. Elements within the contemporary disabled people's movement, such as the National League of the Blind and the Disabled, have been engaged in this type of protest since the 1920s. Nevertheless, at least the balance of 'old' to 'new' style' has shifted in favour of demonstrations and civil protest. Indeed, recent political action has focused on tactics which will attract publicity, and is 'often carefully planned to influence opinion-formers, the media etc.' (Shakespeare, 1993: 258).

What then of the transformative potential of the disabled people's movement? The new social movement literature could scarcely be more optimistic. At the structural level, the most important effect of disabled people's self-organization in this field are legislative victories such as the 1990 Americans with Disabilities Act, Britain's 1995 Disability Discrimination Act, and similar legislation in other parts of the world. Although each of these measures falls well short of what disabled people's organizations had been campaigning for, they do represent significant advances in disability policy. Equal rights for disabled people is now firmly on the political agenda, in complete contrast with the situation thirty years ago. In the UK, other important legislative changes include the 1986 Disabled Persons (Services, Consultations and Representations) Act and the 1996 Community Care (Direct Payments) Act. The 1986 Act required local authorities to include representatives of user-led organizations in the planning and formulation of locally run services for disabled people, while the 1996 legislation overturned previous regulations which prevented local authorities making direct cash payments to individual disabled people to run their own assistance services. When coupled with the spread of user-led initiatives (see chapter 6), the disabled people's movement can claim to have made a significant advance in convincing the general public of the merits of anti-discrimination legislation, and in achieving a wider range of tangible legislative changes. Equally significant in social movement terms, this has been accomplished through being converted simply into a political lobbying group.

However, the establishment of user-led initiatives and service-providing agencies does not guarantee that these measures will be implemented as intended, or that their outcomes will necessarily be as anticipated. The experience of other social movements indicates the potential for incorporation in the political system in ways which effectively neutralize their political goals. These dilemmas will no doubt intensify as the influence of the disabled people's movement extends. As an illustration, the DPI now has consultative status on disability issues within the United Nations, and disabled politicians have achieved national prominence around the world. The risk that the leaders of disabled people's groups will be drawn into the political system and lose touch with the grass roots has been a particular issue in America (Scotch, 1989). Not only may such appointments create divisions within the disabled people's movement but, in addition, such appointments may anyway have more symbolic than practical importance. Thus, in Britain, some activists have expressed serious concern about the BCODP's involvement in 'Rights Now', the campaign for anti-discrimination legislation, exactly because it seemed distanced from local disabled people's organizations and groups (Finkelstein, 1996).

This raises questions about the disabled people's movement's claim to representativeness. Early criticisms centred on the foundations of the American ILM in what Gerben DeJong (1983) refers to as 'radical consumerism' and notions of self-reliance and individual rights. However, Gareth Williams has argued that the faith in consumer sovereignty and self-reliance is misplaced in the context of the economic and political power imbalance which characterizes American society (Williams, 1984a, 1991). There is obvious potential for those 'less disadvantaged' (younger, well-educated, white middle-class) disabled people to reap greater benefits from this approach than the poorest among disabled Americans. In Britain, the emphasis on citizenship is important and developing, but the main efforts have been invested in building a collective organization seeking to advance the general benefit of disabled people (Abberley, 1993; Campbell and Oliver, 1996; Finkelstein and Stuart, 1996).

A related issue is how many individuals with a perceived impairment 'self-identify' as disabled people. The traditional medical focus on functional limitations has been replaced by the notion of 'disabling barriers and attitudes' in the social model approach. Exactly what constitutes a disabled person is not fixed, but is contingent on changing social circumstances and contexts. It is most likely that a significant proportion of the 6.2 million people defined as 'disabled' in national surveys (Martin et al., 1988) do not see themselves in this way, and even fewer actively engage in political activities within the disabled people's movement. Of course, similar conclusions can be applied to other social movements, such as feminism, or anti-poverty movements. Again, not all segments of the disabled population are properly represented in the leadership of the disabled people's movement; but as many disabled people argue, this is better than being represented by non-disabled doctors, politicians, leaders of charity organizations or civil servants.

If the disabled people's movement is to prove an effective force for change, it is essential that these diverse groups consciously adopt a positive 'disabled identity' with the same vigour and sense of purpose as has been achieved in other social movements, such as the women's, black consciousness, or lesbian and gay movements. This necessarily involves the subordination of individual circumstances to a shared sense of identity and experience of social oppression, and a united opposition to a disabling society.

In their recent study of disabled activists in Britain, Jane Campbell and Mike Oliver (1996) conclude that the disabled people's movement in Britain 'is neither one thing nor the other; in fact it is a movement which incorporates both revolutionary and reformist politics' (p. 179). While this debate will continue, it is a more important yardstick that the disabled people's movement is offering disabled people a real political voice than satisfying specific criteria as a new social movement. By the same token, tactics adopted, and specific policies championed, are a means to an end – like anti-discrimination legislation. The ambition is to make representative democracy both more representative and more democratic. The introduction of anti-discrimination legislation is but one step on this journey. It would have to be followed by more dramatic changes in advancing citizenship rights – though even these may be double-edged (F. Williams, 1992). To this extent, a further measure of the value of the disabled people's movement is that it is influencing the thinking and practices of the population at large, and not only of disabled people.

In summary, the claim that the disabled people's movement warrants being described as a new social movement stems from its assertion that it stands apart from conventional politics, uncompromised by traditional party debates or pressure-group bargaining. Its emphasis on consciousness-raising and self-affirmation, along with non-conventional forms of campaigning and protest, has been reinforced by its reconceptualization of disability as a form of social oppression. There has been a significant circulation of ideas between disabled people's organizations, within and most notably between countries. Significant outcomes have been achieved in such areas as Centres for Integrated/Independent Living, with their emphasis on service provision controlled by disabled people, and in the moves towards establishing disabled people's citizenship rights. Disabled people's organizations have also been drawn into more conventional policy negotiations within the state apparatus – although this highlights the 'fine line between marginalisation and incorporation' (Oliver, 1996a: 157). Nevertheless, the potential for linking with other oppressed groups remains unfulfilled (Morris, 1991).

Identity politics

Disabled people's self-organization is a primary source of a strong disability identity. Tactics adopted to achieve political success, such as direct action, can also prove a significant stimulus to constructing a disabled identity.

Many people have stressed the direct action element of disability politics, but this development is important not just instrumentally, in securing specific changes and reforms, but because direct action challenges popular perceptions of disabled people, and empowers and inspires participants. This is an area which enables disabled people to challenge traditional stereotypes of passivity, pathology and weakness most directly. In her book *Pride Against Prejudice*, Jenny Morris writes of the feelings of power that collective action engenders:

> The obvious challenge that we were mounting to people's assumptions was also a source of my sense of power. Indeed, each time I had to explain to a non-disabled friend why I was going on such a demonstration, I was very conscious of the way that this issue challenges the root of our oppression and that even to explain my motivations very briefly brings people up short against the core of their own prejudice. (Morris, 1991: 191)

Direct action by disabled people has a number of important elements. First, it is a way of focusing the general public's attention on the institutions and environments that create disability: the inaccessible transport, the demeaning television charity spectaculars, the inadequacy of the disability benefit system. Second, it is an overtly political act, showing that disability is a matter of social relations, and not simply the outcome of medical conditions.

Third, it is a chance for disabled people to 'do it for themselves', without the help or participation of non-disabled people, thus prefiguring the claims of the disabled people's movement to autonomy, independence and power. Fourth, it is an empowering process for participants, creating a sense of solidarity, purpose and collective strength which enhances and develops the aims of the movement still further. For example, when the Campaign for Accessible Transport blockaded Oxford Street in London in 1990, and on other demonstrations, the police force has been uncertain about how to deal with disabled protesters, especially wheelchairusers. Moreover, proceedings against those arrested at Horseferry Road Magistrates' Court had to be terminated because the building was inaccessible to people with mobility impairments. These examples illustrate the way in which style and method can reinforce the message and content of a protest action. Although to date there have been more than 200 national and local demonstrations in the UK, only seven disabled activists have been prosecuted, and all of these have been given a conditional discharge (Holdsworth, 1998).

It may also be that public opinion finds it difficult to come to terms with disability activism, preferring to think disabled people are happy with their situation. In an editorial in *The Times* coinciding with the Oxford Street demonstrations, it was suggested that, while everyone was sympathetic to disabled people (after all, anyone could become disabled, and it was no one's fault), the militants must be careful not to alienate public opinion: 'militancy, unlawful demonstrations, and the disruption of city life may relieve the feelings of the disabled. But such tactics will eventually alienate the public support on which the disabled have to rely' (*The Times*, 29 Sept. 1990).

Such views are routinely expressed against public demonstrations (Wilson, 1997). Nonetheless, public demonstrations by disabled activists often evince a quite different response from non-politicized disabled individuals. The move towards self-organization and public displays of defiance has encouraged

increasing numbers of disabled people to adopt a 'disabled identity':

> This vocabulary of protest marks a significant shift in consciousness
> from one of almost passive dependence to active involvement in
> raising that consciousness to the point where the minority group is
> no longer one for whom pleas, reforms and changes are made by
> others but where they themselves are instrumental in provoking
> change. (Thomas, 1982: 189)

For the American sociologist Renée Anspach, disability politics
is as much to do with identity formation as it is to do with the
achievement of instrumental goals: 'Not only is the fashioning of
collective identity an explicitly articulated goal of the politicised
disabled, but the very act of political participation in itself induces
others to impute certain characteristics to the activist' (Anspach,
1979: 766). Direct political action is then one part of the wider
process of identity development with the potential to radically
change disabled people's perceptions both of themselves and of
society at large and its treatment of disabled people (Campbell and
Oliver, 1996).

This accords with the emphasis on autonomy, integration and
independence:

> New social movements insist not only on the expansion of direct
> democratic forms of political participation but also on the widening
> of opportunities for social self-organisation. The cultural pluralism
> of the movements and their emphasis on autonomy also suggest a
> more reflexive way of political integration which is more responsive
> to different cultural norms and varying lifestyles. (Brand, 1990: 27)

Here again there is a similarity with analyses of developments in
other liberation struggles such as the civil rights and women's
movements of previous decades. The key to this analysis is that
oppressed groups are seen to be confronting their oppression, and
taking control of their own destiny. Seen as a 'liberation struggle',
the emphasis is on wide-ranging political action and mobilization,
rather than relying on legislative shifts.

In concert with the experience of other oppressed groups, disabled people are subject to 'felt stigma' or internalized oppression.
This denotes the feelings of inadequacy, self-doubt, worthlessness
and inferiority which frequently accompany the onset of impairment. It is important to remember that most disabled people are

not born with an impairment but acquire it as a result of social and economic circumstances, an accident, through illness, and so forth. An initial social identity as 'non-disabled' is overlain by a variety of social forces including gender, social class, ethnicity, age and sexuality, which raises immediate concerns regarding 'biographical disruption' (Bury, 1991) because of the perceived consequences of impairment. Moreover, most congenitally disabled people have non-disabled parents and may grow up believing that they will become non-disabled with the coming of adulthood. The 'formative years' of adolescence are particularly difficult for those coming to terms with a disabled identity (Anderson et al., 1982; Thomas et al., 1989; Hirst and Baldwin, 1994). Furthermore, Western culture is replete with negative images of disabled people. This all adds to the difficulty of establishing a positive 'disabled' identity.

Disabled people's self-organization challenges the myth of passivity and the objectification of disabled people. Disabled people, like children, are meant to be seen, and not heard; they are meant to be grateful, not angry; they are meant to be humble, not proud. In challenging all these preconceptions and discriminatory ideologies, the movement is making progress every day, even before attaining its central political objectives.

Being oppressed is not a sufficient condition for political radicalism; but for growing numbers of disabled people it has been the stimulus to become involved in social protest, which in turn has been a catalyst to a more positive disabled identity:

> Having a hard life and being a member of an exploited group does not in itself lead to political unrest. People often blame themselves for their difficulties. Only when they see that their problems are shared by other people like them, the group, can they attribute the source of their concerns to social conditions, such as discrimination, and look to political solutions. (Klein, 1984: 2)

This emulates Touraine's (1981) analysis of actor and adversary, and the ways in which people develop a self-identity as a member of a collectivity with distinctive interests that set them apart, and which lead to an alternative 'world-view'. For disabled people, personal problems are transformed into political demands because the source of their 'troubles' is seen as social and external – the impairment becomes a series of disabling barriers erected by society.

However, people with accredited impairments often find it particularly hard to adopt a disabled identity, as socially oppressed, compared with women, black people, lesbians or gay men. Unlike, women and black people, their oppression has been generally submerged within the rhetoric of benevolent paternalism, professional altruism and philanthropy. Everyone claims to be on the side of the disabled person, and to be acting in their best interest. The reality of impairment reinforces 'natural' explanations of disability. The possibilities of people with various impairments coming together in a political struggle are reduced by the tendency of medicine and welfare to arbitrarily divide up the constituency: to separate the old from the young, to segregate people with different conditions, and levels of 'severity', even where they share otherwise similar social experiences.

Indeed, the conventional response among traditional welfare and charitable institutions has been to arbitrarily divide up the disabled population into various impairment-specific groups, to separate them on the basis of age, and to incarcerate some and not others in residential institutions (Borsay, 1986). All of which further inhibits the possibility of the disabled population cohering as a unified political force.

In addition, environmental barriers, coupled with a perennial lack of resources, help to explain why the disabled people's movement has been relatively unsuccessful in reaching out to the disabled population as a whole. What little evidence there is suggests that it has proved relatively unsuccessful in developing positive identities and group consciousness beyond specific groups; notably, those with physical and sensory impairments who are both relatively active and relatively young. In America, this was recognized in the early stages of the movement's development: 'Notably absent from the movement's constituency are older persons with severe physical impairments resulting from strokes or other degenerative conditions. While the movement's philosophy may have direct relevance to older disabled persons, the movement has focused its concern elsewhere' (DeJong, 1983: 6).

The disabled people's movement in Britain has also been skewed towards younger people. Whilst there is abundant evidence of the central contribution of disabled women in the movement's development (Barnes, 1996b; Rae, 1996), concern has been expressed regarding their exclusion from positions of power and influence, not least as 'ideologues' (Morris, 1991, 1996). Similar concerns have been expressed with reference to disabled members of minority ethnic groups (Stuart, 1993; Begum et al., 1994), and disabled lesbians and gay men (Shakespeare et al., 1996). There is also a relative silence from what Alan Holdsworth calls 'people left on the plantations', that is, those reliant on day centres and living in residential institutions (Campbell and Oliver, 1996: 131).

Review

As a means of securing citizenship rights, conventional politics and policy-makers have failed the disabled population. Disability politics has been forced outside the mainstream of the liberal parliamentary system, because conventional channels of representation, and traditional forms of lobbying, have not delivered effective reforms for disabled people. None of the British political parties took disability issues seriously until the growth of social protest in the 1980s. The 1970 Chronically Sick and Disabled People's Act arose from a private member's bill, as have all the attempts at achieving anti-discrimination legislation. In Britain, as in America, the campaign for civil rights law has involved extra-parliamentary activity, rather than conventional party political process.

A positive consequence has been the emergence of a burgeoning disabled people's movement. This may be theorized in a variety of different ways: for example, as a new social movement, or as a liberation struggle. However, the significant feature of disability politics is not so much the label attached to what has been happening but the extraordinary growth and impact of the disabled people's movement in the last few decades of the twentieth century. From the most inauspicious beginnings, and with no tradition of collective protest across impairment groups, the disabled people's movement has become a powerful voice arguing for radical changes in the ways in which disabled people are treated by society.

Its tangible achievements rest more on its capacity to transform its own organization and analysis of disability than to overturn the social oppression of disabled people, but some significant advances have been made. Most notably, it has achieved objectives in the formulation and delivery of local user-led services and in the campaign for civil and social rights at national and international levels. However, the benefits and importance of the disabled people's movement are not only defined in instrumental terms.

Individual involvement in the collective struggle for emancipation is an overtly empowering experience. Disabled individuals have access to a newly politicized identity:

> The transformation from tentative affirmation of disability identity to proclamation of disability pride reflects the increasing importance of self-determination. A confident, positive disability identity within a broad, inclusive disability community has emerged. The benefit to disabled people to determine and relate their own stories is increasingly evident. (Gilson et al., 1997: 16)

Exactly how far the movement will be able to maintain this momentum, while also avoiding the possibilities for incorporation, neutralization, and further fragmentation will test the maturity of disabled people's organizations.

8

Culture, Leisure and the Media

The significance of culture, both in the oppression and emancipation of disabled people, is a comparatively recent phenomenon in the field of disability studies (e.g. Davis, 1996, 1997). Its importance was highlighted by disabled people themselves, often outside academic contexts. For example, Paul Hunt's (1966) pioneering work *Stigma* offered the views of a variety of disabled people on the oppressive imagery which dominated their lives. During subsequent decades, a focus on the negative stereotypes promoted through charity advertising and the media, in Europe and North America, led to various calls for a radical reappraisal of cultural representations of disabled people. Disquiet among the disabled community over the prevalence of disablist imagery in popular culture prompted the development of a positive alternative; namely, disability culture, and the disability arts movement. Examples of early initiatives include the production of a television programme specifically for disabled people, entitled *Link*, by a British independent production company, and newsletters and magazines by the disabled people's movement. Examples include *The Disability Rag*, the unofficial newspaper of the American Independent Living Movement, initiated by the Centre for Accessible Living in Louisville, Kentucky in 1980, and *In From the Cold*, the magazine produced by Britain's Liberation Network of Disabled People, which was established in 1981. Further illustrations of this gathering trend include the setting up of the London Disability

Arts Forum in 1986, and a general upsurge in conferences, exhibitions, workshops, cabaret and performance.

The general aim of this chapter is to relate disabled people's achievement in placing disabled imagery firmly on the political agenda to sociological analyses of leisure, media and culture. First, there is a brief introduction to sociological approaches to culture. Second, attention is concentrated on the specific relationship between leisure and disability: how far, and in what ways, do disabled people participate in 'mainstream' leisure activities and establish 'normal' social relationships and contacts? Third, the discussion explores studies of the cultural representation of disabled people in the media and other art forms. The final section examines how disabled people have begun to initiate new meanings and new creative forms, potentially a subculture in opposition to the dominant culture, most notably in the movement known as 'disability arts'.

Sociological approaches to culture

Rather than adopt a restricted definition of culture centring on 'art', sociologists have adopted a broad approach which includes symbolic aspects of human society, such as beliefs, rituals, customs and values, as well as work patterns, leisure activities and material goods: 'Culture consists of the values the members of a given group hold, the norms they follow, and the material goods they create' (Giddens, 1989: 31).

While values are 'abstract ideals', norms encompass the rules or guidelines of what is acceptable in social life. Culture then denotes a 'signifying system' through which practices, meanings and values are, according to Raymond Williams, 'communicated, reproduced, experienced and explored' (Williams, 1981: 13). This diffuse view of culture as a 'way of life' is close to, but distinguished from, the notion of 'society', which refers to a 'system of interrelationships' held in common by those who share a similar culture (Giddens, 1989: 32). To become a member of a society, it is necessary to learn, or be socialized into, its cultural assumptions and rules.

Williams further maintained that:

A culture has two aspects: the known meanings and directions, which its members are trained to; the new observations and meanings, which are offered and tested. These are the ordinary processes of human societies and human minds, and we see through them the nature of a culture: that it is always both traditional and creative; that it is both the most ordinary common meanings and the finest common meanings. (R. Williams, 1989: 4)

Human cultures both set the criteria for, or the boundary lines around, what is considered 'normal' and typical, and the responses to those categorized as 'different'. In exploring disability in culture, the emphasis is on analysing the ways in which the 'common meanings' attached to people with impairments are such that they are perceived as in some way 'deficient', whether not quite 'normal' or perhaps not fully 'human'.

There has been considerable sociological interest in theorizing the relationship between society and culture. The significant variation across cultures in the meaning and representation attached to impairment and disability has already been noted. Traditional Marxist accounts have concentrated on a culture's material basis, where others have ascribed it much greater autonomy. Since the late 1960s, Western Marxist writing has developed more complex notions, taking inspiration from the work of Antonio Gramsci (1971). His notion of 'hegemony' directed attention to the ways in which capitalist domination is achieved not only by coercion, but also by the generation of 'willing consent', through its direction of the production and consumption of culture. This approach has been a major influence on the studies of culture by Stuart Hall and his colleagues (Hall and Jefferson, 1976; Hall et al., 1978; Hall et al., 1980) and has been incorporated into the analysis of disability by Mike Oliver (1990) – see chapter 4.

Another important influence has been Raymond Williams (1980, 1981), who developed the notion of cultural materialism, and bridged the gap between literary criticism and sociology in analysing the relationship between the material means of cultural production and cultural forms. The significance of cultural practices, institutions and representations in the media and other art forms, such as literature, film and photography, is that they are not necessarily derived from a separately constituted social order. Instead, they often contribute significantly to its production and confirmation, while offering scope for alternative possibilities.

Most recently, a burgeoning, often inter-disciplinary, literature on cultural studies has expanded the theoretical bases for debates about cultural representation still further by moving away from the Marxist tradition and engaging with feminist, post-structuralist and postmodernist theories (Inglis, 1993).

Leisure and social life

The rationale for examining leisure stems from claims that this has become an increasingly important aspect of 'lifestyle' and badge of identity and status in late twentieth-century culture and society: 'It is in the sphere of consumption – conspicuous leisure on the basis of adequate disposable income – that many will seek to express their sense of freedom, their personal power, their status and aspirations' (A. Tomlinson, 1990: 6). Whereas a person's job had been widely regarded as the primary source of their social position and identity, a contrasting tendency in recent decades has been to stress patterns of consumption and lifestyle (Giddens, 1993). Identities are produced and regulated in and through consumption and conspicuous leisure practices. It is also an area which amply illustrates the force of analysing disability as a form of social oppression.

In a society and culture much more geared to consumption, the leisure industry has become big business. There has been an extraordinary expansion of personal choice, although leisure is produced, marketed and sold in much the same way as any other commodity. In the early 1990s, total expenditure in the UK on leisure activities accounted for 17 per cent of total household budget, or about £45 per week (CSO, 1994). The most significant items, in terms of time and money spent, spanned holidays, eating out and drinking, buying/renting videos, along with visiting leisure parks such as Alton Towers in Britain or Disney World in Florida.

Nevertheless, the standard definition of leisure is given as 'free time', and is contrasted with the world of paid employment (Parker, 1975; Clarke and Critcher, 1985). In the UK there has been a general decline in the working week, from fifty-four hours in 1901 to under forty-four in the mid-1990s, and a relative augmentation in disposable incomes. This suggests that people have more opportunities to engage in leisure activities. A further assumption is that activities which form part of one's paid employment are largely controlled by others, whereas what is done in non-work time is down to personal choice. While the world of work is thought constraining, leisure provides the occasion to pursue more fulfilling activities.

Where does this leave disabled people? On average, they have more 'free time', but this is simply explained by the relatively higher proportion not in paid employment. In addition, many disabled people, particularly women at home and those who are retired, find that a lot of their 'free time' is taken up with necessary, unpaid activities – such as housework and looking after others in their family. Moreover, this 'free time' is significantly reduced because disabled people often take longer to complete everyday personal and domestic activities such as washing, cooking and eating. There are specific problems for those who require support from a personal assistant or others to complete routine daily tasks. These include the often time-consuming negotiations with local authorities and other agencies in order to maintain and refine their personal assistance packages (Oliver et al., 1988). Disabled women are likely to receive relatively less domestic support than disabled men, which further diminishes their 'free time' (Rae, 1993).

People's ability to make full use of their leisure time is also closely related to their income and employment status (Fagin and Little, 1984). Government figures show that disabled people receive much less than the average national income, and the overwhelming majority do not have sufficient incomes to cover the full cost of impairment-related expenses, let alone leisure pursuits (Martin and White, 1988). The lack of material resources is also a significant constraint on choice of activity and level of involvement. There are also extra costs involved in getting out and about.

Moreover, essential equipment, such as electric wheelchairs and reading aids, which is provided by statutory agencies to disabled people in employment, can also be used in leisure pursuits. However, if they then become unemployed, this equipment may have to be returned; those who are already unemployed cannot apply for equipment or technical aids essential for participating in particular leisure activities. Hence, disabled people's 'free time' can easily become a source of frustration, because they are effectively denied opportunities to 'do their own thing'. This is exacerbated for those not in paid work, since they have a more restricted circle of social contacts. This accentuates the social separation of disabled and non-disabled people.

Disabled people are not simply less well placed to buy into leisure, but they have also been widely ignored, or implicitly discouraged – whether as participants or spectators. For example, disabled people have reported difficulties in taking holidays, often because the cheaper package holidays are less likely to include accessible transport or accommodation (Martin et al., 1989: table 6.4). The gulf has been slightly narrowed in the 1990s, as adverts in the British disability press such as *Disability Now* demonstrate, with the emergence of some specialist companies, although this again perpetuates the social segregation of disabled people.

This disadvantage spans both home-based and outside leisure activities. For example, radio and television are inaccessible to many with visual and hearing impairments, with only 13 per cent of British TV programmes at the end of the 1980s containing subtitles for those with hearing impairments (DBC, 1990; Barnes, 1991). The Broadcasting Act 1990 set a target of subtitled programmes at 50 per cent of total output by 1998, but there is a similar need for routine sign-language translation. This exclusion extends from books to newspapers and magazines, which are rarely available simultaneously in an accessible form for people with visual impairments. Voluntary agencies, such as the Talking Newspaper Association will supply taped summaries, but typically only on a weekly basis, while there is a similar problem with new books (RNIB, 1990).

Socializing with friends is also made problematic by the shortage of accessible housing. Outside the home, participation in leisure activities is severely restricted by an inaccessible physical environment, including key venues such as cinemas, theatres, and swimming pools. Transport is a further constraint for those dependent on specialized systems (Thomas et al., 1989; Heiser, 1995).

Those requiring the services of a personal assistant may find that such help is only available for home-based activities, or for essentials such as shopping for food, rather than for visiting a pub or going to a party, thus intensifying the divide between home and outside activities (Morris, 1993). Similarly, disabled people typically have to wait for special help to use public swimming baths, or have to join 'disabled-only' sessions, although these may be preferred by some in order to avoid the stares of non-disabled people (Edwards, 1995: 24).

The general policy response has consisted of recommending rather than requiring changes. Yet, without enforced sanctions, local practice has been slow to change. Some entertainment venues still refuse admission to wheelchair-users, on safety grounds, or only admit those accompanied by an 'able-bodied' companion.

Even if entrance is allowed, wheelchair-users are urged to telephone first 'to be sure of getting in' (Crouch et al., 1989: 109). Where unaccompanied disabled people are allowed entry, they may be directed to special areas where they can be 'watched over'. Even the most popular tourist attractions impose restrictions: Madame Tussauds in London discourages wheelchair-users at peak times and insists that fire regulations restrict entry to no more than three wheelchair-users at a time. A similar restraint applies to many popular sporting venues. Institutional discrimination is also prevalent in the hotel and catering industry, where disabled people are often shunned because they are perceived as 'bad for business' – despite the introduction of the 1995 Disability Discrimination Act. As an illustration, a zoo manager refused to admit a party of people with learning difficulties on the pretext that they would 'frighten the animals' (*Disability Now*, 1997).

This lack of accessibility extends to arts venues. Although the Carnegie Council (1985) made specific recommendations for policy changes, its own follow-up study, *After Attenborough* (Carnegie Council, 1988), noted that few had been implemented: 'the majority of museums and galleries, cinemas, concert halls and theatres remain inaccessible, at any rate in some respects to wheelchair users and to many other people with disabilities' (p. 15).

A further factor affecting disabled people's leisure in Britain has been local authority provision of facilities. These were signalled in the National Assistance Act 1948, while the Chronically Sick and Disabled Persons Act 1970 identified 'day centres, adult training centres and social clubs whose range of services encompassed "lectures, games, outings or other recreational facilities"'. However, these have often led to segregated recreational and social activities for disabled and older people, which amount to little more than 'company and diversional activities' (Carter, 1981; Barnes, 1990). Reasons for attendance are often not positive: for some, it is an escape from their social isolation at home; others are directed to attend as part of their 'rehabilitation'; while staff in some special schools view day centres (or disability resource centres) as the main alternative for those thought unable to obtain paid employment. Even their location, often outside city centres, or in the grounds of residential institutions, presents travel difficulties and conveys a negative image. Nevertheless, day centres may also facilitate consciousness-raising and building a more positive collective identity (Barnes, 1990).

Most industrialized countries now contain a variety of local and national organizations for disabled people to explore specific leisure pastimes, which are typically run as charities, and as segregated activities. For example, the UK organization Sports for Young Disabled Women organizes climbing and other outdoor activities, while Riding for the Disabled has acquired a high profile. A national network of social clubs, known as Physically Handicapped and Able-Bodied (PHAB), was set up explicitly to bring disabled and 'non-disabled' people together, but there is little evidence that such integration has been achieved. Most of the non-disabled people in attendance are helpers or family and friends of the disabled member, while the wide age-range catered for – from young children to retired people – is often a source of critical comment from users (Barnes, 1990).

Studies of younger disabled people identify particular dissatisfaction with leisure opportunities. Anderson et al. (1982) compared the leisure and social activities of 119 disabled, and thirty-three non-disabled, teenagers. They conclude that disabled teenagers spent more time engaged in passive, solitary activities, such as watching TV or listening to music. They were also less likely to see their friends after school, but more likely than non-disabled children to socialize with other members of their family, thus emphasizing their relative separation from their peer group. Only 21 per cent were rated as having a 'satisfactory' social life compared with 94 per cent of the control group (p. 80), while 41 per cent were rated as having a 'very restricted' social life compared with 3 per cent of disabled teenagers. Such isolation was even greater for those who attended special schools, with over half reporting that they had never been to a friend's house. Brimblecomb et al. (1985) found that, among those aged 16–25 years of age, non-disabled people were three times more likely to be living independently of their parents.

Social isolation and the lack of social relationships are felt very keenly among young people because their peer group look to activities outside the home for social contacts (Dorner, 1976; Markham, 1991). There is also evidence that older people with impairments are even more separated from family and friends (Zarb and Oliver, 1993). Overall, the reality of disability is 'hard for friends to confront' (Morris, 1989: 105). Equally, going out to visit friends needs careful planning, with the result that spontaneity and choice are greatly reduced. This is particularly problematic where the disabled person relies on others for personal support (Oliver et al., 1988).

A further significant aspect of social life is the scope for exploring sexual feelings and encounters (Clarke and Critcher, 1985: 162). Yet this is an area which disabled people find particularly 'closed' (Hurst, 1984; Morris, 1989; Shakespeare et al., 1996). As Alan Holdsworth (1992) points out, disabled youngsters are not regarded as potential partners by their non-disabled peers: 'I was the friend they could trust because my sexuality was denied me by both sexes.' Many disabled people feel disregarded as not attractive to others because they have an impairment. Disabled people are not expected to have sexual feelings or needs. The antagonism towards people with impairments having children, the obsession with the 'body beautiful' (Campling, 1981; Fine and Asch, 1985), and the widespread association of sexual activity with vaginal penetration and orgasm, all reinforce the misgivings and uncertainties experienced by disabled people, who tend to be perceived as asexual. 'Sexuality is often the source of our deepest oppression' (Finger, 1991), much of which may come from family members who see their disabled kin as perpetual children and discourage sexual relationships (Burkitt, 1996). However, contrary stereotypes have also surfaced, such as the perceived tendency towards sexual promiscuity among women with learning difficulties. The sexual abuse of disabled children is also a significant issue (see chapter 5).

Cultural representations of disability

Although the main emphasis within British disability studies has been on material processes of exclusion, there is an important tradition of cultural exploration of disability, within and outwith the disabled people's movement, which can be traced back at least to Louis Battye's (1966) reflections on a disabled identity, and subsequent discussions by Ann Shearer (1981a) and Jo Campling (1981). This also triggered the disability activism which led to protests against disabling imagery in the 1980s, with the formation of the Campaign Against Patronage, and demonstrations at the Telethon fund-raising events (see chapter 7).

The focus on cultural and ideological oppression is widely seen as demonstrating how disability is an all-pervasive experience. The representation of disabled people in the media and other art forms, such as literature, film and photography, is then regarded as confirming what it means to be a disabled person in this society. In this sense, media representations are a primary source of disability as well as a rationalization for treating disabled people as 'deficient'. Initially, the concern was with media stereotypes of disabled people and the experience of disability, and subsequently with the processes by which meanings about normality and bodily difference are produced. There is a further literature, running parallel with these interests, which examines how audiences respond to these media representations.

Media stereotypes

In *Doctoring the Media* (1988), Ann Karpf devotes a chapter to 'crippling images', which develops themes which recur in the literature: for example, the media fondness for cure stories; the role of charity appeals; the invisibility of disabled people on television; the stereotyped portrayal of disabled characters in screen drama; the underemployment of disabled people in broadcasting. Her brief survey summarizes the issues around which disabled people's organizations in Britain continue to campaign. This has achieved some notable outcomes: the ending of the Telethon; the training and employment of disabled people in front of, and behind, the camera; and a growing sensitivity to prejudicial images.

Nevertheless, disabling images continue to reinforce disabled people's everyday experiences. As Jenny Morris argues in *Pride Against Prejudice* (1991):

> The general culture invalidates me both by ignoring me and by its particular representations of disability. Disabled people are missing from mainstream culture. When we do appear, it is in specialized forms – from charity telethons to plays about an individual struck down by tragedy – which impose the non-disabled world's definitions on us and our experience. (Morris, 1991: 85)

Such cultural stereotyping is a form of oppression: with disabled people portrayed as not-powerful and not-attractive, and impairment used as a metaphor for evil. However, culture can also be the site for generating alternative meanings – a theme explored later in the context of disability arts.

Simultaneously, several other researchers were undertaking content analyses of media representation of disabled people. For example, Guy Cumberbatch and Ralph Negrine (1992) undertook a eight-week monitoring of British television during 1988, using content analysis and group discussions. The central finding was not that disabled people were under-represented in television programmes – although this was a general pattern – but that disabled people were misrepresented or represented in a partial way, as was disability. The most prevalent storylines linked disabled people with medical treatment or cure, together with programmes focusing on their 'special achievements'. In contrast, disabled people were much less visible in fictional programmes, where they comprised only 0.5 per cent of all characters. Moreover, these representations were highly stereotypical, showing disabled people as criminal, or only barely human, or powerless and pathetic. They were not depicted as ordinary members of society, but were used to evoke emotions of pity or fear, or to contribute to an atmosphere of mystery, deprivation or menace.

Over recent years, this misrepresentation of disability and disabled people on television has been acknowledged by broadcasters. The Broadcasting Standards Council (BSC) admitted in its Code of Practice, the need for programmes and advertising to give a 'fair reflection of the parts played in the everyday life of the nation of disabled people' (BSC, 1989/94: 45). This would mean, first, a shift away from the portrayal of disabled people in factual programmes in a manner which gives non-disabled viewers 'a sense of the superiority of their condition, or the emotional enjoyment of their generous sympathy' and, second, a concerted effort on the part of writers and producers to include more disabled characters, preferably played by disabled actors, in fictional programmes. These characters should be part of 'the drama of life' and not used 'in either a sinister or a sentimental fashion' (Cumberbatch and Negrine, 1992: 141).

The most recent survey of disabled people suggests that they perceive little change in media practice. The whole thrust of their comments was of a sense of exclusion from, and prejudice within, television (Ross, 1997). The general conclusion was that fictional programming presented a negative portrayal of disabled people, in one-dimensional and stereotypical terms. Disabled characters were not depicted as 'ordinary' people experiencing 'ordinary' problems (p. ii). There was a specific criticism that programme-makers concentrated on 'safe' disabled characters, typically wheelchair-users, for reasons of their own, not least that they could thus avoid those with impairments which were thought 'unappealing'. Mainstream factual TV programmes were condemned as patronizing for the regularity with which non-disabled 'experts' were used to pronounce on the experiences and needs of disabled people. Again, documentary treatment was seen as concentrating on disabled people as either 'tragic but brave' or 'helpless and dependent' (p. iii). Concern was also expressed about the marginalization of specialist disability programmes into 'ghetto-slots', where their potential impact on mainstream audiences was greatly diminished.

Newspaper reporting of disability has attracted similar criticism. The Spastics Society's (now SCOPE) study, *What the Papers Say and Don't Say about Disability* (Smith and Jordan, 1991), included an eight-week survey of newspaper characterizations of disability issues. A limited number of themes dominated newspaper coverage, with health, fund-raising/charity, and personal/individual interest stories accounting for approximately 35 per cent of the total. Tabloids were particularly prone to dramatize and sensationalize, and to ignore other aspects of disabled people's experience. However, broadsheets also presented a one-sided picture and reinforced a medical approach. Language was pejorative and prejudicial, and coverage contravened existing industry codes of practice.

In 1990 the editors of the major national British newspapers agreed on a voluntary Code of Practice to ensure that disabled people are 'fairly represented' in the press and not exploited for their news potential. But this has proven little more than a public relations exercise. A further development has been the appointment to all the major newspapers of a 'readers' representative' or 'Ombudsman' to deal with complaints and to exert pressure for change. However, action can only be instigated after offensive material has been published. The umbrella organization for dealing with complaints is the Press Complaints Commission (previously the Press Council), but it has been notoriously slow in dealing with complaints and has appeared reluctant to exercise its limited powers.

The portrayal of disabled people in advertising also concentrates heavily on disabling stereotypes. Studies indicate that their depiction as pitiable and pathetic is widespread (Rieser and Mason, 1990). The depth of feeling against cynical exploitation by charities has been particularly marked, although Campbell (1990) suggests that there has been a shift in disablist imagery employed by the charity industry. She notes three phases: philanthropic ('fund-raising garden parties'); 'courageous and exceptional'; and 'look at the ability not the disability'. This latest development indicates a shift from a negative focus on impairment to what disabled people can achieve. However, this positive image seems to be defined in terms of what 'normal' people are like, and therefore undermines disabled people's attempts to build their own disability culture (Campbell, 1990: 5–7).

An interest in images of disability in America resulted in a number of studies from the 1970s onwards (Biklen and Bogdan, 1977). Laurie Klobas (1988), for example, collected many examples of disability representations on the small and large screen. Another landmark was John Schuchman's survey of images of deafness in Hollywood films, which concluded: 'Until film makers portray the existence of an active and healthy deaf community, it is improbable that Americans will get beyond the pathological myths that make daily life difficult for disabled individuals' (Schuchman, 1988: 305). The collection *Images of the Disabled, Disabling Images* (Gartner and Joe, 1987) brought together a number of important critiques, exploring the way in which disabled people are objectified in representation. Kriegel's article, examining sources such as *Lady Chatterley's Lover* and *Moby Dick*, suggests that:

> The world of the crippled and disabled is strange and dark, and it is held up to judgement by those who live in fear of it. The cripple is the creature who has been deprived of his ability to create a self . . . He is the other, if for no other reason than that only by being the other will he be allowed to presume upon the society of the 'normals'. He must accept definition from outside the boundaries of his own existence. (Kriegel, 1987: 33)

Paul Longmore points out how even popular cartoon characters like Porky Pig and Elmer Fudd carry messages about impairment and identity. He argues that it is the fear of 'disability' which underlies these presentations: 'What we fear, we often stigmatize and shun and sometimes seek to destroy. Popular entertainments depicting disabled characters allude to these fears and prejudices or address them obliquely or fragmentarily, seeking to reassure us about ourselves' (Longmore, 1987: 66).

Several writers have tried to develop these criticisms into a classification of representations of disabled people. Clogson (1990) identifies five models:

1   medical: disability as illness or malfunction;

2   social pathology: disabled people as disadvantaged, needing
     support;
3   'supercrip': disabled people as deviants, achieving super-
     human feats in spite of impairment;
4   civil rights: disabled people having legitimate grievances, as
     members of a minority group;
5   cultural pluralism: disabled people as multi-faceted, impair-
     ments not the only issue.

Haller (1995) extended this list to include:

6   business: disabled people as costly to society, particularly to
     commerce;
7   legal: disabled people possessing legal rights;
8   consumer: disabled people as an untapped market.

Within this approach, models 4, 5, 7 and 8 would be seen as the
positive representations.

   In Britain, a British Council of Disabled People (BCODP)-
sponsored study also examined the dominant cultural stereotypes
of disability (Barnes, 1992). These comprise images of the disabled
person as: pitiable and pathetic; an object of violence; sinister and
evil; 'atmosphere' or a curio; 'super-cripple'; an object of ridicule;
their own worst and only enemy; burden; sexually abnormal;
incapable of participating fully in community life; and as 'normal'.
While the latter may be viewed as a positive development, it has to
be remembered that the emphasis on 'normality' tends to obscure
the need for change. In a society organized around the needs of a
'non-disabled' majority disabled people are consequently viewed
as 'abnormal'. Moreover, 'if disabled people are viewed as
"normal" then there is little need for policies to bring about a
society free from disablism' (Barnes, 1992: 38).

   The literature on cultural representation considered so far
defines media images as a source of oppression. It not only illustrates the widespread use of disabling images in general, but it also
replicates other sites of social division.

Gendered images

Deborah Kent has reviewed the disabled female in fiction, and suggests: 'Disability seems to undermine the very roots of her womanhood. Not surprisingly, therefore, the disabled women in these

works frequently feel inferior to others and regard themselves with loathing' (Kent, 1987: 63). Moreover, authors appear less concerned with disabled women as subjects, than as vehicles or objects: 'In many instances, the disabled woman is little more than a metaphor through which the writer hopes to address some broader theme' (Kent, 1987: 60).

Jenny Morris's work also explores the gendered nature of disabling imagery: 'the social definition of masculinity is inextricably bound up with a celebration of strength, of perfect bodies. At the same time, to be masculine is not to be vulnerable' (Morris, 1991: 93). Therefore, films such as *Born on the Fourth of July* and *Waterdance* had men trying to cope with their loss of masculinity through impairment. The focus is on disabled men, so as to explore the contradiction between masculine potency, and disabled impotency – on the presumption that the only thing worse than feeling unloved is to feel unlovable. Since women are already seen as vulnerable, passive and dependent, there is less artistic interest in portraying disabled women, unless it is as tragic or saintly figures. While there are images of men as 'supercrips' – characters who triumph over tragedy – there are few similar images of women 'overcoming all odds', with the exception of Helen Keller.

Helen Meekosha and Leanne Dowse (1997b) extend this discussion of the intersection of gender and disability. They note that, while feminists criticize eroticized images of women, disabled women are rarely portrayed as sexual beings. Again, while feminists have objected to the representation of women in conventional domestic roles, disabled women are denied access to these traditional feminine values. However, the use of the disabled climber Lisa O'Nion in a Schweppes poster campaign, veers towards a message that disabled people need to strive to overcome physical limitations – almost to become a 'supercrip'. This raises a potential conflict between the disabled people's movement's general support for images of disabled people in 'normal' roles, and the desire of feminists to challenge traditional gender roles.

> There are also dangers here of the advertising industry moving from selling the beautiful and sculptured non-disabled body to selling the beautiful and sculptured disabled body. For women with degenerative or acquired disabilities, or illnesses not amenable to physical body sculpting, these images can further demoralize and undermine their sense of self-worth. (Meekosha and Dowse, 1997b: 15)

These examples verify two important points: it is vital to include the gender dimension in discussions of disabling imagery, and the notion of a positive, or a negative, image is complex and contradictory.

Media effects

This brings the discussion to the question of media effects. It has been the general conclusion that the preponderance of media imagery is disabling and has a consequential effect on its audience. With so little exposure to contrary messages, this reinforces a straightforward 'hypodermic syringe' model in which the 'naturalness' of disability is seen to be confirmed by the media. Most direct evidence of the effects of media representation comes from charity advertising, where the success of campaigns in generating income and volunteers has been documented (R. Williams, 1989; Hevey, 1992). Nevertheless, not all charity campaigns fulfil their objectives, and there is a considerable debate about the potential for contrasting readings of media representation and the general susceptibility of audiences to media messages.

However, the presumption of an 'inert' or 'passive' audience has been widely challenged. The 'uses and gratifications' approach argued that people actively interpret media materials in accordance with their own needs (McQuail, 1972; Blumler and Katz, 1974). Others have utilized Gramsci's notion of hegemony to explore how the media 'manufacture consent' to the dominant order, while acknowledging that the media may be 'read' in contrary ways, or that different audiences may interpret media materials differently (Hall et al., 1978). Is the impact of the media as pronounced in changing people's views as in confirming existing opinions? People look at the media having already been socialized in a variety of ways, and often with clear views of their own about particular subjects.

This emphasis on an 'active audience' is yet to be fully explored in the context of the media and disability – where media messages are thought unambiguous, but arguably less so than even twenty years ago. To suggest that audiences can be active, and negotiate their own meaning, does not leave the media without any impact. In research conducted by the Glasgow Media Group, the opportunities for audience 'resistance' are highlighted, at the same time as the media are seen as of primary importance in shaping or reinforcing people's views on key social issues, including disability (Philo, 1990, 1996).

In the case of 'mental illness', media coverage has been described as significant, not least because of the repeated association made in headlines between it and unprovoked violence, and because such negative storylines far outnumber more positive reports (Philo, 1996: 112). This had a 'major impact' on audiences, with consequential harmful effects on the users of mental health services and their social relationships. Similarly, studies of the media and HIV/AIDS (Kitzinger, 1993) reported considerable media influence on public opinion. Public attitudes were noticeably affected by information, phrases and images that had their inspiration in media reports. Kitzinger (1993, 1995) argues that key themes owed much to media portrayals, such as the 'ravaged' face of AIDS, the difference between 'guilty' and 'innocent' victims, and the association with 'unnatural' sexual practices. Again, the impact of the media cannot simply be derived from a content analysis but has to be located within people's prior beliefs that enable certain images to take hold more easily, while other messages are rejected, or reinterpreted.

Such research also illustrates how the processes of constructing disabling images are under-theorized:

> Models tend to be static and do not necessarily reflect contradictory representations and change over time. They help us 'fit' media stories into boxes, but do not necessarily aid in a more complex analysis of the processes involved in disability construction. Thus overall, the variety of elements of media analysis necessary to understand disability cannot be reduced to a simple categorization of content, but require a complex sensitivity to multiple dimensions of the process. (Meekosha and Dowse, 1997b: 11)

Cultural studies approaches

The political emphasis, content analyses and schematic classifications which characterize much of the early approaches to understanding disabling representations have been challenged by a multi-disciplinary cultural studies approach – with literary, film studies, neo-Marxist, linguistic and psychoanalytic influences. This has spawned a growing academic disability literature, which engages with specific art works or texts, and develops detailed and multi-layered readings. In contrast to the mainly quantitative or classificatory approach encountered so far, this literature engages in textual critique, and looks at qualitative and aesthetic issues.

With some notable exceptions, cultural studies accounts of disability representations have been most prolific within the American context. The focus has been on the role of disability within literature, film and other art forms. However, these approaches do not make the key social model distinctions between impairment as a property of the body, and disability as a social relationship. While cultural studies writings attribute significance to the disabling impact of society, the political context in which such exclusion is experienced is largely neglected.

Rosemarie Garland Thomson (1997) demonstrates the contribution which literary criticism can make to disability studies, in her interrogation of American sources including the traditional freak show, sentimental novels such as *Uncle Tom's Cabin*, and the contemporary African American fiction of Toni Morrison and Audre Lorde. Her focus is on impaired bodies: 'To denaturalize the cultural encoding of these extraordinary bodies, I go beyond assailing stereotypes to interrogate the conventions of representation and unravel the complexities of identity production within social narratives of bodily differences' (Thomson, 1997: 5). In this project, she draws heavily on contemporary literary and feminist theory, particularly its postmodern versions, in casting light on the construction of normality, by examining how 'corporeal deviance' is a 'product of cultural rules' about 'able-bodiedness': 'Constructed as the embodiment of corporeal insufficiency and deviance, the physically disabled body becomes a repository for social anxieties about such troubling concerns as vulnerability, control and identity' (Thomson, 1997: 6). Thomson's work offers an 'academic' perspective on disabling representation, although her book is also intended as a political intervention in regarding disabled people as akin to a minority ethnic group (see chapter 4). Moreover, while she analyses impaired bodies as 'extraordinary' rather than abnormal, her continued emphasis on the individual body, rather than structural and collective forces, marks out the difference between her approach and most British analyses of culture and disability.

Martin Norden's (1994) comprehensive chronology of disability in film extends the 'image of' approach to the portrayal of social groups in particular social contexts. He shows how, from the earliest days of cinema, stereotypical and distorted representations of disability were the norm – for example, Thomas Edison's 1898 short film, *Fake Beggar*. As a visual medium, cinema used pictures to reveal character, so it became automatic to represent emotional cripples as physical cripples. Moreover, the new technology offered the opportunity for trick photography to represent miracle cures. The cinema also inherited the voyeuristic traditions of the freak-show. As Cecil B. de Mille stated: 'affliction is more saleable' (quoted in Norden, 1994: 71).

Norden traces the development of a range of stereotypes – Elderly Dupe, Saintly Sage, Obsessive Avenger, Sweet Innocent, Comic Misadventurer, Tragic Victim, Noble Warrior. Each, he suggests, is characterized by the isolation experienced by the disabled character: 'We might argue that the movie industry has created physically disabled characters primarily to serve the needs of a society long committed to stifling and exploiting its disabled minority' (Norden, 1994: 314). However, he does detect positive changes of this imagery, as it evolved from the early exploitative phase (1890s–1930s), through the exploratory phase (1930s–1970s) to the incidental phase (1970s to the present). Nevertheless, even in contemporary films, the old stereotypes still surface. While Norden makes connections to broader social, economic and political developments (for instance, the return of disabled veterans from war), he concentrates primarily on psycho-analytic explanations.

The British critic Paul Darke has developed disability analysis through a close reading of specific films, for example, *The Elephant Man* (Darke, 1994). In his own survey of disabling imagery (Darke, 1998), he develops the concept of 'normality drama', arguing that this is a genre which uses abnormal/impaired characters to deal with a perceived threat to the dominant social hegemony of nor-mality. He criticizes the attempt of disabled critics to propose positive images, suggesting this fails to capture the totality and significance of disability within films. Equally, he rejects the psychoanalytical approach taken by Norden. For Darke, normality drama is about the cultural rationalization of the social disable-ment of the person with an impairment.

Lennard Davis' monograph (1996) and subsequent collection on disability studies (Davis, 1997) demonstrates the cultural studies approach in wider artistic and historical arenas. For example, he traces the development of the lexicon of disability, and particularly the social construction of 'normalcy' in the mid-nineteenth century. He argues for analyses not just of the construction of dis-ability, but also of its perceived opposite. This extends a disability critique to work which is not centrally concerned with disability, such as the novels of Flaubert and Conrad:

> My point is that a disabilities studies consciousness can alter the way we see not just novels that have main characters who are disabled but any novel . . . One can find in almost any novel, I would argue, a kind of surveying of the terrain of the body, an attention to difference – physical, mental and national. (Davis, 1997: 23, 26)

This focuses attention primarily on the body, rather than social relations, as the site of struggle. It is the cultural representation of the impaired body, as much as the image of the disabled person, which is of concern. However, there is a danger that the political and social relations which constitute disability may be neglected in the pursuit of academic theorizing.

The British photographer and theorist David Hevey combines an aesthetic and theoretical analysis of bodily representation with a broader concern with its social context and political significance in his study of charity advertising. In *The Creatures Time Forgot* (1992), Hevey demonstrates how charities 'market' their particular impairments in ways which parallel the 'branding' of commercial organizations and their products. The role of charity adverts is to promote the organization, and its approach to impairment, in order to secure public donations. This involves presenting a particularly stark image of disability, usually in black and white, which centres on the physical flaw. The purpose is to evoke fear and sympathy in the viewer. Charity advertising is described as 'the visual flagship for the myth of the tragedy of impairment' (Hevey, 1992: 51), and a highly significant component in the cultural construction of disability: 'It represents the highest public validation of the isolation of disabled people. It presents a solution to the "problem" of disablement by a disguised blaming of the victim. It fails to find a solution because it is itself the problem' (Hevey, 1992: 51).

The role of charitable imagery in the lives of disabled people has been further linked to the role of pornography in women's oppression. In both cases, the imagery serves to subordinate the objectified subject of the image. The focus is on the body, and particularly on parts of the body (the breasts/the impairment). The viewer is manipulated into an emotional response (desire/fear). In both cases, the conditions of production of the image are outside the control of the subject, and involve wider meanings and power relationships (Shakespeare, 1994). More problematic is whether such imagery actively creates social oppression or rather reflects existing inequalities in power relations.

This discussion of charity advertising raises the issue of changing representation: many cultural studies approaches to disability focus on historical images, where the stereotypical or manipulative treatment of disabled people is at its most extreme. Some contemporary films and advertisements have begun to use more complex and subtle images. For example, some British charities have adopted a more political approach: recent campaigns by SCOPE have focused on prejudice and discrimination as constitutive of disability, while still maintaining an individualist style. Recent Mencap advertising has also sought a new image, which is concerned with citizenship and social rights. This transition has thrown up several dilemmas:

> the difficulty of changing image and focus within a conservative organisation; the tensions between the level of empowerment sought by those in the disability movement and that which the charity proposes; the inadequate representation of real images in a desire to market attractive pictures. (Corbett and Ralph, 1994: 11)

Writers on disability culture will need to develop a more sophisticated and less determined analysis of form and content. Many will argue that charity itself is always oppressive, no matter what image is employed. Others will see greater opportunity for recuperating this form of representation, with the analysis of meaning more complex, diverse and contested.

Writers on both sides of the Atlantic have discussed the processes of objectification that disabling images reveal, and drawn on the notion of 'otherness' to explain the ubiquity of representations. Several suggest that disabled people are 'dustbins for disavowal': that non-disabled people's anxieties and denials regarding the body and its limitations are projected onto disabled people through artistic and media imagery (Hevey, 1992; Shakespeare, 1994; Wendell, 1996; Thomson, 1997). Yet broad differences remain between the cultural studies approach to disability representation in America and the more sociological and politically based explanations of disabling imagery provided by British writers. Thus, while the former emphasize the link between corporeal diversity, cultural meanings, and differential privilege, status and power, British writers tend to see imagery as providing an ideological pretext for social discrimination. This directs attention to the ways in which cultural representations reinforce disabling social relations, and are related to the underlying materiality of the oppression of disabled people. While culture may be relatively autonomous, rather than merely an ideological reflection of under-lying social relations, it is nevertheless broadly characterized as an expression of disabling prejudice.

In the future development of disability studies, there is much to gain by drawing on the most beneficial elements of these approaches. The 'cultural studies' approach offers a more theoretic-ally complex analysis, but needs to be supplemented with the dis-tinction between impairment and disability, and greater attention should be accorded to material social relations as the bedrock of disabling representations. Moreover, the concentration on reveal-ing the structures which generate particular readings of media products and practices has been driven by the assumption that subjectivity is conferred on the reader/viewer by the structure of the text/film. This analysis accentuates how a specific 'narrative' locks the reader into an 'able-bodied' view of 'normality' and dis-abled people without exploring this process, and any eventual 'effect', from the perspective of the reader/audience. A further consideration is that, as cultural theories of disability develop, the precedent of feminism's increasing removal from the lives of ordin-ary women and isolation within the academy indicates the press-ing need for disability studies to remain relevant to the broader community of disabled people, and retain its political focus.

Towards a disability culture

In the final part of this chapter we will explore the extent to which disabled people as a group could be said to be developing an alternative culture, or a subculture, in opposition to or separation from the mainstream culture. Given that the dominant culture is suffused with negative images of disability, are disabled people able to develop values and representations which are self-supporting and promote an acceptance of the validity of life with impairment? The discussion will centre on three areas: the experience of those people with congenital hearing impairment who self-define as Deaf, use Sign Language, and consider themselves a cultural minority; the ways in which common experiences create a shared culture of oppression for disabled people; and the positive expression of disability identity through the cultural practices known as disability arts.

In understanding the cultural experience of deafness, it is necessary to distinguish between people with a hearing impairment – who may be described as deaf, or hard of hearing – who have often acquired or developed hearing loss, and are not native users of British Sign Language (BSL), and those people with congenital hearing impairment who have grown up in a BSL environment due to having Deaf parents, who therefore define themselves as Deaf. It is relevant to speak of this second group as constituting a Deaf culture, on the basis of a shared language. However, the community also comprises certain hearing people, who are the children of Deaf adults, and have grown up with sign language and other aspects of Deaf culture (Davis, 1996).

Deaf people explicitly refer to themselves as a cultural or linguistic minority, making the analogy with minority ethnic groups, who are similarly likely to be excluded because English is not their first language. On the same grounds, they resist identification as impaired or disabled people. This has led to considerable resistance to cochlea implants, which have the capacity to restore hearing to some people with hearing loss, or to genetic screening of foetuses who may be affected by genes causing hearing impairment.

This political approach has proved a stumbling-block to relations between Deaf people and the disabled people's movement as a whole: despite the social model understanding of disability as a social relationship, not a deficit, most Deaf people are unwilling to identify with the term. Neither do Deaf people support an assimilationist strategy, preferring to retain their separate cultural identity. For example, while the disabled people's movement campaigns for inclusive schools, the Deaf community, because of a demand for education in the medium of BSL, is likely to support segregated schooling. Nevertheless, there are also those people with a hearing impairment who do not identify in the same way with Deaf culture, or see themselves as part of the broader disabled population (Corker, 1998).

The second way in which it is possible to talk of a disability culture arises out of the experience of separate schooling and other provisions – for example, segregated transport, welfare services, and rehabilitation agencies. Many people born with congenital impairments will experience the same institutionalized educational experiences, just as people who acquire an impairment will often share the same medical experiences. Thus, in the UK, the pattern has been for young adults to attend segregated colleges, such as Herewood College, just as many people with spinal cord injuries have stayed at the National Spinal Injuries Centre at Stoke Mandeville. Equally, many adults with learning difficulties will frequent day centres or adult training centres which are essentially similar in their regimes. To this extent it may be possible to talk of a shared culture, albeit one based on the experience of oppressive institutional settings. ·

There are several examples of the relevance of this shared heritage. Robert Scott (1969), in his study of rehabilitation agencies for visually impaired people in America, shows how blindness is not so much about functional loss as it is about being socialized into a dependent role through the intervention of agencies and professionals (see chapter 3). Although the socialization which he describes is mostly about reproducing dependency, it may also offer the possibility for subversion, and the development of an alternative shared culture of resistance. Thus, the contemporary origins of the disability protest in Britain lay in actions taken by a group of disabled people at the Le Court Cheshire Home in Hampshire, while its American counterpart gathered fresh momentum from the shared experience of veterans of the Vietnam War.

However, the main contemporary arena where a positive cultural conception of disability is fostered is disability arts. While this grows out of shared socialization, it goes beyond the experience of negative social institutions to develop a distinctly political notion of culture. Traditional responses to the issue of disabled people and the arts have been based on paternalism. Those disabled people viewed as inadequate and incapable have been given art as therapy, in the context of segregated institutions and day centres. Such developments have not just individualized and depoliticized creativity, they have also sometimes used it for commercial purposes, such as charity Christmas cards. While there is obviously a place for art therapy, disabled people do not deserve this presumption of perpetual infantilization, and increasingly have refused to put up with it.

Instead, disabled people have demanded a whole new relationship to art and culture. Disability art is not simply about disabled people obtaining access to the mainstream of artistic consumption and production. Nor is it focused primarily on the experience of living with an impairment. Disability art is the development of shared cultural meanings and the collective expression of the experience of disability and struggle. It entails using art to expose the discrimination and prejudice disabled people face and to generate group consciousness and solidarity. Disability cabarets can empower people in much the same way as going on a direct action demonstration.

Developing a more sophisticated approach to the breadth of the disability–art relationship is important when it is remembered that the stereotype of the 'flawed' artist is extremely strong in Western culture: for example Beethoven's deafness or Van Gogh's insanity. More recently, post-punk singer Ian Curtis, from the group Joy Division, owed some of his reputation for tragic extremism to his epilepsy. While impairment may on occasion add to the appeal or the insight of a particular artistic figure, many artists with impairments have denied or ignored this aspect of their lives, or reacted more in a personal rather than a political way: for example, musicians Ray Charles, Jacqueline du Pré, Evelyn Glennie, Hank Williams and Ian Dury. This represents a complete contrast with disability arts, which stresses the importance of the arts in developing cultural (and by inference political) identity:

> Disability arts also provides a context in which disabled people can get together, enjoy themselves and think in some way about issues of common concern. But it goes deeper than that, as disability culture really does offer people a key to the basic process of identifying as a disabled person, because culture and identity are closely linked concepts. (Vasey, 1992b: 11)

Disability arts is therefore about exposing the disabling imagery and processes of society. There is also a role to play alongside conventional political activities:

> Arts practice should also be viewed as much as a tool for change as attending meetings about orange badge provision . . . Only by ensuring an integrated role for disability arts and culture in the struggle can we develop the vision to challenge narrow thinking, elitism and dependency on others for our emancipation. To encourage the growth of a disability culture is no less than to begin the radical task of transforming ourselves from passive and dependent beings into active and creative agents for social change. (Finkelstein and Morrison, 1992: 20, 22)

Disability art is therefore potentially educative, transformative, expressive, emotionally exploratory, participative, and involving. It is a conception of cultural action that owes much to playwrights such as Bertolt Brecht and to educationalists such as Paolo Freire, because it is radical, challenging and progressive at an individual and social level. Such accounts also have their parallels in post-modernist writings within feminist theory, which celebrate a 'politics of signification' in which subversive representations or performances are thought capable of overturning discriminatory barriers and attitudes.

It is a sign of the maturity and confidence of the disabled people's movement that disabled people are able to celebrate difference, and work together to create and discuss images of their own choosing. Mainstream arts have not confronted disability. Moreover, disabled people are often disempowered, if not excluded, by arts training. Therefore developing their own art, in environments controlled by themselves, is seen as critical if disabled people are to develop as creative producers, and compete with artists in the mainstream. It is for this reason that the disability community has started to support and nurture its own artists, and provide opportunities to experiment and develop the necessary experience and confidence (Cribb, 1993). The difficulty has been to avoid imposing a non-disabled view of quality: it is vital to recognize the process in which people are engaged, the struggle against barriers involved in getting there, and the context in which work is presented (Pick, 1992).

There has been a lack of a positive cultural identity for disabled people to draw upon, in the face of cultural oppression: it has had to be created from scratch in the last decades. Yet its emergence contradicts Susan Wendell's (1996) argument that 'It would be hard to claim that disabled people as a whole have an alternative culture or even the seeds of one' (p. 273). Nevertheless, notions such as 'disability pride' and the 'celebration of difference' do seem problematic, in the context of people whose impairments are debilitating, painful, and can result in premature mortality. While other groups may proclaim that 'black is beautiful' or pronounce themselves 'glad to be gay', it is harder for many disabled people to make equivalent claims. While agreeing that the main determinants of disabled people's quality of life are social, not medical, many would contest the optimism of Jenny Morris's suggestion: 'We can celebrate, and take pride in, our physical and intellectual differences, asserting the value of our lives' (Morris, 1991: 189). It may be necessary to develop an attitude of ambivalence towards impairment: on the one hand, asserting the value of people with impairment, on the other hand, refusing to glorify incapacity.

Central to this process is the distinction between impairment and disability. It is possible to celebrate the resistance and strength which the collective movements of disabled people have demonstrated throughout the world in the last few decades, and to take pride in the survival and self-organization of disabled people.

As an illustration, consider the following poems in which two disabled writers engage with impairment and disability. In the first Micheline Mason (1982: 12–13) delivers her 'liberation song':

From the Inside

Our people can be found
In every class and race
Of every age and nation
Our people are awakening

Chorus
We will not beg
We will not hide
We'll come together
To regain our pride

Some of us can be seen
Some as yet cannot
Some recognise themselves
Some as yet do not
Your secrets we reflect
Mirrored in our truth

Chorus
Though we may not walk
We are moving fast
Though we may not see
We are not blind
To the errors of the past
Though we may not hear
We are not deaf
To the sound
of liberty

Chorus
Divided and packaged
We are sold by the charities
Stirring guilt and pity
In the hearts of the people
Silencing our voices
Lest we shatter the image
Upon which our saviours depend

Our babies are threatened
Our elders forgotten
Whilst they spend our wealth
To protect West from East
And East from West
They sacrifice our health

Wound us in wars
Starve us to death
Put pennies in our bowls
Pray for our souls
Hope God will put us right

We'll take our place
Inside the human race.

In the second example, the late Simon Brisenden (1990b: 7), in his poem *Scars*, highlights the experience of surgical invasion which many disabled people share, and the rage at professional domination:

Scars

The man who cut your skin
and delved within
has he got any scars?

the man whose sterile slice
left mind and body in a vice
has he got any scars?

the man who bent your bones
and organised your personal zones
has he got any scars?

the man who laid you flat
and said I'm in charge of that
has he got any scars?

you do not cry alone
in rage
his blood is on this page.

These poems convey the potential of disability arts for affirming individual experience, whether through a publication or the forum of a cabaret event. Both contribute to a social understanding of disability, rather than a medicalized approach, and validate the life experience of people with impairment.

Review

Historically, images of disability have been generated by non-disabled people, and have been more about the prejudices and delusions of mainstream society than the reality of the disability experience. However, these prejudicial stereotypes have had a wide-ranging influence in confirming traditional patterns of social interaction, policy development, and service provision, including the charitable ethos, with its assumptions of disabled people's dependency.

The sheer volume and consistency of disabling images is a barrier not experienced by all other disadvantaged minorities. Yet media audiences are also able to filter or even reject some messages. It is important therefore to highlight how disabled people are currently involved in challenging the dominant meanings of disability in contemporary culture, and in producing new images and art works which reflect their experiences and values. This is akin to the development of a disability subculture, in so far as disability arts is both a way of developing a disabled identity, and also a critique of dominant forms of cultural representation and production.

Disabled scriptwriter and critic Allan Sutherland is positive about this potential: 'The very fact that previous representations of disability have been narrow, confused and unimaginative leaves the way open for disabled writers and film makers. What we can produce can blow the past away' (Sutherland, 1993: 8).

9

Advancing the Sociology
of Disability

This book began with a call for the application of the sociological imagination to the field of disability. This directs attention to exploring the links between structural conditions and people's lived experience of the process of disablement. It is from this location that the argument has been made for analysing disability sociologically, which has relevance to sociologists more generally, as well as those located in the new field of 'disability studies'. The analysis is also intended to inform the perception of disability in the population at large, including disabled and 'non-disabled' people.

The development of a wide-ranging sociological analysis of disability has, in many ways, been obscured by the sometimes acrimonious exchanges between advocates of established approaches and those advocating a more radical 'social model' perspective. Adherents of this 'new paradigm' criticize sociological approaches on theoretical, methodological and political grounds.

Over the last decade, those in the vanguard of the development of disability theory have extended their critique of social science by calling for a new paradigm of disability research. This is presented as an 'emancipatory' approach, which is contrasted with the conventional research strategies and techniques which prevail within sociology. More specifically, it makes an explicit political and moral commitment to securing social justice for disabled people with the development of 'enabling forms of methodology and research practice' (Barton, 1996: 7).

In this concluding chapter, we illustrate the distinctive claims that a 'new' sociology of disability should embrace: first, by considering the critique of mainstream research and the claim of an emancipatory paradigm to offer an alternative way forward and, second, by addressing some of the current and emerging issues surrounding disability and social justice.

Theory: out with the old and in with the new?

Sociology has long been characterized by a diverse array of theoretical perspectives and, if anything, this process seems to have intensified since the late 1960s. In this it reflects the wider social and political changes of recent decades, with the 'retreat' of the welfare state and the greater reliance on market forces, including a shift to the right by many Western governments, and the collapse of state-sponsored socialism in Eastern-bloc countries. The significance of these changes has been reinforced by suggestions of parallel socio-cultural shifts which have encouraged claims of an impending transition to a 'post-industrial' or 'postmodern' society.

Social theory has become divided over the importance of grand theorizing and claims to political relevance. This raises the spectre of academic debates becoming entirely self-serving and inward-looking, and divorced from the concerns of everyday life. It is difficult to otherwise explain the response by sociologists to the growing public clamour by disabled people for recognition of 'disability'. Some of the resistance can be explained by the willingness of sociologists, and medical sociologists in particular, to accept the 'common-sense' view that disability is an individual health problem. While challenging the medical model in other important respects, the analysis of disability has remained a conspicuous exception. Although one of the most active sub-specialisms within sociology in both Europe and North America, medical sociology has consistently failed to respond to calls for a rethink of disability, except to dismiss the disabled people's movement as politically motivated and a threat to sociological values. Indeed, approaches by medical sociologists to 'chronic illness and disability' have typically withdrawn into more politically benign phenomenological or social constructionist approaches in the 1980s and 1990s (Barnes and Mercer, 1996; Williams, 1996).

The emergence of a more overtly political account, widely referred to as the social model of disability, outside academia and rooted in the collective experience of a small but increasingly influential group of activists and writers, demonstrated the clear influence of sociological radicalism. Not surprisingly, Parsons and Goffman figure less prominently than 'critical' and neo-Marxist theorists, although this has been a line of division which has typically separated analyses of disability by American- and British-based writers. The potential impact of the social model approach in developing a sociology of disability is that it points to issues which cannot be dismissed as a minority concern. These include the economic and political dynamics of biological determinism, perceptions of normality, and social exclusion and inclusion – particularly with reference to the social organization of work, the economics and future of welfare, and the politics and culture of interdependence and difference.

A sociological analysis of disability, therefore, cannot be left to the confines of medical sociology, disability studies, nor simply to sociologists, as the following sections on researching disability and disabled people's life chances will demonstrate.

Disabling research

Just as the emergence of the social model of disability has advanced an alternative theoretical analysis of the process and experience of disablement, comparable claims have been made for 'disability research'. The avowed intention has been to overcome the perceived shortcomings of mainstream social research which has been immersed in an individual approach and guided by policy and professional agendas to generate more information on the service needs of disabled people in order to help them better cope with their 'personal tragedy'.

In a scathing critique, Mike Oliver (1992) condemns conventional attitudes to research on disability as a 'rip-off' – a further element of a 'disablist sociology'. They have, he maintains, done little, if anything, to confront the social oppression and isolation experienced by disabled people: 'Disabled people have come to see research as a violation of their experience, as irrelevant to their needs and as failing to improve their material circumstances and quality of life' (Oliver, 1992: 105).

The roots of this disenchantment can be traced back to the 1960s. In what has become a celebrated case in the history of the disabled people's movement in the UK, disabled residents in the Le Court

Cheshire Home, Hampshire, sought the assistance of academic 'experts' to support their struggle against local managers and professionals for greater control over their everyday lives. The residents believed that independent social research would underpin their claims for individual autonomy and more direct and meaningful involvement in the running of the home. Two researchers from the Tavistock Institute, Eric Miller and Geraldine Gwynne, were funded by the Department of Health and Social Security to undertake an in-depth study. Following extensive research in several institutions, including the Le Court Home, over more than three years, Miller and Gwynne rejected the residents' claims as unrealistic. Instead, they recommended a reworking of traditional professional practice, later referred to as the 'enlightened guardianship' model of disability management (Dartington et al., 1981), as the most appropriate approach for those described as existing in circumstances akin to 'social death' (Miller and Gwynne, 1972). The residents felt betrayed and denounced social scientists as 'parasites' (Hunt, 1981).

This rejection of the expressed interests and concerns of disabled people became a continuing complaint against mainstream research: notably, the development of WHO's (1980) *International Classification of Impairments, Disabilities and Handicaps*, and the design and analysis of the Office of Population Censuses and Survey's studies of 'disability' in Britain in the mid-1980s (Martin et al., 1988): 'Consequently, most of this research is considered at best irrelevant, and at worst, oppressive' (Oliver, 1996a: 139).

Seeking a new approach

These negative experiences encouraged a few, predominantly disabled, researchers to explore an alternative research agenda more in sympathy with the theoretical and political foundations of the social model of disability. Examples include: *Walking into Darkness: The Experience of Spinal Cord Injury* (Oliver et al., 1988); *Able Lives: Women's Experience of Paralysis* (Morris, 1989); and *Cabbage Syndrome: The Social Construction of Dependence* (Barnes, 1990). In addition, as noted in chapter 7, the British Council of Organisations of Disabled People commissioned broad-based research in support of its campaign for anti-discrimination legislation.

This established a momentum towards a different kind of disability research. A national symposium on the subject staged in London in 1989 provided an unintentional stimulus. None of those chairing sessions or presenting papers were themselves disabled, and the event ended with a fierce debate on the nature and purpose of disability research (Ward and Flynn, 1994). This led to the organization of a series of seminars on researching disability held at the Policy Studies Institute in 1991 and sponsored by the Joseph Rowntree Foundation (JRF). These events brought together several leading disability activists, disabled and non-disabled researchers, to discuss ways forward for disability research. They generated a new agenda for disability research. At the first of the JRF seminars, Mike Oliver advocated 'what has variously been called critical inquiry, praxis or emancipatory research' (Oliver, 1992: 107). This referred to a growing literature and practice on 'critical social research' which had been initiated by those engaged in political struggles in the 'developing' countries of the majority world, feminists, black writers and educationalists. It is an approach which emphasizes the role of research in promoting the interests of 'oppressed' groups:

> The development of such a paradigm stems from the gradual rejection of the positivist view of social research as the pursuit of absolute knowledge through the scientific method and the gradual disillusionment with the interpretive view of such research as the generation of socially useful knowledge within particular historical and social contexts. The emancipatory paradigm, as the name implies, is about the facilitating of a politics of the possible by confronting social oppression at whatever levels it occurs. (Oliver, 1992: 110)

Although not a unitary body of thought, this quickly achieved a pre-eminent position among disability researchers, at least in its calls for openly partisan and politically committed research. A 'rights' framework is the basis for research: that is, the promotion of citizenship rights, equal opportunities and inclusion. The central objective is phrased in terms of striving for social justice, to enhance disabled people's autonomy over their lives rather than to act out of a compassionate concern for their 'personal tragedy' (Rioux and Bach, 1994). This emphasis is extended into wider claims about the ways in which emancipatory disability research embodies a radical alternative to mainstream contributions – not simply in its political standpoint but also in its procedures.

The guiding force is provided by the maxims of the social model of disability. Hence, the primary focus of disability research is on the mechanisms and processes which influence people's understanding of disability, and the factors which inhibit disabled people's participation in the economic and social life of the community. It rejects, therefore, the assumptions of the traditional individualistic approach to disability research with its emphasis, whether explicit or implicit, on impairment as the principal cause of disabled people's individual and collective disadvantage. In contrast, disability research should encourage 'reciprocity, gain and empowerment' (Oliver, 1992: 111).

Translating emancipatory theory into research practice

How then is the broad commitment to an emancipatory approach translated into day-to-day research practice? A number of themes appear consistently through the disability literature, which are best summed up as attempts to transform the material and social relations of research production, including the role of funding bodies and the relationship between researchers and those being researched (Oliver, 1992; Zarb, 1992).

A key criticism advanced by disabled people and their organizations has been that control of the material resources necessary to undertake research projects rests directly in the hands of funding bodies and, perhaps more indirectly, with policy-makers. They are able to set the parameters within which projects must be conducted. This includes decisions about how research agendas are established, and the basis on which funding of individual proposals is decided. Needless to say, most of the established groups which fund research (including, in Britain, the NHS, the Benefits Agency, and large 'impairment-specific' charities such as the Royal National Institute for the Blind and the Multiple Sclerosis Society) remain locked into a medical approach to disability, notwithstanding formal commitments to 'user involvement' and 'user-led' services (Oliver, 1997). In this way, the main funding bodies also help to sustain traditionally organized studies of 'disability'.

Similar concerns have been expressed about the role of the research councils and institutes which dominate 'contract' policy research. However, there are important funders of disability research – notably the Joseph Rowntree Foundation – which have recently shown a commitment to funding research which adopts a social-model-led disability approach (Ward, 1997). The Economic and Social Research Council has also been persuaded to fund a large-scale project on measuring disablement (Zarb, 1997).

Beyond these material relations, the emancipatory paradigm

further seeks to change the established social relations of research production which presume an asymmetrical relationship between researcher and researched. The power of the researcher-as-expert is enshrined in their control over the design, implementation, analysis and dissemination of research findings. The end result is that the 'subjects' of research are treated as 'objects', who are simply conduits for supplying information required by the researcher. A classic of traditional research on 'disability' – both in its conceptual and methodological bases – is the OPCS *Surveys of Disability in Great Britain* (Martin et al., 1988). Their focus was fixed on individual functional limitations without reference to society's disabling barriers, while it did little to include disabled people in the design of the study, and ignored their published criticism (Abberley, 1991, 1992). A further feature of this instrumental attitude towards research has been the way in which so many practitioners move between research fields like 'academic tourists', using disability as a means of advancing their own status and interests. This has led to calls from disabled people for 'no participation without representation' (Finkelstein, cited in Oliver, 1992: 105).

For those adhering to the emancipatory paradigm, the intention is to break with the primacy attached to the researcher-as-expert. Instead, researchers are expected to place their skills and knowledge at the disposal of those being researched, who become active participants in the process. Nevertheless, where such proposals have been adopted, whether in disability or other research, several uncertainties have been identified. For example: is the elimination of power differences always necessary or feasible? Is the relationship reversed or equalized? How is accountability to research subjects guaranteed? An equally contentious presumption is that the social world is divided neatly between oppressors and oppressed, and that each is a cohesive grouping (Stone and Priestley, 1996; Barnes and Mercer, 1997; Moore et al., 1998).

Not all those working from a social model perspective are pessimistic about the progress, albeit slow and partial, being made in overturning old orthodoxies in disability research. A positive note about the ways in which disability research is being changed, covering both the material and social relations of production, is provided by Linda Ward (1997). A key demand of the emancipatory paradigm has been that there should be a meaningful input by research subjects, at all stages of the investigation process, including adequate monitoring and accountability. Here, the JRF has been active in supporting innovative studies that have made significant advances in involving people with learning difficulties, and disabled children, for example, in all stages of the research process – such as developing research issues, and as consultants/advisers. In addition, final conclusions and recommendations increasingly reflect this collective input. These are ways of confirming both that disabled people are entitled to be involved in research which affects their lives, and that this leads to more 'relevant' research.

Linda Ward (1997) concludes that an organization which is idealistic in its goals, and open to persuasion about new ways of doing research, can be a catalyst for changes in the social and material relations of research. She illustrates this by the JRF's efforts to shift the balance of power between researchers and those being researched. Other disability researchers have also expressed grounds for partial optimism about revising the social relations of research production through participatory research (Zarb, 1992).

A further issue has been the lack of agreement among disability researchers on whether an emancipatory approach demands a distinctive set of research techniques. In contrast, feminist criticism of main(male)stream research has opened up a debate about feminist 'ways of knowing'. This highlights the validity of personal experience as opposed to 'scientific methods'. In much feminist research, this has been translated into an emphasis on unstructured data-collection methods, with personal experiences shared between interviewer and interviewee (Oakley, 1981). The underlying philosophy is that research subjects have a privileged access to knowledge which researchers should respect. Such 'feminist methods' have struck a sympathetic chord among some disabled female researchers (Vernon, 1997). However, this focus on experience has also provoked sharp disagreements about whether impairment is properly considered part of the overall experience of disability (Morris, 1991, 1996; Crow, 1996; Shakespeare et al., 1996; see also chapter 4 above). The contrary opinion, expressed forcefully by Vic Finkelstein (1996), holds that disability research and political activity should not be deflected from the barriers 'out there' to explore disabled people's personal experience of physical pain, fatigue and depression – although this still leaves open how experience of those disabling barriers is best explored.

While some disability researchers had opted for what is generally described as a more 'qualitative' approach, the overall picture suggests a willingness to draw on a wide range of research strategies and techniques, both quantitative and qualitative. Oliver acknowledges his own uncertainties on this count: 'I am not sure whether interviews, questionnaires, participant observation, transcript analysis, etc., are compatible or incompatible with emancipatory research' (Oliver, 1997: 21). There is a broad consensus about rejecting mainstream claims to objectivity, but beyond that, disability researchers have adopted widely used forms of data collection and analysis. Indeed, Oliver (1997) has questioned the relevance of offering a checklist of methodological criteria for those wishing to follow an emancipatory approach. From this perspective, the whole emphasis is on the outcomes of the research. Disability research should be judged solely in terms of whether it has contributed to the process of enabling disabled people to empower themselves.

The relationship between disability research and policy initiatives is another contentious issue. Social research generally does not have the best of records in impressing policy-makers, but disability researchers have argued that the dismal record to date is exactly the reason why a new way forward is required. Hence the shifting emphasis towards informing political struggle, rather than expecting 'findings' and policy recommendations to be acted upon. Again, the JRF is offered as an exception (Morris, 1993; Ward, 1997). It has a demonstrated commitment both to funding projects which have a definite policy relevance for disabled people, such as its programme around independent living and direct payments, and to disseminating results to those involved in policy-making and implementation. This offers a rare counterpoint to the general reception of emancipatory disability research on the part of government policy-makers.

For the most part, the 'committed' standpoint adopted by disability researchers has attracted a lot of criticism from policy-makers and professionals. It also runs counter to traditional claims to value freedom and objectivity espoused by social scientists and researchers working in a university setting. Exchanges between mainstream researchers and those engaged in disability research have found little common ground (Barnes, 1996a; Bury, 1996a; Shakespeare, 1996c). In their review of the differing demands of the academic community and the disabled people's movement, Emma Stone and Mark Priestley conclude that

> if disablement studies, as well as disability politics, are to be taken seriously then there is a need to satisfy the rigorous demands of academe (the research establishment) at the same time as furthering

the political campaign for emancipation and equality. That these twin goals have been held as inherently conflictual by many within both the research establishment and the disabled people's movement is perhaps not surprising given the current political and research context. This should not dissuade the researcher from seeking to achieve both. (Stone and Priestley, 1996: 715)

The evidence to date demonstrates both the difficulties and pitfalls, as well as the potential, of such an emancipatory approach (Woodill, 1992; Rioux and Bach, 1994; Barnes and Mercer, 1997; Moore et al., 1998). Much more disability research needs to be completed in order to sustain a considered evaluation – both from the standpoint of researchers and the disabled subjects/collaborators. Moreover, it is important to reflect on conclusions drawn by mainstream and feminist researchers about the potential divergence between the 'theory' and 'practice' to social research (Bell and Newby, 1977; Roberts, 1981). Disability research which takes an emancipatory standpoint should be similarly self-critical.

Life chances

Social justice is at the heart of disability theory and research. Although the struggles for civil, political and social rights are sometimes represented as largely resolved, they have remained contentious, certainly for a group such as disabled people, throughout the twentieth century (Giddens, 1982b). Citizenship rights have existed side by side with the continuing exclusion of others (see chapter 7).

Most significantly, for disabled people, and for research into their social oppression, disability has retained a marginalized status. The rhetoric of social justice in the individual model of disability eschewed all talk of 'rights', and emphasized disabled people's deficiencies and dependence. Despite recent policy initiatives, the notion of a disabled citizen is still regarded by large sections of the population as a contradiction in terms (Meekosha and Dowse, 1997a). Irrespective of any changes in the post-1945 years from 'state-guaranteed' citizenship, to a more market-led approach, the social oppression of disabled people – in respect of their material circumstances and quality of life – endures to fuel campaigns for equality and social justice.

Most recently, a conference of disabled Europeans recommended that the list of basic human rights compiled by Disabled People's International (DPI, 1982) should be extended to include the 'right to life' and the 'right to parenthood' (CSCE, 1992). Why have these become such pressing issues for disabled people?

Abortion, euthanasia and the new genetics

In many Western societies assumptions about perceived impairment, and by implication biological and social inferiority, are used to legitimate selective abortion, the withholding of life-saving medical treatments and 'mercy killing'. The eugenic 'solution' is as powerful today as it was in the ancient world of Greece and Rome. Indeed, it has been given a significant impetus by current developments in genetic medicine. Changing morality has intertwined with changing medical knowledge and technology to throw up new variants on old ethical dilemmas: genetic engineering, pre-natal screening, selective abortion, definition of 'death', quality of life/death, and rationing of medical resources (Morris, 1991). Yet the 'disability' dimension to these issues has only really become explicit since the 1980s.

It has been disabled people who have taken the lead in challenging 'taken-for-granted' assumptions that an impairment greatly reduces a person's quality of life and devalues them as a human being:

> What is the point of keeping a road accident victim on a life-support system for years on end? What is the value of providing for the care of a paralysed person who will always require care and attention simply to stay alive in the technical sense? Why should we go to the expense of adapting our local library so that one or two people in wheelchairs can have access? Surely it is better to kill (sorry, allow to die) infants with congenital malformations since we can predict that the 'quality of life' for such children will be impoverished? (Thomas, 1982: 17)

The most conspicuous threat posed in recent times has been Nazi policies to eliminate many people with physical and 'mental' impairments, as part of their racist programme to 'purify' the German 'race' (Burleigh, 1995). Yet liberal democratic regimes in Europe and North America have also embraced eugenic ambitions to force women with 'mental' impairments to be sterilized. At the present time, such policies lack support, but disabled people's fear is that they will resurface, albeit in other guises.

Since the 1960s, there has been a general trend in Western societies towards the legalization of abortion on broad social grounds. It has been stimulated by a shift in moral views which has coincided with a period of social and sexual liberation and change. If abortion is accepted, is it the woman's right to decide? Are there other extenuating or special circumstances to consider? The solution arrived at in the 1967 Abortion Act in Britain was that: 'A pregnancy may be lawfully terminated if continuance would culminate in harm to the pregnant woman, or if there is substantial risk that if the child were born it would suffer from such physical or mental abnormalities as to be seriously handicapped.' Moreover, the extraordinary pace of technological innovation has greatly increased medicine's ability to identify impairments in the foetus. Diagnostic procedures such as amniocentesis and ultrasound scanning have all gained widespread usage. Their impact is evidenced by the decline in births of those with spina bifida by up to three-quarters in the last twenty years in Britain. As Davis (1989) argues: 'Once handicap has been detected, abortion is not only seen as acceptable, but is often positively encouraged' (p. 83).

While it is not legitimate to abort a foetus because of its sex or 'race', termination because of anticipated impairment is permissible. Indeed, women come under considerable professional and family pressure to have an abortion where an impairment is identified (C. Thomas, 1997). The justification offered is that a disabled child places an excessive burden on the woman/family/society – both in terms of additional time needed to support the child as well as the financial and emotional resources that must be devoted to its well-being – with a consequent deterioration in the quality of family life and relationships. Yet to many disabled people this confirms a general public hostility towards those with impairments. The person with spina bifida or with cerebral palsy is made to feel devalued or threatened by societal readiness to allow abortion on these grounds. It is hard to justify equal rights to those alive while denying such rights to the new generation of disabled people: 'For if it is decided that it is both right and proper to kill someone because they have a particular condition, why should others with that same condition be accorded rights simply because they are older?' (Davis, 1989: 83).

The birth of a child with an impairment is widely regarded as a tragic and negative event which changes significantly the lives of other family members. There is a widespread lay concern that the baby should be 'all right'. Parents of a child (likely to be) born with an impairment experience a mixture of emotions, including shock, guilt, shame, and helplessness (Oliver, 1983). Micheline Mason, a disabled woman, remembers professional intervention in the following way:

> My father and mother, like so many other people, had very little experience of disability or of disabled people. They believed most of what they were told, at first anyway. They were told that I would always be severely 'handicapped'. That I would become increasingly deformed as a result of numerous fractures. That I would always be dependent on them, and that I would be wanted only by them. (Mason, 1992: 113)

The legalization of euthanasia, unlike abortion, has been much more contentious. The British Medical Association remains hostile to any suggestion that doctors should actively hasten death. In practice, individual doctors may collude with patients, or their families, so that there is an understanding that nothing more is done to prolong life (where the prognosis suggests that the quality of life is likely to be intolerable). Again, the moral dilemma for doctors and society generally has been heightened because technological and clinical advances have greatly extended the capacity of medicine to keep people alive.

What particularly concerns disabled people is the way in which calculations are made about the quality of people's lives. As an illustration, health economists have explored the production of a QALY (quality-adjusted life years) measure whose intention is to allow comparison of treatments/services for different conditions (Culyer et al., 1972). Four aspects of life quality have been stressed: physical mobility; capacity for self-care; freedom from pain and distress; and social adjustment. While it is emphasized that these are social judgements, it encourages calculation of a person's quality of life and social contribution to provide a league table of those able to benefit most from medical interventions, or who are more 'costly' to keep alive. With public understanding of impairment so negative, disabled people understandably feel threatened.

Disabled people's fears are magnified with the promise of the new genetics to identify the likelihood of transmitting impairment and disease. This 'reinforces a biological determinist explanation of disablement; threatens eugenic elimination of impairment; undermines the authenticity of disabled lives; and reinforces the hegemony of biomedicine over disability' (Shakespeare, 1995: 24).

Medical science is now, more than ever, poised to engage in wide-ranging preventive intervention (Hood, 1992). It is not simply the rights of disabled people that are at issue. Genetic medicine may soon be able to decipher the very structures and functions of the genes that form the building-blocks of individual human development – what are called genetic markers. This will, it is argued, facilitate the identification and modification of those genes which make an individual most susceptible to those conditions which result in perceived impairment – whether physical, sensory or intellectual. New techniques such as genetic re-implantation and screening will be able to offer prospective parents the embryo of their choice and, by implication, the opportunity to reject any which might manifest a perceived impairment, irregularity or imperfection. It may also soon be possible for 'corrective' gene therapy to 'normalize' what is regarded as 'abnormal'. Given the recent and intensifying marketization of health and welfare support services, as well as the cultural emphasis on 'healthy minds and healthy bodies', those who choose not to intervene may find themselves denigrated as socially irresponsible. The implications for our understanding of what it means to be human, and what form of 'difference' is socially acceptable, are profound.

Not that innovations in genetic medicine, by themselves, guarantee the means of eradicating disability, since so much impairment is acquired well after birth – through working conditions, accidents, violence, and the ageing process. Soon, one in five of the general population in Western societies will be of retirement age or over. Unprecedented environmental changes, with significant air and water pollution, signal new health hazards which will increase the prevalence of impairment. The sharp divide which formally exists between 'disabled' and 'non-disabled' people does not tally with the actual distribution of impairment:

> The idea that physicality involves impairment and increasing impairment, and ultimately death may not seem positive, but a view of life which embraced that fact would be healthier, would probably lessen prejudice against disabled people and older people, and would certainly warrant doctors radically altering their view of their role, and of what it is to be human. (Shakespeare, 1995: 28)

Just as new medical knowledge and treatments may seriously impact on the lives of those with impairments, so too the changing character of capitalism and the welfare state creates uncertainties about the form and extent of disability. Various claims have been made about the arrival of a qualitatively different form of 'post-industrial', 'post-capitalist', and 'postmodern' economy and society (Giddens, 1989). Disability theory and research has paid too little attention to the detail of these changes or their potential impact on disabled people. Whereas in the nineteenth, and most of the twentieth, century an 'able body' was an essential prerequisite for inclusion in the workforce and a non-disabled status, in the twenty-first century an 'able mind' may be far more important. The growth of information technology, and more flexible production systems, may prove enabling to some, but to others may bring worsening social isolation and new or enhanced forms of disablement.

The situation is even more complex, and alarming, when the spotlight is turned on to the problems faced by disabled people in the under-resourced countries of the majority world. Here the issues for disabled people are often more about survival than citizenship rights. With so many poor people already, the presence of a family member with an impairment places an additional economic strain on the entire family:

> These persons frequently live in deplorable conditions, owing to the presence of physical and social barriers which prevent their integration and full participation in the community. As a result, millions of disabled people throughout the world are segregated and deprived of virtually all their social rights, and lead a wretched and marginal life. (Despouy, 1991: 1)

What is also very important to remember is the way in which Western-style 'disability business' – its institutions and ideologies – have been imposed, initially by the colonial powers, and more recently through the increasing globalization of markets. Hence the pressure on poorer countries to develop medical and 'rehabilitation' services. This is evident in the forms of support supplied by Western governments, charities and international organizations and agencies (Coleridge, 1993). Yet just as under-resourced countries have sought ways to develop economically which do not necessarily replicate the Western experience, so too the policies and institutions that support disabled people must emerge from local knowledge and expertise, indigenous resources and cultures. Rather than simply exporting rehabilitation experts, Western governments could contribute far more by stopping the export of products which actually generate impairment – such as arms, 'injurious' and 'inferior' drugs, or industries which harm workers and are an environmental hazard (Doyal, 1979).

Moving forward

As successive chapters in this book have argued, there is a pressing need for a comprehensive sociological theory of disability founded in the collective and individual experiences of disabled people which provides a stimulus for further research and policy formulation. This should also be sustained by a moral and political agenda: to advance the interests of disabled people by confronting disability in all its forms. Hence, the enterprise outlined here insists on a continuing engagement with the concerns of those who experience impairment and disability on a daily basis.

This does not mean that the social model of disability should simply be incorporated into the canons of existing sociology of health and illness approaches. On the contrary, what is needed is a re-evaluation of the insights of medical sociology from the perspective of a social model framework. This offers a more positive way forward for developing a sociological analysis that includes consideration of both disability and impairment, and that addresses an interested lay public as well as academic debates.

As the processes of differentiation become more complex, and traditional social divisions based on geographic location, social class, gender, sexuality, and ethnicity become ever more blurred, the demand for a greater sociological insight into the complex process of disablement, and the moral dilemmas which it creates, will intensify. In the brave new world of the twenty-first century, this is a task, albeit a formidable one, that the sociological imagination must confront.

The search for a new paradigm in disability research highlights one specific instance of this determination to break with 'disabling' academic practice. What distinguishes the 'emancipatory' approach is its commitment to advancing social justice for disabled people. In this ambition, it sits easily with a general socio-political approach to disability. However, the high expectations set for an emancipatory approach, whether in changing the social and material relations of research production, or in enabling disabled people to gain more autonomy in their lives, will be difficult to sustain, unless short- as well as long-term progress is demonstrated. The experience of translating such theory into practice is only now beginning to accumulate.

The targets for disability theory and research are clearly identified as the structures and processes of a disablist society. It is important to disabled people that research should retain its location in the moral outrage against disability. Hence, the emphasis on how exclusion is manifested and how inclusion may be facilitated. While the voice of disabled people and their organizations is being heard more often and more distinctly than before, the struggle for improved socio-economic conditions, for a better quality of life, and for citizenship rights generally goes on. Recent policy debates ranging across welfare benefits and services to abortion and euthanasia have increased the suspicions of disabled people. There is generally a much-changed political rhetoric in responding to disabled people's claims, and in considering research evidence and making policy proposals, but promised improvements all too often fail to materialize.

A sociological approach that is of value to disabled people must expect to make a similar commitment to contesting disability:

> An adequate sociology of disability will entail an exploration of the issues of power, social justice, citizenship and human rights . . . What vision do you have with regard to your society and to what extent is your concern over the question of disability inspired by a human rights approach? (Barton, 1996: 14)

This is the challenge – but it also carries potential benefits to sociology in achieving a richer understanding of social oppression and, more specifically, of the complex process of disablement, and the moral dilemmas which it poses. As we enter the twenty-first century, these are tasks which mainstream sociology should no longer ignore.

Bibliography

Abberley, P. (1987) 'The Concept of Oppression and the Development of a Social Theory of Disability', *Disability, Handicap and Society*, 2 (1), 5–19.

Abberley, P. (1991) 'The Significance of the OPCS Disability Surveys', in M. Oliver, ed., *Social Work: Disabled People and Disabling Environments*, London: Jessica Kingsley.

Abberley, P. (1992) 'Counting Us Out: A Discussion of the OPCS Disability Surveys', *Disability, Handicap and Society*, 7 (2), 139–55.

Abberley, P. (1993) 'Disabled People and Normality', in J. Swain, V. Finkelstein, S. French and M. Oliver, eds., *Disabling Barriers – Enabling Environments*, London: Sage, in association with the Open University.

Abberley, P. (1995) 'Disabling Ideology in Health and Welfare: The Case of Occupational Therapy', *Disability and Society*, 10 (2), 221–32.

Abberley, P. (1996) 'Work, Utopia and Impairment', in L. Barton, ed., *Disability and Society: Emerging Issues and Insights*, London: Longman.

Abbott, P. and Wallace, C., eds. (1990) *The Sociology of the Caring Professions*, Basingstoke: Falmer Press.

Ablon, J. (1981) 'Stigmatized Health Conditions', *Social Science and Medicine*, 15B, 5–9.

Ackers, L. and Abbott, P. (1996) *Social Policy for Nurses and the Caring Professions*, Buckingham: Open University Press.

Albrecht, G. (1976) *The Sociology of Physical Disability and Rehabilitation*, Pittsburgh: The University of Pittsburgh Press.

Albrecht, G. (1992) *The Disability Business: Rehabilitation in America*, London: Sage.

Anderson, E. M., Clarke, L. and Spain, B. (1982) *Disability in Adolescence*, London: Methuen.

Anderson, R. and Bury, M., eds. (1988) *Living With Chronic Illness: The Experience of Patients and their Families*, London: Unwin Hyman.

Andrews, K. and Jacobs, J. (1990) *Punishing the Poor*, London: Macmillan.

Anspach, R. (1979) 'From Stigma to Identity Politics', *Social Science and Medicine*, 13A, 765–73.

Apple, M. (1990) *Ideology and Curriculum*, London: Routledge and Kegan Paul.

Armstrong, D. (1983) *Political Anatomy of the Body: Medical Knowledge in Britain in the Twentieth Century*, Cambridge: Cambridge University Press.

Armstrong, D. (1984) 'The Patient's View', *Social Science and Medicine*, 18 (9), 737–44.

Armstrong, D. (1987) 'Silence and Truth in Death and Dying', *Social Science and Medicine*, 24 (8), 651–7.

Atkin, K. and Rollins, J. (1991) *Informal Care and Black Communities*, York: Social Policy Research Unit, University of York.

Audit Commission (1986) *Making a Reality of Community Care*, London: HMSO.

Audit Commission (1992a) *Getting in on the Act: Provision for Pupils with Special Educational Needs: The National Picture*, London: HMSO.

Audit Commission (1992b) *Getting the Act Together: Provision for Pupils with Special Educational Needs*, London: HMSO.

Baldwin, S. (1985) *The Costs of Caring*, London: Routledge and Kegan Paul.

Baldwin, S. and Glendinning, C. (1981) 'Employment, Women and their Disabled Children', in J. Finch and D. Groves, eds., *A Labour of Love*, London: Routledge and Kegan Paul.

Barnes, C. (1990) *Cabbage Syndrome: The Social Construction of Dependence*, Lewes: Falmer Press.

Barnes, C. (1991) *Disabled People in Britain and Discrimination*, London: Hurst and Co., in association with the British Council of Organisations of Disabled People.

Barnes, C. (1992) *Disabling Imagery and the Media: An Exploration of Media Representations of Disabled People*, Belper: British Council of Organisations of Disabled People.

Barnes, C., ed. (1993) *Making Our Own Choices: Independent Living, Personal Assistance, and Disabled People*, Belper: British Council of Organisations of Disabled People.

Barnes, C. (1995) *From National to Local: An Evaluation of National Disablement Information Provider Services to Local Disablement Information Providers*, Derby: British Council of Organisations of Disabled People.

Barnes, C. (1996a) 'Disability and the Myth of the Independent Researcher', *Disability and Society*, 11 (1), 107–10.

Barnes, C. (1996b) 'The Social Model of Disability: Myths and Misrepresentations', *Coalition*, August, 25–30.

Barnes, C. (1996c) 'What Next? Disability, the 1995 Disability Discrimination Act and the Campaign for Disabled People's Rights', *The Skill Journal*, 55, 7–10.

Barnes, C. and Mercer, G., eds. (1996) *Exploring the Divide: Illness and Disability*, Leeds: The Disability Press.

Barnes, C. and Mercer, G., eds. (1997) *Doing Disability Research*, Leeds: The Disability Press.

Barnes, C. and Oliver, M. (1995) 'Disability Rights: Rhetoric and Reality in the UK', *Disability and Society*, 10 (4), 111–16.

Barnes, M. and Shardlow, P. (1996) 'Identity Crisis: Mental Health User Groups and the "Problem of Identity"', in C. Barnes and G. Mercer, eds., *Exploring the Divide: Illness and Disability*, Leeds: The Disability Press.

Barton, L., ed. (1989a) *Disability and Dependence*, Lewes: Falmer Press.

Barton, L., ed. (1989b) *Integration: Myth or Reality*, Lewes: Falmer Press.

Barton, L. (1993) 'The Struggle for Citizenship: The Case of Disabled People', *Disability and Society*, 8 (3), 236–48.

Barton, L. (1995) 'Segregated Special Education: Some Critical Observations', in G. Zarb, ed., *Removing Disabling Barriers*, London: Policy Studies Institute.

Barton, L. (1996) 'Sociology and Disability: Some Emerging Issues', in L. Barton, ed., *Disability and Society: Emerging Issues and Insights*, London: Longman.

Barton, L. and Oliver, M., eds. (1997) *Disability Studies: Past, Present and Future*, Leeds: The Disability Press.

Barton, R. (1959) *Institutional Neurosis*, Bristol: Wright.

Battye, L. (1966) 'The Chatterley Syndrome', in P. Hunt, *Stigma*, London: Geoffrey Chapman.

Bauman, Z. (1990) *Thinking Sociologically*, Oxford: Blackwell.

Bayley, M. (1973) *Mental Handicap and Community Care*, London: Routledge and Kegan Paul.

BCODP (1986) *Disabled Young People Living Independently*, London: British Council of Organisations of Disabled People.

BCODP (1997) Personal communication, 24 September.

Beardshaw, V. (1988) *Last on the List: Community Services for People with Physical Disabilities*, London: King's Fund Institute.

Beazley, S. and Moore, M. (1995) *Deaf Children, their Families and Professionals*, London: David Fulton Publishers.

Becker, H. (1963) *Outsiders: Studies in the Sociology of Deviance*, New York: Free Press.

Begum, N. (1992a) *Something to be Proud of: The Lives of Asian Disabled People in Waltham Forest*, London: Waltham Forest Race Relations Unit.

Begum, N. (1992b) 'Disabled Women and The Feminist Agenda', *Feminist Review*, 40, 70–84.

Begum, N. (1993) 'Independent Living, Personal Assistance and Black Disabled People', in C. Barnes, ed., *Making Our Own Choices: Independ-*

ent *Living, Personal Assistance and Disabled People,* Belper: British Council of Organisations of Disabled People.

Begum, N. (1996) 'General Practitioners' Role in Shaping Disabled Women's Lives', in C. Barnes and G. Mercer, eds., *Exploring the Divide,* Leeds: The Disability Press.

Begum, N., Hill, M. and Stevens, A., eds. (1994) *Reflections: Voices of Black Disabled People on their Lives and Community Care,* London: Central Council on the Education and Training of Social Workers.

Bell, C. and Newby, H., eds. (1977) *Doing Sociological Research,* London: Routledge and Kegan Paul.

Beresford, P., Gifford, G. and Harrison, C. (1996) 'What Has Disability Got To Do With Psychiatric Survivors?', in J. Read and J. Reynolds, eds., *Speaking Our Minds: An Anthology,* Basingstoke: Macmillan.

Beresford, P. and Wallcraft, J. (1997) 'Psychiatric System Survivors and Emancipatory Research: Issues, Overlaps and Differences', in C. Barnes and G. Mercer, eds., *Doing Disability Research,* Leeds: The Disability Press.

Berger, P. (1963) *Invitation to Sociology: A Humanistic Perspective,* New York: Anchor Books.

Berthoud, R. (1995) 'Social Security, Poverty and Disabled People' in G. Zarb, ed., *Removing Disabling Barriers,* London: Policy Studies Institute.

Berthoud, R., Lakey, J. and McKay, S. (1993) *The Economic Problems of Disabled People,* London: Policy Studies Institute.

Beveridge, W. (1942) *Social Insurance and Allied Services* (The Beveridge Report), London: HMSO, Cmnd 6404.

Bewley, C. and Glendinning, C. (1994) *Involving Disabled People in Community Care Planning,* York: Joseph Rowntree Foundation.

Bickenbach, J. (1993) *Physical Disability and Social Policy,* Toronto: University of Toronto Press.

Biklen, D. and Bogdan, R. (1977) 'Media Portrayals of Disabled People: A Study of Stereotypes', *Interracial Books for Children Bulletin,* 8 (6 and 7), 4–7.

Blaxter, M. (1976) *The Meaning of Disability,* London: Heinemann.

Blaxter, M. (1984) 'Letter in Response to Williams', *Social Science and Medicine,* 17 (15), 104.

Blaxter, M. (1990) *Health and Lifestyles,* London: Routledge.

Bloch, M. (1965) *Feudal Society,* 2 vols., trans. by L. A. Manyon, London: Routledge and Kegan Paul.

Bloor, M. J. (1976) 'Professional Autonomy and Client Exclusion: A Study in ENT Clinics', in M. Wadsworth and D. Robinson, eds., *Studies in Everyday Medical Practice,* London: Martin Robertson.

Bloor, M. J. and Horobin, G. (1975) 'Conflict and Conflict Resolution in Doctor–Patient Interactions', in C. Cox and A. Mead, eds., *A Sociology of Medical Practice,* London: Collier-Macmillan.

Blumler, J. and Katz, E., eds. (1974) *The Uses of Mass Communications,* Beverly Hills, Ca.: Sage.

Bogdan, R. and Taylor, S. (1987) 'Toward a Sociology of Acceptance: The Other Side of the Study of Deviance', *Social Policy*, 34–9.

Bogdan, R. and Taylor, S. (1989) 'Relationships with Severely Disabled People: The Social Construction of Humanness', *Social Problems*, 36 (2), 135–48.

Bone, M. and Meltzer, H. (1989) *OPCS Surveys of Disability in Great Britain: Report 3 – The Prevalence of Disability Among Children*, London: HMSO.

Booth, T. (1985) *Home Truths*, Aldershot: Gower.

Booth, T. and Booth, W. (1994) *Parenting Under Pressure: Mothers and Fathers with Learning Difficulties*, Buckingham: Open University Press.

Borsay, A. (1986) *Disabled People in the Community*, London: Bedford Square Press.

Borsay, A. (1990) 'Disability and Attitudes to Family Care in Britain: Towards a Sociological Perspective', *Disability, Handicap and Society*, 5 (2), 107–22.

Bowe, F. (1978) *Handicapping America*, New York: Harper and Rowe.

Bowles, S. and Gintis, H. (1976) *Schooling in Capitalist America*, London: Routledge and Kegan Paul.

Bracking, S. (1993) 'An Introduction to the Idea of Independent/Integrated Living', in C. Barnes, ed., *Cashing in on Independence*, Derby: British Council of Organisations of Disabled People.

Bradshaw, J. (1991) 'Social Security', in D. Marsh and R. Rhodes, eds., *Implementing Thatcherite Policies: Audit of an Era*, Buckingham: Open University Press.

Brand, K. W. (1990) 'Cyclical Aspects of New Social Movements', in R. J. Dalton and M. Keuchler, eds., *Challenging the Political Order*, Cambridge: Polity Press.

Brechin, A. and Liddiard, P. (1981) *Look at it This Way: New Approaches to Rehabilitation*, London: Hodder and Stoughton.

Brechin, A., Liddiard, P. and Swain, J., eds. (1981) *Handicap in a Social World*, Sevenoaks: Hodder and Stoughton, in association with the Open University.

Brimblecomb, F. S. W. et al. (1985) *The Needs of Handicapped Young Adults*, Exeter: Paediatric Research Unit, Royal Devon and Exeter Hospital.

Brisenden, S. (1986) 'Independent Living and the Medical Model of Disability', *Disability, Handicap and Society*, 1 (2), 173–8.

Brisenden, S. (1989) 'A Charter for Personal Care', in Disablement Income Group, *Progress London*, No. 16.

Brisenden, S. (1990a) 'Independent Living: A Case of Human Rights', in R. Rieser and M. Mason, eds., *Disability Equality in the Classroom: A Human Rights Issue*, London: Inner London Education Authority.

Brisenden, S. (1990b) *Poems for Perfect People*, Hampshire: Hampshire Coalition of Disabled People.

Brittan, A. and Maynard, M. (1984) *Sexism, Racism and Oppression*, Oxford: Blackwell.

Brown, H. and Smith, H., eds. (1992) *Normalisation: A Reader for the Nineties*, London: Tavistock.

BSC (1989/94) *Code of Good Practice* (2nd edn.), London: Broadcasting Standards Council.

Burkitt, B. (1996) 'Believe in Yourself – Get Sexy', *Coalition*, April, 5–9.

Burleigh, M. (1995) *Death and Deliverance: Euthanasia in Germany c.1900–1945*, Cambridge: Cambridge University Press.

Burns, T. (1992) *Erving Goffman*, London: Routledge.

Burrell, E. (1989) 'Fostering Children with Disabilities: The Lessons of the Last Ten Years', *Foster Care*, 59, September, 22–3.

Bury, M. (1982) 'Chronic Illness as Biographical Disruption', *Sociology of Health and Illness*, 4 (2), 167–92.

Bury, M. (1987) 'The International Classification of Impairments, Disabilities and Handicaps: A Review of Research and Prospects', *International Disability Studies*, 9 (3), 118–22.

Bury, M. (1988) 'Meanings at Risk: The Experience of Arthritis', in R. Anderson and M. Bury, eds., *Living with Chronic Illness: The Experience of Patients and their Families*, London: Unwin Hyman.

Bury, M. (1991) 'The Sociology of Chronic Illness: A Review of Research and Prospects', *Sociology of Health and Illness*, 13 (4), 451–68.

Bury, M. (1992) 'Medical Sociology and Chronic Illness: A Comment on the Panel Discussion', *Medical Sociology News*, 18 (1), 29–33.

Bury, M. (1996a) 'Disability and the Myth of the Independent Researcher: A Reply', *Disability and Society*, 11 (1), 111–13.

Bury, M. (1996b) 'Defining and Researching Disability: Challenges and Responses', in C. Barnes and G. Mercer, eds., *Exploring the Divide: Illness and Disability*, Leeds: The Disability Press.

Bury, M. (1997) *Health and Illness in a Changing Society*, London: Routledge.

Bynoe, I., Oliver, M. and Barnes, C. (1991) *Equal Rights for Disabled People: The Case for a New Law*, London: Institute for Public Policy Research.

Calnan, M. (1984) 'Clinical Uncertainty: Is It a Problem in the Doctor–Patient Relationship?', *Sociology of Health and Illness*, 6 (1), 74–85.

Campbell, J. (1990) 'Who's in Control', paper presented at the Cap in Hand conference, February.

Campbell, J. and Oliver, M. (1996) *Disability Politics: Understanding Our Past, Changing Our Future*, London: Routledge.

Campbell, P. (1996) 'The History of the User Movement in the United Kingdom', in T. Heller, J. Reynolds, R. Gomm, R. Muston and S. Pattison, eds., *Mental Health Matters: A Reader*, Basingstoke: Macmillan.

Campion, M. J. (1995) *Who's Fit to be a Parent?*, London: Routledge.

Campling, J. (1979) *Better Lives for Disabled Women*, London: Virago.

Campling, J. (1981) *Images of Ourselves: Women with Disabilities Talking*, London: Routledge and Kegan Paul.

Carby, H. (1982) 'Black Feminism and the Boundaries of Sisterhood', in Centre for Contemporary Cultural Studies, *The Empire Strikes Back: Race and Racism in 70s Britain*, London: Hutchinson.

Carnegie Council (1985) *Arts and Disabled People: The Attenborough Report*, London: Bedford Square Press.

Carnegie Council (1988) *After Attenborough: Arts and Disabled People*, London: Bedford Square Press.

Carter, J. (1981) *Day Centres for Adults: Somewhere to Go*, London: Allen and Unwin.

Cawson, A. (1982) *Corporatism and Welfare: Social Policy and State Intervention in Britain*, London: Heinemann.

Chappell, A. L. (1992) 'Towards a Sociological Critique of the Normalisation Principle', *Disability, Handicap and Society*, 7 (1), 35–53.

Charlton, J., Patrick, D. and Peach, H. (1983) 'Use of Multivariate Measures of Disability in Health Surveys', *Journal of Epidemiology and Health*, 37, 296–304.

Charmaz, K. (1983) 'Loss of Self: A Fundamental Form of Suffering in the Chronically Ill', *Sociology of Health and Illness*, 5, 168–95.

Charmaz, K. (1987) 'Struggling for Self: Identity Levels of the Chronically Ill', in J. A. Roth and P. Conrad, eds., *Research in the Sociology of Health Care*, vi: *The Experience and Management of Chronic Illness*, Greenwich, Conn.: JAI Press.

Clarke, J. and Critcher, C. (1985) *The Devil Makes Work: Leisure in Capitalist Britain*, Basingstoke: Macmillan.

Clarke, J. and Newman, J. (1997) *The Managerialist State*, London: Sage.

Clogson, J. (1990) *Disability Coverage in Sixteen Newspapers*, Louisville, Ky.: Avocado Press.

Coleridge, P. (1993) *Disability, Liberation and Development*, Oxford: Oxfam.

Confederation of Indian Organisations (1987) *Double Bind: To Be Disabled and Asian*, London: Confederation of Indian Organisations.

Conrad, F. and Schneider, J. (1980) *Deviance and Medicalisation: From Deviance to Badness*, St Louis, Mo.: C. V. Mosby.

CORAD (1982) *Report of the Committee on Restrictions Against Disabled People*, London: HMSO.

Corbett, J. and Ralph, S. (1994) 'Empowering Adults: The Changing Imagery of Charity Advertising', *Australian Disability Review*, 1, 5–14.

Corbin, J. and Strauss, A. (1985) 'Managing Chronic Illness at Home: Three Lines of Work', *Qualitative Sociology*, 8 (3), 224–47.

Corbin, J. and Strauss, A. (1991) 'Comeback: The Process of Overcoming Disability', in G. L. Albrecht and J. A. Levy, eds., *Advances in Medical Sociology*, vol. ii, Greenwich, Conn.: JAI Press.

Corker, M. (1998) *Deaf and Disabled, or Deafness Disabled?*, Buckingham: Open University Press.

Cousins, C. (1987) *Controlling Social Welfare*, Brighton: Wheatsheaf Books.

Craig, G., ed. (1989) *Your Flexible Friend? Voluntary Organisations and the Social Fund*, London: Social Security Commission.

Crawford, R. (1977) 'You are Dangerous to Your Health: The Ideology and Politics of Victim Blaming', *International Journal of Health Services*, 7, 663–80.

Crewe, N. and Zola, I., eds. (1983) *Independent Living For Physically Disabled People*, London: Jossey Bass.

Cribb, S. (1993) 'Are Disabled Artists Cotton-woolled?', *Disability Arts Magazine*, 3/2 (Summer), 10–11.

Croft, S. and Beresford, P. (1990) *From Paternalism to Participation: Involving People in Social Services*, London: Open Services Project.

Crook, S., Pakluski, J. and Waters, M. (1992) *Postmodernization: Change in Advanced Society*, London: Sage.

Cross, M. (1994) 'Abuse', in L. Keith, ed., *Mustn't Grumble*, London: The Women's Press.

Crouch, G., Forrester, W. and Mayhew-Smith, P. (1989) *Access in London*, London: Nicholson.

Crow, L. (1992) 'Renewing the Social Model of Disability', *Coalition*, July, 5–9.

Crow, L. (1996) 'Including All of Our Lives: Renewing the Social Model of Disability', in C. Barnes and G. Mercer, eds., *Exploring the Divide: Illness and Disability*, Leeds: The Disability Press.

CSCE (1992) *The Helsinki Statement on Human Rights and Disabled People*, Helsinki: The Cooperation and Security Conference of Europe.

CSIE (1997) *Inclusive Education: A Framework for Change*, Bristol: Centre for Studies on Inclusive Education.

CSO (1994) *Social Trends 24*, London: Central Statistical Office.

Culyer, A. J., Lavers, R. J. and Williams, A. (1972) 'Health Indicators', in A. Schonfield and S. Shaw, eds., *Social Indicators*, London: Heinemann Educational.

Cumberbatch, G. and Negrine, R. (1992) *Images of Disability on Television*, London: Routledge.

DA (1988) *The Financial Circumstances of Disabled Adults in Private Households: A Disability Alliance Briefing on the Second OPCS Report*, London: Disability Alliance Educational and Research Association.

DA (1998) *Disability Rights Handbook* (23rd edn.), London: Disability Alliance Educational and Research Association.

Dalley, G. (1988) *Ideologies of Caring: Re-thinking Community and Collectivism*, London: Macmillan.

Dalley, G., ed. (1991a) *Disability and Social Policy*, London: Policy Studies Institute.

Dalley, G. (1991b) 'Disability and Social Policy', in G. Dalley, ed., *Disability and Social Policy*, London: Policy Studies Institute.

Daly, M. and Noble, M. (1996) 'The Reach of Disability Benefits: An Examination of the Disability Living Allowance', *Journal of Social Welfare and Family Law*, 18, 37–51.

Darke, P. (1994) '*The Elephant Man* (David Lynch, EMI Films, 1980): An Analysis from a Disabled Perspective', *Disability and Society*, 9 (3), 327–42.

Darke, P. (1998) 'Understanding Cinematic Representations of Disability', in T. Shakespeare, ed., *The Disability Reader*, London: Cassell.

Dartington, T., Miller, E. J. and Gwynne, G. V. (1981) *A Life Together: The Distribution of Attitudes around the Disabled*, London: Tavistock.

Daunt, P. (1991) *Meeting Disability: A European Response*, London: Cassell.

Davis, A. (1989) *From Where I Sit: Living With Disability in an Able-Bodied World*, London: Triangle.

Davis, F. (1961) 'Deviance Disavowal: The Management of Strained Inter-action by the Visibly Handicapped', *Social Problems*, 9, 121–32.

Davis, K. (1981) '28–38 Grove Road: Accommodation and Care in a Community Setting' in A. Brechin, P. Liddiard and J. Swain, eds., *Handicap in a Social World*, Sevenoaks: Hodder and Stoughton, in association with the Open University.

Davis, K. (1990) *Activating the Social Model of Disability: The Emergence of the Seven Needs*, Derby: Derbyshire Coalition of Disabled People.

Davis, K. (1993) 'On the Movement', in J. Swain, V. Finkelstein, S. French and M. Oliver, eds., *Disabling Barriers – Enabling Environments*, London: Sage, in association with the Open University.

Davis, K. and Mullender, A. (1993) *Ten Turbulent Years: A Review of the Work of the Derbyshire Coalition of Disabled People*, Nottingham: University of Nottingham Centre for Social Action.

Davis, L. J. (1996) *Enforcing Normalcy: Disability, Deafness, and the Body*, London and New York: Verso.

Davis, L. J., ed. (1997) *The Disability Studies Reader*, London: Routledge.

DBC (1990) *Pre-recorded Teletext Subtitles on Television*, Coventry: Deaf Broadcasting Council.

Deegan, M. J. and Brooks, N. A., eds. (1985) *Women and Disability: The Double Handicap*, New Brunswick, NJ: Transaction Books.

DeJong, G. (1981) 'The Movement for Independent Living: Origins, Ideology and Implications for Disability Research', in A. Brechin, P. Liddiard and J. Swain, eds., *Handicap in a Social World*, Sevenoaks: Hodder and Stoughton, in association with the Open University.

DeJong, G. (1983) 'Defining and Implementing the Independent Living Concept', in N. Crewe and I. Zola, eds., *Independent Living for Physically Disabled People*, London: Jossey Bass.

DeJong, G. (1984) 'Independent Living: From Social Movement to Analytic Paradigm', in R. P. Marinelli and A. E. Dell Orto, eds., *The Psychological and Social Impact of Physical Disability*, New York: Springer.

Dench, S., Meager, N. and Morris, S. (1996) *The Recruitment and Retention of People with Disabilities*, Brighton: The Institute for Employment Studies.

Despouy, L. (1991) *Human Rights and Disability*, New York: United Nations Economic and Social Council.

De Swann, A. (1990) *The Management of Normality*, London: Routledge.

DfEE (1998) *Excellence for All Children. Meeting Special Educational Needs*, Cm. 3785, London: HMSO.

DHSS (1971) *Better Services for the Mentally Handicapped*, Cmnd. 4683, London: HMSO.

DHSS (1974) *Social Security Provision for Chronically Sick and Disabled People*, HC276, London: HMSO.

DHSS (1975) *Better Services for the Mentally Ill*, Cmnd. 6233, London: HMSO.

DHSS (1976) *Priorities for Health and Personal Social Services in England*, London: HMSO.

DHSS (1981a) *Care in Action*, London: HMSO.

DHSS (1981b) *Growing Older*, London: HMSO.

DIG (1987) *DIG's National Disability Income*, London: Disablement Income Group.

DIG (1988) *Not the OPCS Survey: Being Disabled Costs More than They Said*, London: Disablement Income Group.

Disability and Society (1996) 'Announcement: Disability Research on E-Mail', *Disability and Society*, 10 (1), 136.

DoH (1989) *Caring for People*, London: HMSO.

DoH (1990) *Community Care in the Next Decade and Beyond: Policy Guidance*, London: HMSO.

Dorner, S. (1976) 'Adolescents with Spina Bifida: How They See their Situation', *Archives of Diseases in Childhood*, 51, 439–44.

DoT (1992) *Co-ordinated Planning of Accessible Public Transport*, London: Department of Transport.

Douglas, M. (1966) *Purity and Danger*, London: Routledge and Kegan Paul.

Douglas, M. (1970) *Natural Symbols: Explorations in Cosmology*, London: Cresset Press.

Doyal, L. with Pennell, I. (1979) *The Political Economy of Health*, London: Pluto Press.

Doyle, B. (1995) *Disability, Discrimination and Equal Opportunities: A Comparative Study of the Employment Rights of Disabled Persons*, London: Mansell.

Doyle, B. (1996) *Disability Discrimination: The New Law*, London: Jordan.

DPI (1982) *Disabled People's International: Proceedings of the First World Congress Singapore*, Singapore: Disabled People's International.

DPI (1992) *Disabled People's International: Proceedings of the Third World Congress of the Disabled People's International*, Winnipeg: Disabled People's International.

DPI (1994) 'Agreed Statement', at Human Rights Plenary Meeting in Support of European Day of Disabled Persons, London: Disabled People's International.

DPTAC (1989) *Public Transport and the Missing Six Millions: What Can be Learned?*, London: Disabled Persons' Transport Advisory Committee.

Drake, R. (1994) 'The Exclusion of Disabled People from Positions of Power in British Voluntary Organisations', *Disability and Society*, 9 (4), 461–80.

Drake, R. F. (1996) 'A Critique of the Role of the Traditional Charities', in L. Barton, ed., *Disability and Society: Emerging Issues and Insights*, London: Longman.

Driedger, D. (1989) *The Last Civil Rights Movement: Disabled People's International*, London: Hurst and Co.

DSS (1990) *The Way Ahead: Benefits for Disabled People*, Cm. 917, London: HMSO.

DSS (1994) *A Consultation on Government Measures to Tackle Discrimination Against Disabled People*, Bristol: Enable/HMSO.

Dwoskin, S. (1992) 'DAM Film: Tragedy Chaired', *Disability Arts Magazine*, 2/4 (Winter), 14–17.

Edwards, J. (1995) 'Theorising Leisure and Disability', *Australian Disability Review*, 1, 17–30.

Eldridge, J., Kitzinger, J. and Williams, K. (1997) *The Mass Media and Power*, Oxford: Oxford University Press.

Elias, N. (1978) *The Civilising Process*, vol. i, Oxford: Blackwell.

Emerson, E. (1992) 'What is Normalisation?', in H. Brown and H. Smith, eds., *Normalisation: A Reader for the Nineties*, London: Tavistock.

Enticott, J., Graham, P. and Lamb, B. (1992) *Polls Apart: Disabled People and the 1992 General Election*, London: The Spastics Society.

EOC (1991) *Women and Men in Britain: A Statistical Profile*, London: Equal Opportunities Commission.

EOR (1995) 'The Disability Discrimination Bill', *Equal Opportunities Review*, 60 (March/April), 25–35.

Evans, C. (1995) 'Disability, Discrimination and Local Authority Social Services 2: Users' Perspectives', in G. Zarb, ed., *Removing Disabling Barriers*, London: Policy Studies Institute.

Evans, C. and Hughes, M. (1993) *Tall Oaks from Little Acorns: The Wiltshire Experience of Involving Users in the Training of Professionals*, Wiltshire: Wiltshire Community Care Involvement Network.

Evans, J. (1993) 'The Role of Centres of Independent/Integrated Living and Networks of Disabled People', in C. Barnes, ed., *Making Our Own Choices*, Belper: British Council of Organisations of Disabled People.

Evans-Pritchard, E. E. (1937) *Witchcraft, Oracles and Magic among the Azande*, Oxford: Clarendon Press.

Fagan, T. and Lee, P. (1997) 'New Social Movements and Social Policy: A Case Study of the Disability Movement', in M. Lavalette and A. Pratt, eds., *Social Policy: A Conceptual and Theoretical Introduction*, London: Sage.

Fagerhaugh, S. Y. and Strauss, A. (1977) *Politics of Pain Management: Staff–Patient Interaction*, Menlo Park: Addison Wesley.

Fagin, L. and Little, M. (1984) *The Forsaken Families: The Effects of Unemployment on Family Life*, Harmondsworth: Penguin.

Fielder, B. (1988) *Living Options Lottery: Housing and Support Services for People with Severe Physical Disabilities*, London: Prince of Wales Advisory Group on Disability.

Fielder, B. (1991) 'Housing and Independence', in M. Oliver, ed., *Social Work: Disabled People and Disabling Environments*, London: Jessica Kingsley.

Fine, M. and Asch, A. (1985) 'Disabled Women: Sexism Without the Pedestal?', in M. J. Deegan and N. A. Brooks, eds., *Women and Disability: The Double Handicap*, New Brunswick, NJ: Transaction Books.

Fine, M. and Asch, A. (1988) *Women with Disabilities: Essays in Psychology, Culture, and Politics*, Philadelphia: Temple University Press.

Finger, A. (1991) *Past Due: A Story of Disability, Pregnancy and Birth*, London: The Women's Press.

Finkelstein, V. (1980) *Attitudes and Disabled People*, New York: World Rehabilitation Fund.

Finkelstein, V. (1981) 'Disability and the Helper/Helped Relationship: An Historical View', in A. Brechin, P. Liddiard and J. Swain, eds., *Handicap in a Social World*, Sevenoaks: Hodder and Stoughton, in association with the Open University.

Finkelstein, V. (1991) 'Disability: An Administrative Challenge (The Health and Welfare Heritage)', in M. Oliver, ed., *Social Work: Disabled People and Disabling Environments*, London: Jessica Kingsley.

Finkelstein, V. (1993a) 'The Commonality of Disability', in J. Swain, V. Finkelstein, S. French and M. Oliver, eds., *Disabling Barriers – Enabling Environments*, London: Sage, in association with the Open University.

Finkelstein, V. (1993b) 'Disability: A Social Challenge or an Administrative Responsibility?', in J. Swain, V. Finkelstein, S. French and M. Oliver, eds., *Disabling Barriers – Enabling Environments*, London: Sage, in association with the Open University.

Finkelstein, V. (1996) 'Outside: "Inside Out"', in *Coalition*, April, 31–6.

Finkelstein, V. and Morrison, E. (1992) 'Culture as Struggle: Access to Power', in S. Lees, ed., *Disability Arts in London*, London: Shape Publications.

Finkelstein, V. and Stuart, O. (1996) 'Developing New Services', in G. Hales, ed., *Beyond Disability: Towards an Enabling Society*, London: Sage.

Ford, J., Mongon, D. and Whelan, E. (1982) *Special Education and Social Control*, London: Routledge and Kegan Paul.

Foster, P. (1989) 'Improving the Doctor/Patient Relationship', *Journal of Social Policy*, 18 (3), 337–61.

Foucault, M. (1965) *Madness and Civilisation: A History of Insanity in the Age of Reason*, London: Tavistock.

Foucault, M. (1976) *The Birth of the Clinic*, London: Tavistock.

Foucault, M. (1979) *Discipline and Punish*, Harmondsworth: Peregrine.

Foucault, M. (1980) 'The Eye of Power', in C. Gordon, ed., *Power/Knowledge: Selected Interviews and Other Writings 1972–1977*, Brighton: Harvester.

Foucault, M. (1981) *History of Sexuality*, vol. i, Harmondsworth: Penguin.

Fowkes, A., Oxley, P. and Heiser, E. (1993) *Cross-Sector Benefits of Accessible Public Transport*, Cranfield: Cranfield University School of Management.

Frank, A. W. (1990) 'Bringing Bodies Back In: A Decade Review', *Theory, Culture and Society*, 7, 131–62.

Frank, A. W. (1991) *At the Will of the Body: Reflections on Illness*, Boston, Mass.: Houghton Mifflin.

Freeman, A. and Gray, H. (1989) *Organising Special Educational Needs: A Critical Approach*, London: Paul Chapman.

Freidson, E. (1965) 'Disability as Deviance', in M. Sussman, ed., *Sociology and Rehabilitation*, Washington, DC: American Sociological Association.

Freidson, E. (1970a) *Profession of Medicine: A Study of the Sociology of Applied Knowledge*, New York: Harper and Row.

Freidson, E. (1970b) *Professional Dominance*, New York: Atherton.

French, S. (1993) 'Disability, Impairment or Something In-between', in J. Swain, V. Finkelstein, S. French and M. Oliver, eds., *Disabling Barriers – Enabling Environments*, London: Sage, in association with the Open University.

French, S., ed. (1994) *On Equal Terms: Working with Disabled People*, Oxford: Butterworth-Heinemann.

Fry, E. (1987) *Disabled People and the 1987 General Election*, London: Spastics Society.

Gabe, J. and Calnan, M. (1989) 'The Limits of Medicine: Women's Perception of Medical Technology', *Social Science and Medicine*, 28 (3), 223–31.

Garland, R. R. J. (1995) *The Eye of the Beholder: Deformity and Disability in the Graeco-Roman World*, London: Duckworth.

Gartner, A. and Joe, T., eds. (1987) *Images of the Disabled, Disabling Images*, New York: Praeger.

Gerhardt, U. (1989) *Ideas About Illness: An Intellectual and Political History of Medical Sociology*, London: Macmillan.

Giddens, A. (1982a) *Sociology: A Brief but Critical Introduction*, London: Macmillan.

Giddens, A. (1982b) *Profiles and Critiques in Social Theory*, London: Macmillan.

Giddens, A. (1989) *Sociology*, Cambridge: Polity.

Giddens, A. (1991) *Modernity and Self-Identity: Self and Society in the Late Modern Age*, Cambridge: Polity.

Giddens, A. (1993) *Sociology* (2nd edn.), Cambridge: Polity.

Gillespie-Sells, K. (1993) 'Sing if You're Happy That Way', *Rights Not Charity*, 1 (2), 23–4.

Gilman, S. L. (1995) *Picturing Health and Illness: Images of Identity and Difference*, Lincoln: University of Nebraska.

Gilson, S. F., Tusler, A. and Gill, C. (1997) 'Ethnographic Research in Disability Identity: Self-determination and Community', *Journal of Vocational Rehabilitation*, 9, 7–17.

Ginsburg, N. (1992) *Divisions in Welfare: A Critical Introduction to Comparative Social Policy*, London: Sage.

Girlin, T. (1994) 'From Universality to Difference', in C. Calhoun, ed., *Social Theory and the Politics of Identity*, Cambridge, Mass.: Blackwell.

GLAD (1988) *The Impact of Transport on the Quality of Life and Lifestyle of*

Young People with Disabilities, London: Greater London Association of Disabled People.

Gleeson, B. J. (1997) 'Disability Studies: A Historical Materialist View', *Disability and Society*, 12 (2), 179–204.

Glendinning, C. (1983) *Unshared Care: Parents and their Disabled Children*, London: Routledge and Kegan Paul.

Glendinning, C. (1986) *A Single Door: Social Work with the Families of Disabled Children*, London: Allen and Unwin.

Glendinning, C. (1991) 'Losing Ground: Social Policy and Disabled People in Great Britain 1980–90', *Disability, Handicap and Society*, 6 (1), 3–20.

Glendinning, C. (1992) 'Residualism vs. Rights: Social Policy and Disabled People', in N. Manning and R. Page, eds., *Social Policy Review 4*, Canterbury: Social Policy Association.

GMCDP (1995) *Information Bulletin Manchester*, Manchester: Greater Manchester Coalition of Disabled People, August.

GMCDP (1996) *Coalition: Relationships in Focus*, Manchester: Greater Manchester Coalition of Disabled People, April.

Goffman, E. (1961) *Asylums*, Harmondsworth: Penguin.

Goffman, E. (1968) *Stigma: Notes on the Management of Spoiled Identity*, Harmondsworth: Penguin.

Goldsmith, S. (1976) *Designing for the Disabled* (3rd edn.), London: Riba Publications.

Gooding, C. (1994) *Disabling Laws: Enabling Acts*, London: Pluto.

Gooding, C (1995) 'Employment and Disabled People: Equal Rights or Positive Action', in G. Zarb, ed., *Removing Disabling Barriers*, London: Policy Studies Institute.

Gooding, C. (1996) *Disability Discrimination Act 1995*, London: Blackstone Press.

Gordon, C. (1966) *Role Theory and Illness: A Sociological Perspective*, New Haven: Connecticut College and University Press.

Graham, P., Jordan, A. and Lamb, B. (1990) *An Equal Chance or No Chance*, London: Spastics Society.

Gramsci, A. (1971) *Selections from the Prison Notebooks of Antonio Gramsci*, ed. and trans. Q. Hoare and G. Nowell-Smith, London: Lawrence and Wishart.

Gramsci, A. (1985) *Selections from the Cultural Writings*, ed. and trans. D. Forgacs and G. Nowell-Smith, London: Lawrence and Wishart.

Gregory, S. and Hartley, G., eds. (1991) *Constructing Deafness*, London: Pinter/The Open University.

Griffiths, R. (1988) *Community Care: Agenda for Action*, London: HMSO.

Groce, N. (1985) *Everyone Here Spoke Sign Language: Hereditary Deafness on Martha's Vineyard*, Cambridge, Mass.: Harvard University Press.

Gussow, Z. and Tracey, G. (1968) 'Status, Ideology and Adaptation to Stigmatised Illness', *Human Organisation*, 27, 873–84.

Gwaltney, J. (1970) *The Thrice Shy: Cultural Accommodation to Blindness and*

Other Disabilities in a Mexican Community, New York: Columbia University Press.

Haber, L. and Smith, R. (1971) 'Human Deviance: Normative Adaptation and Role Behaviour', *American Sociological Review*, 36 (1), 87–97.

Haffter, C. (1968) 'The Changeling: History and Psychodynamics of Attitudes to Handicapped Children in European Folklore', *Journal of the History of Behavioural Studies*, 4, 55–61.

Hahn, H. (1985) 'Towards a Politics of Disability: Definitions, Disciplines and Policies', *Social Science Journal*, 22 (4), 87–105.

Hahn, H. (1986) 'Public Support for Rehabilitation Programs: The Analysis of US Disability Policy', *Disability, Handicap and Society* 1 (2), 121–38.

Hahn, H. (1988) 'The Politics of Physical Differences: Disability and Discrimination', *Journal of Social Issues*, 44 (1), 39–47.

Hahn, H. (1989) 'Disability and the Reproduction of Bodily Images: The Dynamics of Human Appearances', in J. Wolch and M. Dear, eds., *The Power of Geography*, Boston: Unwin Hyman.

Hales, G., ed. (1996) *Beyond Disability: Towards an Enabling Society*, London: Sage.

Hall, S. et al., eds. (1980) *Culture, Media, Language: Working Papers in Cultural Studies 1972–79*, London: Hutchinson, in association with the Centre for Contemporary Cultural Studies, University of Birmingham.

Hall, S., Critcher, C., Jefferson, T., Clarke, J. and Roberts, B. (1978) *Policing the Crisis*, London: Macmillan.

Hall, S. and Jefferson, T., eds. (1976) *Resistance through Rituals*, London: Hutchinson.

Haller, B. (1995) 'Rethinking Models of Media Representations of Disability', *Disability Studies Quarterly*, 15 (2), 26–30.

Hanks, J. and Hanks, L. (1948) 'The Physically Handicapped in Certain Non-Occidental Societies', *Journal of Social Issues*, 4 (4), 11–20; reprinted (1980) in W. Phillips and J. Rotenberg, eds., *Social Scientists and the Physically Handicapped*, London: Arno Press.

Hanna, W. J. and Rogovsky, B. (1991) 'Women with Disabilities: Two Handicaps Plus', *Disability, Handicap and Society*, 6 (1), 49–63.

Hansard (1992) Parliamentary Debates, 31 January, 1251.

Harris, A., Cox, E. and Smith, C. (1971) *Handicapped and Impaired in Great Britain*, vol. i, London: HMSO.

Harris, J., Sapey, B. and Stewart, J. (1997) *Wheelchair Housing and the Estimation of Need*, Preston: University of Central Lancashire.

HCIL (1986) *Project 81: One Step On*, Hampshire: The Hampshire Centre for Independent Living.

HCIL (1990) *Working Papers*, Hampshire: The Hampshire Centre for Independent Living.

HCIL (1991) *Source Book. Towards Independent Living: Care Support Ideas*, Hampshire: The Hampshire Centre for Independent Living.

Hearn, K. (1991) 'Disabled Lesbians and Gays are Here to Stay', in T. Kaufman and P. Lincoln, eds., *High Risk Lives: Lesbian and Gay Politics after the Clause*, Bridport: Prism Press.

Heiser, B. (1995) 'The Nature and Causes of Transport Disability in Britain and How to Remove It', in G. Zarb, ed., *Removing Disabling Barriers*, London: Policy Studies Institute.

Helander, E. (1993) *Prejudice and Dignity: An Introduction to Community-Based Rehabilitation*, Geneva: World Health Organization.

Hertz, M., Endicott, J. and Spitzer, R. (1977) 'Brief Hospitalisation: A Two-year Follow-up', *American Journal of Psychiatry*, 134, 502–7.

Herzlich, C. and Pierret, J. (1987) *Illness and Self in Society*, Baltimore: Johns Hopkins University Press.

Hevey, D. (1992) *The Creatures that Time Forgot: Photography and Disability Imagery*, London: Routledge.

Hewitt, M. (1993) 'Social Movements and Social Need: Problems with Postmodern Political Theory', *Critical Social Policy*, 37, 52–74.

Higgins, P. (1981) *Outsiders in a Hearing World*, London: Sage.

Hill, M. (1994) 'They are not our Brothers; The Disability Movement and the Black Disability Movement', in N. Begum, M. Hill and A. Stevens, eds., *Reflections*, London: Central Council for the Education and Training of Social Workers.

Hills, J. (1993) *The Future of Welfare: A Guide to the Debate*, York: Joseph Rowntree Foundation.

Hirst, M. and Baldwin, S. (1994) *Unequal Opportunities: Growing up Disabled*, York: Social Policy Research Unit, University of York.

Holdsworth, A. (1992) 'Hot Legs . . . and Coming Out', *Coalition*, July, 13–15.

Holdsworth, A. (1998) personal communication, 16 March.

Honey, S., Meagar, N. and Williams, M. (1993) *Employers' Attitudes Towards People with Disabilities*, Sussex: University of Sussex, Manpower Studies Institute.

Hood, L. (1992) 'Biology and Medicine in the 21st Century', in D. J. Kevles and L. Hood, eds., *The Code of Codes: Scientific and Social Issues in the Human Genome Project*, London: Routledge.

House of Commons Commission on Citizenship (1990) *Encouraging Citizenship: Report of the House of Commons Commission on Citizenship*, London: HMSO.

Hudson, B. (1989) 'Michael Lipsky and Street-Level Bureaucracy: A Neglected Perspective', in L. Barton, ed., *Disability and Dependence*, Lewes: Falmer Press.

Hughes, B. and Paterson, K. (1997) 'The Social Model of Disability and the Disappearing Body: Towards a Sociology of Impairment', *Disability and Society*, 12 (3), 325–40.

Hugman, R. (1991) *Power and the Caring Professions*, Basingstoke: Macmillan.

Humphries, S. and Gordon, P. (1992) *Out of Sight: The Experience of Disability 1900–1950*, London: Northcote House.

Hunt, P. (1966) *Stigma: The Experience of Disability*, London: Geoffrey Chapman.

Hunt, P., ed. (1981) 'Settling Accounts with the Parasite People: A Critique of "A Life Apart" by E. J. Miller and G. V. Gwynne', *Disability Challenge*, 1, 37–50.

Hurst, A. (1984) 'Adolescence and Physical Disability: An Introduction', in L. Barton and S. Tomlinson, eds., *Special Education and Social Interests*, London: Croom Helm.

Hyde, M. (1996) 'Fifty Years of Failure: Employment Services for Disabled People in the UK', *Work, Employment and Society*, 10 (4), 683–700.

Hyde, M. and Armstrong, E. (1995) 'Underclass or Underdogs: Britain's Poor in the 1990s', *Public Policy Review*, 3 (4), 44–6.

Illich, I. (1975) *Medical Nemesis: The Expropriation of Health*, London: Marion Boyars.

Illich, I. et al. (1977) *Disabling Professions*, London: Marion Boyars.

Imrie, R. (1996) *Disability and the City: International Perspectives*, London: Paul Chapman.

Imrie, R. and Wells, P. (1993) 'Disablism, Planning and the Built Environment', *Environment and Planning C: Government and Policy*, 11, 213–31.

Inglehart, R. (1990) 'Values, Ideology and Cognitive Mobilisations in New Social Movements', in R. J. Dalton and M. Kuechler, eds., *Challenging the Political Order*, Cambridge: Polity Press.

Inglis, F. (1993) *Cultural Studies*, Oxford: Blackwell.

Ingstad, B. and Whyte, S. R., eds. (1995) *Disability and Culture*, Berkeley, Ca.: University of California Press.

Jenkins, R. (1991) 'Disability and Social Stratification', *British Journal of Sociology*, 42 (4), 557–80.

Jewson, N. (1976) 'The Disappearance of the Sick Man from Medical Cosmology 1770–1870', *Sociology*, 10, 225–44.

Johnson, T. (1972) *Professions and Power*, London: Macmillan.

Johnson, W. G., ed. (1997) 'The Americans With Disabilities Act: Social Contract or Special Privilege?', *The Annals*, special issue, 549 (January), 1–220.

Jones, K., Brown, J. and Bradshaw, J. (1978) *Issues in Social Policy*, London: Routledge and Kegan Paul.

Jones, K. and Fowles, A. (1984) *Ideas on Institutions*, London: Routledge and Kegan Paul.

Karpf, A. (1988) *Doctoring the Media*, London: Routledge.

Kassebaum. G. and Baumann, B. (1965) 'Dimensions of the Sick Role in Chronic Illness', *Journal of Health and Social Behaviour*, 6, 16–25.

Keith, L., ed. (1994) *Mustn't Grumble*, London: The Women's Press.

Keith, L. (1996) 'Encounters with Strangers: The Public's Response to Disabled Women and how this Affects our Sense of Self', in J. Morris, ed., *Encounters with Strangers: Feminism and Disability*, London: The Women's Press.

Keith, L. and Morris, J. (1996) 'Easy Targets: A Disability Rights Perspective on the "Children as Carers" Debate', in J. Morris, ed., *Encounters with Strangers: Feminism and Disability*, London: The Women's Press.

Kelleher, D. (1988) *Diabetes*, London: Tavistock.

Kelly, M. P. (1991) 'Coping with an Ileostomy', *Social Science and Medicine*, 33 (2), 115–25.

Kelly, M. P. (1992a) 'Self, Identity and Radical Surgery', *Sociology of Health and Illness*, 14 (3), 390–415.

Kelly, M. P. (1992b) *Colitis*, London: Routledge.

Kelly, M. and May, D. (1982) 'Good and Bad Patients: A Review of the Literature and a Theoretical Critique', *Journal of Advanced Nursing*, 7, 221–9.

Kennedy, M. (1989) 'Child Abuse: Child Sexual Abuse', *Deafness*, 3 (2), 47.

Kennedy, M. (1996) 'Sexual Abuse and Disabled Children', in J. Morris, ed., *Encounters with Strangers: Feminism and Disability*, London: The Women's Press.

Kent, D. (1987) 'Disabled Women: Portraits in Fiction and Drama', in A. Gartner and T. Joe, eds., *Images of the Disabled, Disabling Images*, New York: Praeger.

Kestenbaum, A. (1993a) *Making Community Care a Reality*, Nottingham: Independent Living Fund.

Kestenbaum, A. (1993b) *Taking Care in the Market*, Nottingham: Independent Living Fund.

Kestenbaum, A. (1995) 'Independent Living: A Review of Findings and Experience', draft paper for the Joseph Rowntree Foundation.

Kevles, D. J. (1985) *In the Name of Eugenics*, Berkeley, Ca.: University of California Press.

Killin, D. (1993) 'Independent Living, Personal Assistance, Disabled Lesbians and Disabled Gay Men', in C. Barnes, ed., *Making Our Own Choices*, Belper: British Council of Organisations of Disabled People.

King, R., Raynes, N. and Tizard, J. (1971) *Patterns of Residential Care*, London: Routledge and Kegan Paul.

Kitzinger, J. (1993) 'Media Messages and What People Know about Acquired Immune Deficiency Syndrome', in Glasgow University Media Group, *Getting the Message*, London: Routledge.

Kitzinger, J. (1995) *Child Sexual Abuse and the Media: Summary Report to the Economic and Social Research Council*, Glasgow: Glasgow Media Group.

Klein, E. (1984) *Gender Politics: From Consciousness to Mass Politics*, Cambridge, Mass.: Harvard University Press.

Klobas, L. E. (1988) *Disability Drama in Television and Film*, Jefferson, NC: McFarland.

Kriegel, L. (1987) 'The Cripple in Literature', in A. Gartner and T. Joe, eds., *Images of the Disabled, Disabling Images*, New York: Praeger.

Ladd, P. (1988) 'Hearing Impaired or British Sign Language Users: Social Policies and the Deaf Community', *Disability, Handicap and Society*, 3 (2), 195–200.

Lakey, J. (1994) *Caring about Independence: Disabled People and the Independent Living Fund*, London: Policy Studies Institute.

Lakoff, R. T. (1989) 'Women and Disability', *Feminist Studies*, 15 (2), 365–75.

Lamb, B. and Layzell, S. (1994) *Disabled in Britain: A World Apart*, London: SCOPE.

Lamb, B. and Layzell, S. (1995) *Disabled in Britain: Counting on Community Care*, London: SCOPE.

Lane, H. (1995) 'Constructions of Deafness', *Disability and Society*, 10 (2), 171–89.

Langan, M. and Clarke, J. (1993) 'The British Welfare State: Foundation and Modernisation', in A. Cochrane and J. Clarke, eds., *Comparing Welfare States: Britain in International Context*, London: Sage.

Larson, M. (1977) *The Rise of Professionalism*, Berkeley, Ca.: University of California Press.

Lawler, J. (1991) *Behind the Screens: Nursing, Somology and the Problem of the Body*, London: Churchill Livingstone.

Layder, D. (1997) *Modern Social Theory*, London: UCL Press.

Leach, B. (1989) 'Disabled People and the Implementation of Local Authorities Equal Opportunities Policies', *Public Administration*, 67, 65–77.

Lecouturier, J. and Jacoby, A. (1995) *Study of User Satisfaction with Wheelchair Provision in Newcastle*, Newcastle: Centre for Health Services Research, University of Newcastle.

Lees, S., ed., *Disability Arts and Culture Papers*, London: Shape Publications.

Lemert, E. (1951) *Social Pathology*, New York: McGraw-Hill.

Liggett, H. (1988) 'Stars are not Born: An Interpretive Approach to the Politics of Disability', in *Disability, Handicap and Society*, 3 (3), 263–76.

Lindoe, J. and Morris, J. (1995) *Service User Involvement Synthesis of Findings and Experience in the Field of Community Care*, York: Joseph Rowntree Foundation.

Linton, S. (1998a) 'Disability Studies: Not Disability Studies', *Disability and Society*, 13 (4), 525–41.

Linton, S. (1998b) *Reclaiming Disability: Knowledge and Identity*, New York: New York University Press.

Lloyd, M. (1992) 'Does She Boil Eggs? Towards a Feminist Model of Disability', *Disability Handicap and Society*, 7 (3), 207–21.

Locker, D. (1983) *Disability and Disadvantage*, London: Tavistock.

Longmore, P. (1987) 'Screening Stereotypes: Images of Disabled People in Television and Motion Pictures', in A. Gartner and T. Joe, eds., *Images of the Disabled, Disabling Images*, New York: Praeger.

Lonsdale, S. (1990) *Women and Disability*, London: Macmillan.

Lowe, R. (1993) *The Welfare State in Britain since 1945*, London: Macmillan.

Lunt, N. and Thornton, P. (1993) *Employment Policies for Disabled People: A Review of Legislation and Services in Fifteen Countries*, Sheffield: Department of Employment.

Lupton, D. (1994) *Medicine as Culture*, London: Sage.

McCarthy, A. E. (1984) 'Is Handicapped External to the Person and There-fore "Man Made"?', *British Journal of Mental Subnormality*, 30 (1), 3–7.

McCormack, M. (1992) *Special Children, Special Needs: Families Talk about Living with Mental Handicap*, Wellingborough: Thorson.

McDonald, P. (1991) 'Double Discrimination Must Be Faced Now', *Disability Now*, 8 March, 7–8.

MacDonald, R. (1995) 'Disability and Planning Policy Guidance', paper for the Access Sub-Committee, Oxford City Council, 7 March, Oxford: School of Planning, Oxford Brookes University.

McGinnis, B. (1991) 'Income Maintenance for People with Disabilities', in G. Dalley, ed., *Disability and Social Policy*, London: Policy Studies Institute.

McIntosh, J. (1976) *Communication and Awareness in a Cancer Ward*, London: Croom Helm.

Mack, J. and Lansley, S. (1985) *Poor Britain*, London: Allen and Unwin.

McQuail, D., ed. (1972) *Sociology of Mass Communications: Selected Readings*, Harmondsworth: Penguin.

Markham, N. (1991) 'Parents and Independence', *Coalition*, September, 10–13.

Marshall, T. H. (1950) *Citizenship and Social Class*, Cambridge: Cambridge University Press.

Martin, J., Meltzer, H. and Elliot, D. (1988) *OPCS Surveys of Disability in Great Britain: Report 1 – The Prevalence of Disability Among Adults*, London: HMSO.

Martin, J. and White, A. (1988) *OPCS Surveys of Disability in Great Britain: Report 2 – The Financial Circumstances of Disabled Adults in Private House-holds*, London: HMSO.

Martin, J., White, A. and Meltzer, H. (1989) *OPCS Surveys of Disability in Great Britain: Report 4 – Disabled Adults: Services, Transport and Employ-ment*, London: HMSO.

Mason, M. (1982) 'From the Inside', *In From the Cold*, Summer, 12–13.

Mason, M. (1992) 'A Nineteen-Parent Family', in J. Morris, ed., *Alone Together: Voices of Single Mothers*, London: The Women's Press.

Mason, P. (1992) 'The Representation of Disabled People: A Hampshire Centre for Independent Living Discussion Paper', *Disability, Handicap and Society*, 7 (1), 79–85.

Mathieson, C. M. and Stam, H. J. (1995) 'Renegotiating Identity: Cancer Narratives', *Sociology of Health and Illness*, 17, 283–306.

Meekosha, H. and Dowse, L. (1997a) 'Enabling Citizenship: Gender, Dis-ability and Citizenship in Australia', *Feminist Review*, 57 (Autumn), 45–72.

Meekosha, H. and Dowse, L. (1997b) 'Distorting Images, Invisible Images: Gender, Disability and the Media', *Media International Australia*, 84 (May), 91–101.

Melluci, A. (1980) 'The Symbolic Challenge of Contemporary Move-ments', *Social Research*, 52 (4), 789–816.

Meltzer, H., Smyth, M. and Robus, N. (1989) *OPCS Surveys of Disability in Great Britain: Report 6 – Disabled Children: Services, Transport and Education*, London: HMSO.

Meredith Davies, B. (1982) *The Disabled Child and Adult*, London: Ballière Tindall.

Miller, E. J. and Gwynne, G. V. (1972) *A Life Apart*, London: Tavistock.

MIND (1989) *The Right to Vote*, Preston, MIND (North-West).

Minde, K. S. (1972) 'How They Grow Up; Forty-one Physically Handicapped Children and their Families', *American Journal of Psychiatry*, 126, 1154–60.

Moore, M., Beazley, S. and Maelzer, J. (1998) *Researching Disability Issues*, Buckingham: Open University Press.

Moore, N. (1995) *Access to Information: A Survey of the Provision of Disability Information*, London: Policy Studies Institute.

Morgan, M., Calnan, M. and Manning, N., eds. (1985) *Sociological Approaches to Health and Medicine*, London: Routledge.

Morrell, J. (1990) *The Employment of People with Disabilities: Research into the Policies and Practices of Employers*, Sheffield: Department of Employment, Employment Services.

Morris, J. (1989) *Able Lives: Women's Experience of Paralysis*, London: The Women's Press.

Morris, J. (1990a) 'Progress with Humanity: The Experience of a Disabled Lecturer', in R. Rieser and M. Mason, eds., *Disability Equality in the Classroom: A Human Rights Issue*, London: Inner London Education Authority.

Morris, J. (1990b) *Our Homes Our Rights*, London: Shelter.

Morris, J. (1991) *Pride Against Prejudice*, London: The Women's Press.

Morris, J., ed. (1992a) *Alone Together: Voices of Single Mothers*, London: The Women's Press.

Morris, J. (1992b) 'Personal and Political: A Feminist Perspective in Researching Physical Disability', *Disability, Handicap and Society*, 7 (2), 157–66.

Morris, J. (1993) *Independent Lives: Community Care and Disabled People*, Basingstoke: Macmillan.

Morris, J. (1994) *The Shape of Things to Come? User-Led Services*, London: National Institute for Social Work.

Morris, J., ed. (1996) *Encounters with Strangers: Feminism and Disability*, London: The Women's Press.

Morris, P. (1969) *Put Away*, London: Routledge and Kegan Paul.

Morrison, E. and Finkelstein, V. (1993) 'Broken Arts and Cultural Repair: The Role of Culture in the Empowerment of Disabled People', in J. Swain, V. Finkelstein, S. French and M. Oliver, eds., *Disabling Barriers – Enabling Environments*, London: Sage, in Association with the Open University.

Murphy, R. (1987) *The Body Silent*, London: Phoenix House.

Murphy, R., Scheer, J., Murphy, Y. and Mack, R. (1988) 'Physical Disability and Social Liminality: A Study of the Rituals of Adversity', *Social Science and Medicine*, 26 (2), 235–42.

NACAB (1994) *NACAB Evidence on Discrimination in Employment*, London: National Association of Citizens' Advice Bureaux.

Navarro, V. (1978) *Class Struggle, the State and Medicine*, London: Martin Robertson.

NCHAFC (1994) *Unequal Opportunities: Children with Disabilities and their Families Speak Out*, London: National Children's Home Action For Children.

Nettleton, S. (1995) *The Sociology of Health and Illness*, Cambridge: Polity Press.

Nicolaisen, I. (1995) 'Persons and Nonpersons: Disability and Personhood among the Punan Bah of Central Borneo', in B. Ingstad and S. R. Whyte, eds., *Disability and Culture*, Berkeley, Ca.: University of California Press.

Noble, M., Platt, L., Smith, G. and Daly, M. (1997) 'The Spread of Disability Living Allowance', *Disability and Society*, 12 (5), 741–51.

NOG (1996) *The Disability Discrimination Act: A Policy and Practice Guide for Local Government and Disabled People*, Sheffield: Northern Officers Group.

Norden, M. (1994) *The Cinema of Isolation: A History of Disability in the Movies*, New Brunswick, NJ: Rutgers University Press.

Norwich, B. (1994) *Segregation and Inclusion: English LEA Statistics 1988–92*, Bristol: Centre for Studies on Inclusive Education.

Norwich, B. (1997) *A Trend Towards Inclusion*, Bristol: Centre for Studies on Inclusive Education.

Oakley, A. (1981) 'Interviewing Women: A Contradiction in Terms', in H. Roberts, ed., *Doing Feminist Research*, London: Routledge and Kegan Paul, 30–61.

Offe, C. (1984) *Contradictions of the Welfare State*, London: Hutchinson.

Offe, C. (1985) 'New Social Movements: Challenging the Boundaries of Institutional Politics', *Social Research*, 52 (4), 817–68.

Oliver, J. (1995) 'Counselling Disabled People: A Counsellor's Perspective', *Disability and Society*, 10 (3), 261–79.

Oliver, M. (1983) *Social Work with Disabled People*, Basingstoke: Macmillan.

Oliver, M. (1986) 'Social Policy and Disability: Some Theoretical Issues', *Disability, Handicap and Society*, 1 (1), 5–18.

Oliver, M. (1990) *The Politics of Disablement*, Basingstoke: Macmillan.

Oliver, M. (1992) 'Changing the Social Relations of Research Production?', *Disability, Handicap and Society*, 7 (2), 101–14.

Oliver, M. (1995) 'Disability, Empowerment and the Inclusive Society', in G. Zarb, ed., *Removing Disabling Barriers*, London: Policy Studies Institute.

Oliver, M. (1996a) *Understanding Disability: From Theory to Practice*, London: Macmillan.

Oliver, M. (1996b) 'A Sociology of Disability or a Disablist Sociology?', in L. Barton, ed., *Disability and Society: Emerging Issues and Insights*, London: Longman.

Oliver, M. (1996c) 'Defining Impairment and Disability: Issues at Stake', in C. Barnes and G. Mercer, eds., *Exploring the Divide: Illness and Disability*, Leeds: The Disability Press.

Oliver, M. (1997) 'Emancipatory Research: Realistic Goal or Impossible Dream?', in C. Barnes and G. Mercer, eds., *Doing Disability Research*, Leeds: The Disability Press.

Oliver, M. and Barnes, C. (1991) 'Discrimination, Disability and Welfare: From Needs to Rights', in I. Bynoe, M. Oliver, and C. Barnes, eds., *Equal Rights and Disabled People: The Case for a New Law*, London: Institute for Public Policy Research.

Oliver, M. and Barnes, C. (1998) *Social Policy and Disabled People: From Exclusion to Inclusion*, London: Longman.

Oliver, M. and Hasler, F. (1987) 'Disability and Self-help: A Case Study of the Spinal Injuries Association', *Disability, Handicap and Society*, 2 (2), 113–25.

Oliver, M. and Zarb, G. (1989) 'The Politics of Disability: A New Approach', *Disability, Handicap and Society*, 4 (3), 221–40.

Oliver, M. and Zarb, G. (1992) *Personal Assistance Schemes in Greenwich: An Evaluation*, London: University of Greenwich.

Oliver, M., Zarb, G., Silver, J., Moore, M. and Salisbury, V. (1988) *Walking into Darkness: The Experience of Spinal Cord Injury*, Basingstoke: Macmillan.

Pagel, M. (1988) *On Our Own Behalf: An Introduction to the Self-Organisation of Disabled People*, Manchester: Greater Manchester Coalition of Disabled People Publications.

Palfreyman, T. (1993) *Designing for Accessibility: An Introductory Guide*, London: Centre for Accessible Environments.

Parker, G. (1990) *With Due Care and Attention* (2nd edn.), London: Family Policy Studies Institute.

Parker, G. (1993) *With this Body: Caring and Disability in Marriage*, Buckingham: Open University Press.

Parker, R. A. (1988) 'An Historical Background', in I. Sinclair, ed., *Residential Care: The Research Reviewed*, London: HMSO.

Parker, S. (1975) 'The Sociology of Leisure: Progress and Problems', *British Journal of Sociology*, 26, 91–101.

Parsons, T. (1951) *The Social System*, New York: Free Press.

Parsons, T. (1958) 'Definitions of Health and Illness in the Light of American Values and Social Structure', in E. G. Jaco, ed., *Patients, Physicians, and Illness*, New York: Free Press.

Parsons, T. (1975) 'The Sick Role and the Role of the Physician Reconsidered', *Milbank Memorial Fund Quarterly: Health and Society*, 53 (3), 257–78.

Patrick, D. and Peach, H., eds. (1989) *Disablement in the Community*, Oxford: Oxford Medical Publications.

Patten, C. (1990) 'Big Battalions and Little Platoons', 7th Annual Goodmans Lecture (unpublished), London: Charities Aid Foundation.

Pfeiffer, D. (1994) 'The Americans with Disabilities Act: Costly Mandates or Civil Rights', *Disability and Society*, 9 (4), 533–42.

Pfeiffer, D. and Yoshida, K. (1995) 'Teaching Disability Studies in Canada and the USA', *Disability and Society*, 10 (4), 475–500.

Philips, V. L. (1993) *Caring for Severely Disabled People: Care Providers and their Costs*, Nottingham: Independent Living Fund.

Philo, G. (1990) *Seeing and Believing*, London: Routledge.

Philo, G., ed. (1996) *Media and Mental Distress*, Harlow: Addison Wesley Longman.

Pick, J. (1992) 'Why have there been no Great Disabled Artists?', *Disability Arts Magazine*, 2/4 (Winter), 18–20.

Prescott Clarke, P. (1990) *Employment and Handicap*, London: Social and Community Planning Research.

Quinn, G., McDonagh, M. and Kimber, C. (1993) *Disability Discrimination Laws in the United States, Australia and Canada*, Dublin: Oak Tree Press in association with the National Rehabilitation Board.

RADAR (1993) *Disability and Discrimination in Employment*, London: Royal Association for Disability and Rehabilitation.

Radley, A. (1994) *Making Sense of Illness*, London: Sage.

Rae, A. (1993) 'Independent Living, Personal Assistance and Disabled Women', in C. Barnes, ed., *Making Our Own Choices: Independent Living, Personal Assistance and Disabled People*, Belper: British Council of Organisations of Disabled People.

Rae, A. (1996) 'Social Model Under Attack?', *Coalition*, August, 37–40.

Ratska, A. (1992) 'Independent Living', in *World Congress III: Disabled People's Equalisation of Opportunities*, Vancouver: Disabled People's International.

Read, J. and Reynolds, J., eds. (1996) *Speaking Our Minds: An Anthology of Personal Experiences of Mental Distress and its Consequences*, Basingstoke: Macmillan.

Rieser, R. (1990a) 'Resource Cards 12 A and B: History – Disabled People in Nazi Germany', in R. Rieser and M. Mason, eds., *Disability Equality in the Classroom: A Human Rights Issue*, London: Inner London Education Authority.

Rieser, R. (1990b) 'Internalised Oppression: How it Seems to Me', in R. Rieser and M. Mason, eds., *Disability Equality in the Classroom: A Human Rights Issue*, London: Inner London Education Authority.

Rieser, R. and Mason, M., eds. (1990) *Disability Equality in the Classroom: A Human Rights Issue*, London: Inner London Education Authority.

Rioux, M. H. and Bach, M., eds. (1994) *Disability Is Not Measles*, North York, Ontario: Roeher Institute.

Rioux, M. H., Crawford, C., Ticoll, M. and Bach, M. (1997) 'Uncovering the Shape of Violence: A Research Methodology Rooted in the Experience of People with Disabilities', in C. Barnes and G. Mercer, eds., *Doing Disability Research*, Leeds: The Disability Press.

Rizvi, F. and Lingard, B. (1996) 'Disability, Education and Discourses of Justice', in C. Christensen and F. Rizvi, eds., *Disability and the Dilemmas of Education and Justice*, Buckingham: Open University Press.

RNIB (1990) *Thomas Rhodes Armitage: RNIB's Founder*, London: Royal National Institute for the Blind.

RNIB (1996) *Blind in Britain: The Employment Challenge*, London: Royal National Institute for the Blind.

Roberts, H., ed. (1981) *Doing Feminist Research*, London: Routledge and Kegan Paul.

Robinson, D. and Henry, S. (1977) *Self Help and Health: Mutual Aid for Modern Problems*, London: Martin Robertson.

Robinson, I. (1988) *Multiple Sclerosis*, London: Routledge.

Roeher Institute (1995) *Harms's Way: The Many Faces of Violence and Abuse Against Persons with Disabilities*, North York, Toronto: Roeher Institute.

Rogers, A., Pilgrim, D. and Lacey, R. (1993) *Experiencing Psychiatry: Users' Views of Services*, Basingstoke: Macmillan.

Ross, K. (1997) *Disability and Broadcasting: A View from the Margins*, Cheltenham: Cheltenham and Gloucester College of Higher Education.

Roth, A. (1984) 'Staff–Inmate Bargaining Tactics in Long-term Treatment Institutions', *Sociology of Health and Illness*, 6 (2), 111–31.

Roth, J. (1963) *Timetables: Structuring the Passage of Time in Hospital Treatment*, New York: Bobbs-Merrill.

Roulstone, A. (1998) *Enabling Technology. Disabled People, Work and New Technology*, Buckingham: Open University Press.

Rowe, A., ed. (1990) *Lifetime Homes*, London: Helen Hamlyn Foundation.

Rutter, M. (1979) *Changing Youth in a Changing Society*, London: Nuffield Provincial Hospitals Trust.

Ryan, J. and Thomas, F. (1980) *The Politics of Mental Handicap*, Harmondsworth: Penguin.

Sacks, O. (1984) *A Leg to Stand On*, New York: Summit Books.

Safilios-Rothschild, C. (1970) *The Sociology and Social Psychology of Disability and Rehabilitation*, New York: Random House.

Safilios-Rothschild, C. (1976) 'Disabled Persons' Self-Definitions and their Implications for Rehabilitation', in G. Albrecht, ed., *The Sociology of Physical Disability and Rehabilitation*, Pittsburgh: The University of Pittsburgh Press.

Sainsbury, R., Hirst, M. and Lawton, D. (1995) *Evaluation of Disability Living Allowance and Attendance Allowance*, London: HMSO.

Sainsbury, S. (1973) *Measuring Disability*, Occasional Papers on Social Administration, No. 54, London: Bell.

Saunders, S. (1994) 'The Residential School: A Valid Choice', *British Journal of Special Education*, 21 (2), 64–6.

Sayers, J. (1982) *Biological Politics: Feminist and Anti-feminist Perspectives*, London: Tavistock.

Scambler, G. (1989) *Epilepsy*, London: Tavistock and Routledge.

Scambler, G. and Hopkins, A. (1986) 'Being Epileptic: Coming to Terms with Stigma', *Sociology of Health and Illness*, 8, 26–43.

Scheer, J. and Groce, N. (1988) 'Impairment as a Human Constant: Cross-cultural and Historical Perspectives', *Journal of Social Issues*, 44 (1), 23–37.

Scheff, T. J. (1966) *Being Mentally Ill*, New York: Aldine.

Scheper-Hughes, N. and Lock, M. (1987) 'The Mindful Body: A Prolegomenon to Future Work in Medical Anthropology', *Medical Anthropology Quarterly*, 1, 6–41.

Schneider, J. W. and Conrad, P. (1983) *Having Epilepsy: The Experience and Control of Epilepsy*, Philadelphia: Temple University Press.

Schuchman, J. (1988) *Holywood Speaks: Deafness and the Film Entertainment Industry*, Urbana: University of Illinois Press.

Scotch, R. (1988) 'Disability as the Basis for a Social Movement: Advocacy and the Politics of Definition', *Journal of Social Issues*, 44 (1), 159–72.

Scotch, R. (1989) 'Politics and Policy in the History of the Disability Rights Movement', *Milbank Memorial Quarterly*, 67 (2: 2), 380–401.

Scott, A. (1990) *Ideology and New Social Movements*, London: Unwin Hyman.

Scott, R. A. (1969) *The Making of Blind Men*, London: Sage.

Scott, S. and Morgan, D., eds. (1993) *Body Matters: Essays on the Sociology of the Body*, London: Falmer Press.

Scull, A. (1979) *Museums of Madness*, London: Allen Lane.

Scull, A. (1984) *Decarceration* (2nd edn.), Cambridge: Polity Press.

Shakespeare, T. (1992) 'A Response to Liz Crow', *Coalition*, September, 40–2.

Shakespeare, T. (1993) 'Disabled People's Self-organisation: A New Social Movement?', *Disability, Handicap and Society*, 8 (3), 249–64.

Shakespeare, T. (1994) 'Cultural Representations of Disabled People: Dustbins for Disavowal', *Disability and Society*, 9 (3), 283–301.

Shakespeare, T. (1995) 'Back to the Future? New Genetics and Disabled People', *Critical Social Policy*, 44 (5), 22–35.

Shakespeare, T. (1996a) 'Disability, Identity, Difference', in C. Barnes, and G. Mercer, eds., *Exploring the Divide: Illness and Disability*, Leeds: The Disability Press.

Shakespeare, T. (1996b) 'Power and Prejudice: Issues of Gender, Sexuality and Disability', in L. Barton, ed., *Disability and Society: Emerging Issues and Insights*, London: Longman.

Shakespeare, T. (1996c) 'Rules of Engagement: Doing Disability Research', *Disability and Society*, 11 (1), 115–19.

Shakespeare, T. and Watson, N. (1995) 'Defending the Social Model', *Disability and Society*, 12 (2), 293–300.

Shakespeare, T., Gillespie-Sells, K. and Davies, D. (1996) *The Sexual Politics of Disability*, London: Cassell.

Shearer, A. (1981a) *Disability: Whose Handicap?*, Oxford: Blackwell.

Shearer, A. (1981b) 'A Framework for Independent Living', in A. Walker and P. Townsend, eds., *Disability in Britain: A Manifesto of Rights*, Oxford: Martin Robertson.

Shearer, A. (1983) *Living Independently*, London: Kings Fund.

Shilling, C. (1993) *The Body and Social Theory*, London: Sage.

Sieglar, M. and Osmond, M. (1974) *Models of Madness: Models of Medicine*, London: Collier Macmillan.

Silburn, L. (1993) 'A Social Model in a Medical World', in J. Swain, V. Finkelstein, S. French and M. Oliver, eds., *Disabling Barriers – Enabling Environments*, London: Sage, in association with the Open University.

Silverman, D. (1987) *Communication and Medical Practice: Social Relations in the Clinic*, London: Sage.

Singer, P. (1993) *Practical Ethics*, Cambridge: Cambridge University Press.

SJAC (1979) *Can Disabled People Go Where You Go?*, London: The Silver Jubilee Access Committee, Department of Health and Social Security.

Sly, F. (1996) 'Disability and the Labour Market', *Labour Market Trends*, September, 413–24.

Smith, S. and Goddard, T. (1994) *Wheel Power? Case Studies of Users and Providers of NHS Wheelchair Services*, London: SCOPE.

Smith, S. and Jordan, A. (1991) *What the Papers Say and Don't Say about Disability*, London: Spastics Society.

Smyth, M. and Robus, N. (1989) *OPCS Surveys of Disability in Great Britain: Report 5 – The Financial Circumstances of Disabled Children living in Private Households*, London: HMSO.

Sontag, S. (1978) *Illness as Metaphor*, London: Pelican.

Sontag, S. (1991) *Illness as Metaphor/AIDS and its Metaphors*, London: Pelican.

Stimson, G. and Webb, B. (1975) *Going to See the Doctor: The Consultation Process in General Practice*, London: Routledge.

Stockholder, F. E. (1994) 'Naming and Renaming Persons with Intellectual Disabilities', in M. H. Rioux and M. Bach, eds., *Disability Is Not Measles*, North York, Ontario: Roeher Institute.

Stone, D. A. (1985) *The Disabled State*, London: Macmillan.

Stone, E. and Priestley, M. (1996) 'Parasites, Pawns and Partners: Disability Research and the Role of Non-disabled Researchers', *British Journal of Sociology*, 47 (4), 699–716.

Strauss, A. L. and Glaser, B. (1975) *Chronic Illness and the Quality of Life*, St Louis, Mo.: C. V. Mosby and Co.

Strong, P. (1979a) *The Ceremonial Order of the Clinic*, London: Routledge and Kegan Paul.

Strong, P. (1979b) 'Sociological Imperialism and the Profession of Medicine: A Critical Examination of the Thesis of Medical Imperialism', *Social Science and Medicine*, 13A (2), 199–215.

Stuart, O. (1992) 'Race and Disability: Just a Double Oppression?', *Disability, Handicap and Society*, 7 (2), 177–88.

Stuart, O. (1993) 'Double Oppression: An Appropriate Starting Point', in J. Swain, V. Finkelstein, S. French and M. Oliver, eds., *Disabling Barriers – Enabling Environments*, London: Sage in association with the Open University.

Sullivan, M. and Munford, R. (1998) 'The Articulation and Practice: Critique and Resistance in Aotearoa New Zealand', *Disability and Society*,

13 (2), 183–98.

Sutherland, A. (1981) *Disabled We Stand*, London: Souvenir Press.

Sutherland, A. (1993) 'Black Hats and Twisted Bodies', *Disability Arts Magazine*, 3/1 (Spring), 3–8.

Swain, J., Finkelstein, V., French, S. and Oliver, M., eds. (1993) *Disabling Barriers – Enabling Environments*, London: Sage, in association with the Open University.

Swann, W. (1992) *Segregation Statistics: English LEAS 1988–91*, London: Centre for Studies on Inclusive Education.

Szasz, T. S. (1970) *The Manufacture of Madness*, New York: Harper and Row.

Szasz, T. S. (1990) *Insanity: The Idea and Its Consequences*, New York: Wiley.

Szasz, T. S. and Hollender, M. H. (1956) 'A Contribution to the Philosophy of medicine', *AMA Archives of Internal Medicine*, 97, 585–92.

Talle, A. (1995) 'A Child is a Child: Disability and Equality among the Kenya Masai', in B. Ingstad and S. R. Whyte, eds., *Disability and Culture*, Berkeley, Ca.: University of California Press.

Taylor, S. J. and Bogdan, R. (1989) 'On Accepting Relationships Between People with Mental Retardation and Non-disabled People: Towards an Understanding of Acceptance', *Disability, Handicap and Society*, 4 (1), 21–36.

Taylor-Gooby, P. (1994) 'Postmodernism and Social Policy: A Great Leap Backwards', *Journal of Social Policy*, 23 (3), 285–404.

Thomas, A. P., Bax, M. C. O. and Smith, D. P. L. (1989) *The Health and Social Needs of Young Adults with Physical Disabilities*, Oxford: Blackwell Scientific Publications.

Thomas, C. (1997) 'The Baby and the Bath Water: Disabled Women and Motherhood in Social Context', *Sociology of Health and Illness*, 19 (3), 622–43.

Thomas, D. (1982) *The Experience of Handicap*, London: Methuen.

Thomas, G. (1997) *Exam Performance in Special Schools*, Bristol: Bristol Centre for Studies on Inclusive Education.

Thomas, H. (1992) 'Disability, Politics, and the Built Environment', *Planning Practice and Research*, 7 (1), 22–5.

Thomas, K. (1977) 'The Place of Laughter in Tudor and Stuart England', *Times Literary Supplement*, 21 January, 77–81.

Thomson, R. G. (1996) *Freakery: Cultural Spectacles of the Extraordinary Body*, New York: Columbia University Press.

Thomson, R. G. (1997) *Extraordinary Bodies: Figuring Physical Disability in American Culture and Literature*, New York: Columbia University Press.

Thornton, P. and Lunt, N. (1995) *Employment for Disabled People: Social Obligation or Individual Responsibility*, York: Social Policy Research Unit, University of York.

Titmuss, R. (1958) *Essays on the Welfare State*, London: Unwin.

Tomlinson, A., ed. (1990) *Consumption, Identity and Style: Marketing, Meanings and the Packaging of Pleasure*, London: Routledge.

Tomlinson, S. (1982) *A Sociology of Special Education*, London: Routledge and Kegan Paul.

Tomlinson, S. (1996) 'Conflicts and Dilemmas for Professionals in Special Education', in C. Christensen and F. Rizvi, eds., *Disability and the Dilemmas of Education and Justice*, Buckingham: Open University Press.

Topliss, E. (1979) *Provision for the Disabled*, Oxford: Blackwell/Martin Robertson.

Topliss, E. and Gould, B. (1981) *A Charter for the Disabled*, Oxford: Blackwell.

Touraine, A. (1977) 'An Introduction to the Study of Social Movements', *Social Research*, 52 (4), 749–88.

Touraine, A. (1981) *The Voice and the Eye: An Analysis of Social Movements*, Cambridge: Cambridge University Press.

Townsend, P. (1967) *The Last Refuge*, London: Routlege and Kegan Paul.

Townsend, P. (1979) *Poverty in the United Kingdom*, Harmondsworth: Penguin.

Townsend, P. (1993) *The International Analysis of Poverty*, Hemel Hempstead: Harvester Wheatsheaf.

Townsend, P., Davidson, N. and Whitehead, M. (1988) *Inequalities in Health: The Black Report, The Health Divide*, Harmondsworth: Penguin.

Tremain, S. (1996) *Pushing the Limits: Disabled Dykes Produce Culture*, Toronto: Women's Press.

Turner, B. (1984) *The Body and Society*, Oxford: Blackwell.

Turner, B. (1987) *Medical Power and Social Knowledge*, London: Sage.

Turner, B. (1992) *Regulating Bodies: Essays in Medical Sociology*, London: Routledge.

Twigg, J. (1989) 'Models of Caring: How do Social Care Agencies Conceptualise their Relationship with Informal Carers?', *Journal of Social Policy*, 18 (1), 53–66.

UN (1988) *A Compendium of Declarations on the Rights of Disabled Persons*, New York: United Nations.

UN (1990) *Disability Statistics Compendium*, New York: United Nations.

UPIAS (1976) *Fundamental Principles of Disability*, London: Union of the Physically Impaired Against Segregation.

Vasey, S. (1992a) 'A Response to Liz Crow', *Coalition*, September, 42–4.

Vasey, S. (1992b) 'Disability Arts and Culture: An Introduction to Key Issues and Questions', in S. Lees, ed., *Disability Arts and Culture Papers*, London: Shape Publications.

Verbrugge, L. M. and Jette, A. M. (1994) 'The Disablement Process', *Social Science and Medicine*, 38 (1), 1–14.

Vernon, A. (1996) 'A Stranger in Many Camps: The Experience of Disabled Black and Ethnic Minority Women', in J. Morris, ed., *Encounters with Strangers: Feminism and Disability*, London: The Women's Press.

Vernon, A. (1997) 'Reflexivity: The Dilemmas of Researching from the Inside', in C. Barnes and G. Mercer, eds., *Doing Disability Research*,

Leeds: The Disability Press.

Voysey, M. (1975) *A Constant Burden*, London: Routledge and Kegan Paul.

Wade, B. and Moore, M. (1993) *Experiencing Special Education: What Young People with Special Education Needs Can Tell Us*, Buckingham: Open University Press.

Waitzkin, H. (1984) 'The Micropolitics of Medicine: A Contextual Analysis', *International Journal of Health Services*, 14 (3), 339–77.

Waitzkin, H. (1989) 'A Critical Theory of Medical Discourses', *Journal of Health and Social Behaviour*, 30, 220–39.

Walker, A. (1981a) 'Disability and Income', in A. Walker and P. Townsend, eds., *Disability in Britain: A Manifesto of Rights*, Oxford: Martin Robertson.

Walker, A. (1981b) 'The Industrial Preference in State Compensation for Industrial Injury and Disease', *Social Policy and Administration*, 15, 54–71.

Walker, A. (1982) *Unqualified and Underemployed*, Basingstoke: Macmillan.

Walker, A. (1990) 'The Benefits of Old Age?', in E. McEwan, ed., *Age: The Unrecognised Discrimination*, Mitcham: Age Concern.

Walker, A. and Townsend, P., eds. (1981) *Disability in Britain: A Manifesto of Rights*, Oxford: Martin Robertson.

Walker, A. and Walker, C. (1990) 'The Structuring of Inequality: Poverty and Income Distribution in Britain 1979–89', in I. Taylor, ed., *The Social Effects of Free Market Policies*, Hemel Hempstead: Harvester Wheatsheaf.

Walker, A. and Walker, L. (1991) 'Disability and Financial Need: The Failure of the Social Security System', in G. Dalley, ed., *Disability and Social Policy*, London: Policy Studies Institute, 20–56.

Walker, Andrew (1995) 'Universal Access and the Built Environment: Or From Glacier to Garden Gate', in G. Zarb, ed., *Removing Disabling Barriers*, London: Policy Studies Institute.

Warburton, W. (1990) *Developing Services for Disabled People*, London: Department of Health.

Ward, L. (1987) *Talking Points: The Right to Vote*, London: Values Into Action.

Ward, L. (1997) 'Funding for Change: Translating Emancipatory Disability Research from Theory to Practice', in C. Barnes and G. Mercer, eds., *Doing Disability Research*, Leeds: The Disability Press.

Ward, L. and Flynn, M. (1994) 'What Matter Most: Disability Research and Empowerment', in M. H. Rioux and M. Bach, eds., *Disability Is Not Measles*, North York, Ontario: Roeher Institute.

Warnock (1978) *Report of the Committee of Enquiry into the Education of Handicapped Children and Young People*, London: HMSO.

Warnock (1982) *Special Educational Needs*, London: HMSO.

Wates, M. (1997) *Disabled Parents: Dispelling the Myths*, Cambridge: National Childbirth Trust.

Weller, D. J. and Miller, P. M. (1977) 'Emotional Reactions of Patients, Family and Staff in Acute Care Period of Spinal Cord Injury: Part 1',

Social Work in Health Care, 2 (4), 369–77.

Wendell, S. (1996) *The Rejected Body*, London: Routledge.

West, J., ed. (1991) *The Americans With Disabilities Act: From Policy to Practice*, New York: Milbank Memorial Fund.

West, P. (1979) 'An Investigation into the Social Construction of Consequences of the Label Epilepsy', *Sociological Review*, 27 (4), 719–41.

Westcott, H. and Cross, M. (1996) *This Far and No Further: Towards the Ending of the Abuse of Disabled Children*, Birmingham: Venture Press.

Which? (1989) 'No Entry', *Which?*, October, 498–501.

WHO (1976) *International Classification of Disease*, Geneva: World Health Organisation.

WHO (1980) *International Classification of Impairments, Disabilities and Handicaps*, Geneva: World Health Organisation.

Wiener, C. L. (1975) 'The Burden of Rheumatoid Arthritis: Tolerating the Uncertainty', *Social Science and Medicine*, 9, 97–104.

Wilding, P. (1982) *Professional Power and Social Welfare*, London: Routledge and Kegan Paul.

Williams, F. (1989) *Social Policy, a Critical Introduction: Issues of Class, Race and Gender*, Cambridge: Polity Press.

Williams, F. (1992) 'Somewhere Over the Rainbow: Universality and Diversity in Social Policy' in N. Manning and R. Page, eds., *Social Policy Review No. 4*, Canterbury: Social Policy Association.

Williams, F. (1993) 'Gender, "Race" and Class in British Welfare Policy', in A. Cochrane and J. Clarke, eds., *Comparing Welfare States: Britain in International Context*, London: Sage.

Williams, F. (1996) 'Postmodernism, Feminism and the Question of Difference', in N. Parton, ed., *Social Theory, Social Change and Social Work*, London: Routledge.

Williams, G. (1984a) 'The Movement for Independent Living: An Evaluation and Critique', *Social Science and Medicine*, 17 (15), 1000–12.

Williams, G. (1984b) 'The Genesis of Chronic Illness: Narrative Reconstruction', *Sociology of Health and Illness*, 6, 175–200.

Williams, G. (1991) 'Disablement and the Ideological Crisis in Health Care', *Social Science and Medicine*, 32, 517–24.

Williams, G. (1996) 'Representing Disability: Some Questions of Phenomenology and Politics', in C. Barnes and G. Mercer, eds., *Exploring the Divide: Illness and Disability*, Leeds: The Disability Press.

Williams, G. and Wood, P. (1988) 'Coming to Terms with Chronic Illness: The Negotiation of Autonomy in Rheumatoid Arthritis', *International Disability Studies*, 10, 128–32.

Williams, I. (1989) *The Alms Trade*, London: Unwin Hyman.

Williams, R. (1980) *Problems in Materialism and Culture*, London: New Left Books.

Williams, R. (1981) *Culture*, Glasgow: Fontana.

Williams, R. (1989) *Resources of Hope*, London: Verso.

Williams, S. (1993) *Chronic Respiratory Illness*, London: Routledge.

Williams, S. and Calnan, M. (1995) *Modern Medicine: Lay Perspectives and Experiences*, London: UCL Press.

Wilson, A. (1997) 'How Not to Win Friends', *The Sunday Telegraph*, 28 December, p. 16.

Wolfensberger, W. (1980) 'The Definition of Normalisation: Update, Problems, Disagreements and Misunderstandings', in R. J. Flynn and K. E. Nitsch, eds., *Normalisation, Social Integration and Community Service*, Baltimore: University Park Press.

Wolfensberger, W. (1983) 'Social Role Valorisation: A Proposed New Term for the Principle of Normalisation', *Mental Retardation*, 21 (6), 234–9.

Wolfensberger, W. (1989) 'Human Service Policies: The Rhetoric versus the Reality', in L. Barton, ed., *Disability and Dependence*, Lewes: Falmer Press.

Wolfensberger, W. (1994) 'The Growing Threat to the Lives of Handicapped People in the Context of Modernistic Values', *Disability and Society*, 9 (3), 395–413.

Wolfensberger, W. and Thomas, S. (1983) *Program Analysis of Service Systems Implementation of Normalisation Goals: Normalisation and Ratings Manual* (2nd edn.), Toronto: National Institute of Mental Retardation.

Wood, R. (1991) 'Care of Disabled People', in G. Dalley, ed., *Disability and Social Policy*, London: Policy Studies Institute.

Woodill, G. (1992) *Independent Living: Participation in Research*, Toronto: Centre for Independent Living in Toronto.

Woodill, G. (1994) 'The Social Semiotics of Disability', in M. H. Rioux and M. Bach, eds., *Disability Is Not Measles*, North York, Ontario: Roeher Institute.

Wright Mills, C. (1970) *The Sociological Imagination*, Harmondsworth: Penguin.

Young, I. M. (1990) *Justice and the Politics of Difference*, Princeton, NJ: Princeton University Press.

Younghusband, E. et al., eds. (1970) *Living with Handicap*, London: National Children's Bureau.

Zarb, G. (1992) 'On the Road to Damascus: First Steps towards Changing the Relations of Research Production', *Disability, Handicap and Society*, 7 (2), 125–38.

Zarb, G., ed. (1995) *Removing Disabling Barriers*, London: Policy Studies Institute.

Zarb, G. (1997) 'Researching Disabling Barriers', in C. Barnes and G. Mercer, eds., *Doing Disability Research*, Leeds: The Disability Press.

Zarb, G. and Nadash, P. (1994) *Cashing in on Independence*, Derby: British Council of Organisations of Disabled People.

Zarb, G. and Oliver, M. (1993) *Ageing with a Disability: What Do They Expect After All These Years?*, London: University of Greenwich.

Zola, I. K. (1972) 'Medicine as an Institution of Social Control', *Sociological Review*, 20, 487–504.

Zola, I. K. (1973) 'Pathways to the Doctor: From Person to Patient', *Social Science and Medicine*, 7, 677–89.

Zola, I. K. (1982) *Missing Pieces: A Chronicle of Living with a Disability*, Philadelphia: Temple University Press.

Zola, I. K. (1983a) *Socio-Medical Enquiries: Recollections, Reflections and Reconsiderations*, Philadelphia: Temple University Press.

Zola, I. K. (1983b) 'Developing New Self-Images and Interdependence', in N. Crewe and I. K. Zola, eds., *Independent Living For Physically Disabled People*, London: Jossey Bass.

Zola, I. K. (1989) 'Toward the Necessary Universalizing of Disability Policy', *The Milbank Memorial Fund Quarterly*, 67 (Supplement 2), 401–28.

Zola. I. K. (1991) 'Bringing Our Bodies and Ourselves Back In: Reflections on Past, Present and Future Medical Sociology', *Journal of Health and Social Behaviour*, 32, 1–16.

Zola, I. K. (1994) 'Towards Inclusion: The Role of People with Disabilities in Policy and Research Issues in the United States – A Historical and Political Analysis', in M. Rioux and M. Bach, eds., *Disability Is Not Measles*, North York, Ontario: Roeher Institute.

Index